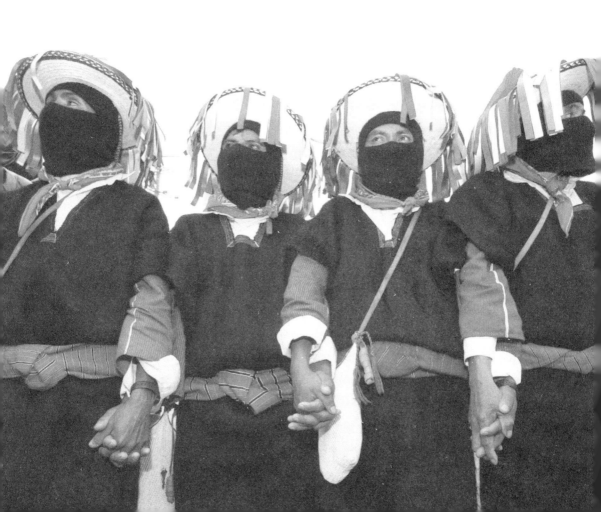

The Fire and the Word

A History of the Zapatista Movement

Gloria Muñoz Ramírez

Translated by Laura Carlsen with Alejandro Reyes Arias

City Lights Books
San Francisco

All royalties from this book will directly benefit the
autonomous communities in Chiapas.

Illustrations by Antonio Ramírez and Domi.

Original text design Efraín Herrera.

Additional typography and layout by Harvest Graphics.

Original cover design: Yuriria Pantoja Millán

Cover image: Creación Gráfica
            Arnulfo Aquino

Library of Congress Cataloging-in-Publication Data

Muñoz Ramírez, Gloria.
  [EZLN. English]
  The fire and the word : a history of the Zapatista
movement / Gloria Muñoz Ramírez ; translated by Laura
Carlsen with Alejandro Reyes Arias.
      p.   cm.
  ISBN 978-0-87286-488-7
1. Chiapas (Mexico)—History—Peasant Uprising, 1994-
2. Ejército Zapatista de Liberación Nacional (Mexico)—
History.   I. Carlsen, Laura, 1957-   II. Reyes Arias,
Alejandro.   III. Title.
  F1256.M8613 2008
  972'.750836—dc22
                                                2007052477

City Lights Books are published at the City Lights Bookstore,
261 Columbus Avenue, San Francisco, CA 94133.

Visit our Web site: www.citylights.com

CONTENTS

The Fire and the Word
in the United States

On November 10, 2003, the book *EZLN: 20 y 10, el fuego y la palabra* was published in Mexico. The Zapatista Army of National Liberation (EZLN) was in the midst of celebrating the twenty-year anniversary of its founding on November 17, 1983, and its ten years of public life since the armed uprising of January 1, 1994. The book was born as part of a series of events with the same name, organized by the magazine *Rebeldía* to commemorate these two important Zapatista anniversaries.

Three months prior to its publication, the *Caracoles* were inaugurated in the Zapatista territories of southern Mexico. The *Caracoles* are centers for political and cultural meetings and exchange between the Zapatista communities and national and international civil society. They are also the headquarters of the Good Government Boards, recently formed as a crucial building block of Zapatista autonomy. The Good Government Boards provide a living example to the world that it is possible to build alternative forms of truly participatory democracy.

In the years since its first Mexican edition, *The Fire and the Word* has traveled the world. It has been translated into French, Italian, German, Turkish, Persian and Greek, and published in separate Spanish-language editions in Spain, Argentina, Chile and Uruguay.

This new edition of the book, updated to include developments through 2007, couldn't be better timed for a U.S. readership. Indignation with the disastrous effects of the U.S. war in Iraq, the use of "rendition" and torture, the deterioration of civil liberties in the face of national security policies, and the growing marginalization of immigrants and minorities have led to a serious credibility crisis and to a disenchantment with the political system on the part of a good portion of the U.S. public. At the same time, immigrant communities, primarily Mexican, are facing a wave of increasing racism, intolerance and repression. The militarization of the border and the criminalization of immigration, with the deportation of thousands of "undocumented" people and the forced separation of innumerable families, have led to an unprecedented climate of fear and repression among Latin American populations living and working in the United States.

These factors help explain the recent increase in the number of groups related to or inspired by Zapatismo in the United States. In December 2006, the U.S. was the country with the second largest number of adherents to the Sixth Declaration of the Lacandón Jungle—the Zapatista Army's most recent initiative. The Sixth Declaration seeks precisely to build common ground and weave contacts among the many struggles in Mexico and the world. It is in this context that we are publishing *The Fire and the Word* here in the United States, in both English and Spanish editions.

The book paints a landscape of the history of the Zapatista movement from its creation, in November 1983, to the birth of the Good Government Boards in August 2003. The introduction and the prologue were written by Subcomandante Insurgente Marcos, military chief and spokesman of the EZLN, who also evaluates the first decade of Zapatista struggle and resistance in an extensive interview. This edition includes an additional text that brings the book up to date and helps to answer the question "What are the Zapatistas doing now?"

The new epilogue was co-written in 2007 by Gloria Muñoz and Hermann Bellinghausen, the renowned Mexican writer and journalist who has been covering the war in Chiapas since its beginning. After years of following the movement, from remote mountain villages to massive urban demonstrations, Bellinghausen knows and understands Mexico's indigenous Zapatista communities very well.

The epilogue tells the story of the Other Campaign and the Zezta Internazional. After the Sixth Declaration of the Lacandón Jungle was published in June 2005, the Zapatistas initiated a tour through what anthropologist Guillermo Bonfil Batalla called "deep Mexico"—Mexico

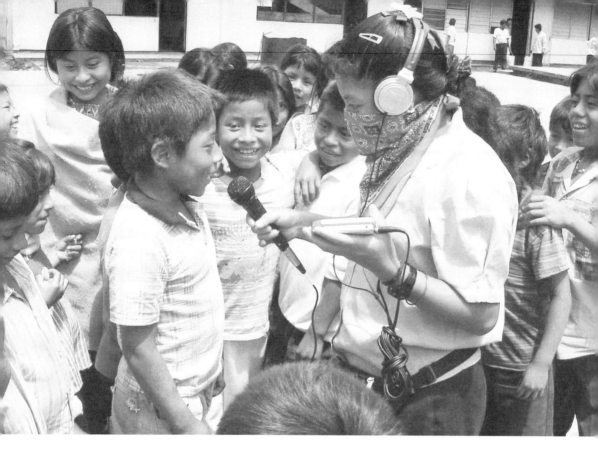

from the lower classes and on the political left. The objective was to develop a national plan of struggle and a new Constitution. The Other Campaign traveled across Mexico and crossed the northern border to reinvent the map, creating what the Zapatistas call the Other Geography—a new territory where Mexicans and Chicanos encounter one another across artificially imposed barriers and generations of common history. This Other Geography finds echoes around the globe: by refusing to recognize borders, it recognizes systemic problems that affect all who struggle from below for justice and dignity in any country of the world. This is basis of the international component of the Sixth Declaration, better known as the Zezta Internazional.

Without further ado, we present you, the reader, the first English translation of the *Fire and the Word*—a tapestry and a mirror, as

Subcomandante Marcos would say, and perhaps you will see yourself therein, finding reflections of your own resistance, threads of connection with other struggles, and even a glimmer of hope.

—Greg Ruggiero and Elaine Katzenberger
November 17, 2007

17

Audio Message
by Subcomandante Insurgente Marcos

The following text is a transcript of an audio recording by *Subcomandante Insurgente Marcos. The message was made to be played at a book launch event in Mexico City celebrating the publication of the original Mexican edition.*

Zapatista Army of National Liberation
Mexico

November 10, 2003

We're here to begin celebrating a history and to present a book that tells a good part of that history. Contrary to what one might think, the history we're celebrating and telling is not that of the twenty and ten years of the EZLN. I mean, not only that. Many people will feel a part of those twenty and those ten. And I'm not referring only to the thousands of indigenous peoples in rebellion, but also to thousands of men, women, children and elders in Mexico and the world. The history that we begin celebrating today is also their history.

These words are directed to all of those people who, without belonging to the EZLN, share, live and struggle with us for an idea: to build a world in which many worlds fit. Or to put it another way, we want to have a birthday that celebrates many birthdays.

So we begin our celebration the same way all birthday parties used to start in the mountains of the Mexican southeast twenty years ago—telling stories.

According to our calendar, the history of the EZLN prior to the beginning of the war had seven stages.

The first was when those who would be part of the EZLN were chosen. This was around 1982. One- or two-month training sessions were organized in the jungle, where the participants were evaluated to see who qualified. The second stage was what we called "implantation;" in other words, the actual founding of the EZLN.

Today is November 10, 2003.

I ask you to imagine that on a day like today, but twenty years ago, in 1983, a group of people in some clandestine house were preparing the tools they would take to the mountains of southeast Mexico. Perhaps twenty years ago today the day was spent checking equipment, gathering information about the roads, alternative routes, the weather, and specifying itineraries, orders, arrangements. Perhaps twenty years ago today, at this time of day, the group was boarding a vehicle and starting their trip to Chiapas. If we could be there now, perhaps we would ask those people what they were up to. And they would have undoubtedly answered: "We're going to found the Zapatista Army of National Liberation." They had waited fifteen years to say those words.

Let us suppose, then, that they begin their trip on November 10,

20

1983. Some days later they reached the end of a dirt road, picked up their equipment, said goodbye to the driver, put on their backpacks and began climbing one of the mountains that, facing westward, traverse the Lacandón Jungle. After walking many hours, carrying fifty-five pounds on their backs, they set up their first camp in the sierra. Yes, it's quite possible that it was cold that day, and perhaps it even rained.

Twenty years ago, night came early under the large trees and the men and women turned on their flashlights, set up plastic roofs held up with ropes, hung their hammocks, looked for dry firewood and made a bonfire, lighting it with a plastic bag. Lit by the bonfire, the leader of the group wrote in his campaign diary something like:

"November 17, 1983. So many feet above sea level. Rainy. We set up camp. No news."

On the upper left-hand part of the sheet he wrote the name that they gave to this first stop on a voyage that everyone knew would be very long. There was no special ceremony, but on that day and at that time the Zapatista Army of National Liberation was founded.

Someone probably proposed a name for that camp, we don't know for sure. What we do know is that the group was made up of six people, the first six insurgents—five men and one woman. Of those six, three were mestizo and three were indigenous. The ratio of 50 percent mestizo and 50 percent indigenous members has never been seen again in these twenty years of the EZLN. Neither has the proportion of women (less than 20 percent in those early years). Today, twenty years after that November 17, the percentage is probably 98.9 percent indigenous and 1 percent mestizo. The proportion of women is close to 45 percent.

What was the name of the first camp of the EZLN? Those first six insurgents can't agree about it. As I learned later, camp names were chosen without any particular logic and in a very natural way, avoiding apocalyptic or prophetic names. None of them, for example, was called "January 1, 1994."

According to those first six, one day they sent an insurgent to explore an area to see if it was suitable for camping. The insurgent returned saying that the place was "a dream." The compañeros marched in that direction and when they got there they found a swamp. They told the compañero: "This isn't a dream, it's a nightmare." *Ergo*, the camp was named "The Nightmare." It must have been in the early months of 1984. The name of that insurgent was Pedro. Later, he would become sublieutenant, lieutenant, second captain, first captain and subcomandante. With that degree, and acting as Chief of the General Staff of the EZLN, he fell in combat ten years later, on January 1, 1994, during the offensive on Las Margaritas, Chiapas, Mexico.

The third stage prior to the uprising began when we applied ourselves to the tasks of survival: hunting, fishing, collecting wild fruits and plants. During this time we studied the terrain through orientations, walking, topography. And during this period we also studied military strategies and tactics in the manuals of the U.S. and Mexican armies, as well as handling and maintenance of various sorts of weapons, and the so-called martial arts. We also studied Mexican history and, in fact, we led a very active cultural life.

I arrived at the Lacandón Jungle during this third stage, around August or September 1984, some nine months after the arrival of the first group. I got there together with two other compañeros: an indigenous Chol compañera and an indigenous Tzotzil compañero. If I remember correctly, when I arrived the EZLN had seven stable members and two more that "went up and down" to the city with messages and for supplies. They passed through the villages at night, disguised as engineers.

The camps at that time were relatively simple. They had an administrative area or a kitchen, a sleeping area, an area for exercising, surveillance points, the area for twenty-five and fifty, and the security areas for the defense of the camp. Perhaps some of my listeners might be wondering what in the world is "the area for twenty-five and fifty." Well, it turns out

22

that, in order to take care of "primary" needs, one had to go a certain distance away from the camp. In order to urinate, one had to walk a distance of twenty-five meters; to defecate, it was fifty meters, in addition to making a hole with one's machete and then covering the "product." Of course, these rules applied when we were just a handful of men and women; that is, when we were fewer than ten. Some time later, we built latrines located further away, but the terms "twenty-five" and "fifty" stuck.

There was a camp called "The Wood Stove," because it was the first place where we built a rustic wood stove. Before that, we made our bonfires on the ground and we hung two pots—one for beans and another one for whatever animal we might have hunted or fished—on a crossbar with reeds. Afterwards, when there were more of us, we entered the "wood-stove age." In those days the EZLN had twelve combatants.

Sometime later, at a camp called "Recruits," we entered the "wheel age." It was there that new combatants were trained, and that we used a machete to carve a wooden wheel and built a wheelbarrow to carry stone for the trenches. It must have been the times, because the wheel was pretty square and we ended up carrying the stones on our backs.

Another camp was called "Baby Doc" in honor of the man who, with the United States' approval, ravaged Haiti. It seems that, with a column of recruits, we were on our way to set up camp near a village. On the way we ran across a pack of boars. In other words, a shitload of wild pigs. The guerrilla column positioned itself with great discipline and ability. The combatant in the vanguard shouted "pigs!" and, with panic as an engine and fuel, he climbed a tree with extraordinary skillfullnes and we didn't see him again. Others ran valiantly. . . but in the opposite direction from the enemy, that is, the wild boars. Others aimed and shot two of them. During the enemy's retreat—that is, when the wild boars ran off—a little pig was left behind, barely the size of a domestic cat. We adopted him and we named him "Baby Doc" because it was around that time that Papa Doc Duvalier died and passed the carnage on to his son.

23

We camped there to prepare the meat and eat. The little pig took a liking to us, I think because of the smell.

Another camp during those years was called "Of the Youth," because it was there that we formed the first group of insurgent young people, which was called the "Young Rebels of the South." Once a week the young insurgents would get together to sing, dance, read, practice sports and participate in contests.

Nineteen years ago, on November 17, 1984, was the first time we celebrated the EZLN's anniversary. There were nine of us. I think it was at a camp called "Margaret Thatcher," because we had caught a little monkey that, I swear, was a clone of the "Iron Lady."

A year later, in 1985, we celebrated at a camp called "Watapil," which is the name of a plant whose leaves we used to build a shed for food.

I was second captain, when we were at the so-called "Almond Sierra," and the main column had stayed behind. I was in command of three insurgents. If my math is correct, that made four of us at that camp. We celebrated with *tostadas*, coffee, *pinole* with sugar and a *cójola* (pheasant) we killed that morning. There were songs and poetry. One of us would sing or declaim and the others would clap with a boredom worthy of a better cause. When it was my turn, I gave a solemn speech and I told them, with no more arguments than the mosquitoes and the solitude that surrounded us, that one day we would be thousands and that our word would travel the world. The other three agreed that the *tostada* was probably moldy and that I must have gotten sick and that the illness most likely explained why I was delirious. I remember it rained that night.

During the fourth stage, we made our first contact with people living in the region. First we would talk to one of them, and that person would talk with his or her family. From the family we moved on to the village. From the village to the region. And so, little by little, our presence became a well-known secret and a widespread conspiracy. At this stage the EZLN was no longer what we had conceived when we arrived. By then we had been defeated by the indigenous communities, and as a product of that defeat, the EZLN started to grow exponentially and to become "very otherly." In other words, the wheel kept on wearing down the edges until, finally, it was round and could do what wheels do—roll.

The fifth stage was the period of explosive growth for the EZLN. Political and social conditions led us to grow beyond the Lacandón Jungle and we reached the regions of Los Altos and Norte. The sixth stage was when we voted on the war and prepared for it, including the so-called Battle of Corralchén in May 1993 when we had our first combats with the Mexican Federal Army.

Two years ago, in some of the places we went through during the March for Indigenous Dignity, I saw a sort of fat bottle, like a pot with a narrow mouth. I think it was made of clay and it was covered with little pieces of mirrors. When it reflected the light, each little mirror of the pot gave forth a particular image. Everything around it found in it a singular reflection, and at the same time the whole resembled a rainbow of images. It was as if many small histories came together to compose a larger history, but without losing their own distinct selves. I thought that perhaps the history of the EZLN could be told, looked at, and analyzed like that mirrored pot.

Today, November 10, 2003, twenty years after the beginning of that voyage by the founders of our organization, a campaign starts, as an initiative of the magazine *Rebeldía*, to celebrate the twentieth birthday of the EZLN, the tenth anniversary of the start of the war against oblivion, and this book by Gloria Muñoz. If I could synthesize this book in an image, I could think of nothing better than the pot covered in little pieces of mirror.

In one of the book's parts Gloria gathers the testimonies of some of the compañeros from the bases of support, committee members and insurgents, who speak their little piece of mirror during the last five stages previous to the uprising; that is, stages three, four, five, six and seven. This is the first time that compañeros who have been struggling as Zapatistas for

28

over nineteen years open their hearts and their memories of those years of silence. Thus, Gloria manages to turn those pieces of mirror into crystal pieces that allow us to gaze a little at those first ten years of the EZLN.

We can thus catch a glimpse of another history, one very different to the one created by the governments of Carlos Salinas de Gortari and Ernesto Zedillo with lies, altered police reports, and the complicity of intellectuals who, under the cover of supposedly "serious" research, disguised the check and the caresses they got from Power to exercise their "scientific objectivity."

With the pieces of mirrors and crystals that Gloria put together, the reader will realize that he or she is looking at only small parts of a giant puzzle. A puzzle whose key piece is the first day of 1994, when Mexico entered the North American Free Trade Agreement, when it entered the "First World."

The days before that January 1 were the seventh stage of the EZLN.

I remember that on the night of December 30, 1993, I was traveling on the highway between Ocosingo and San Cristóbal de las Casas. That day I had been at the positions we held around Ocosingo. I had checked via radio the situation of our troops, which were concentrating at various points along the highway, in the canyons of Patiwitz, Monte Líbano and Las Tazas. These troops belonged to the Third Infantry Regiment. They were around 1,500 combatants. The Third Regiment's mission was to take Ocosingo. But on the way there they were to take the large ranches of the region and gather the weapons of the ranchers' private, paramilitary guards—*guardias blancas*. I was informed that a helicopter of the Federal Army had been flying over the town of San Miguel, probably in response to the many vehicles that were gathering there. Since the early morning of December 29, no vehicle that entered the canyons was allowed to leave; all of them had been "borrowed" to transport the troops of the Third Regiment. The Third Regiment was entirely made up of indigenous Tzeltal combatants.

On my way, I had checked the positions of the Eighth Battalion, which formed part of the Fifth Regiment. The Eighth Battalion was in charge of taking the municipal seat of Altamirano as its first action. Afterwards, as it moved on, it would take Chanal, Oxchuc and Huixtán, before participating in the attack on the Rancho Nuevo military base, on the outskirts of San Cristóbal. The Eighth was a reinforced battalion. Six hundred combatants took part in the attack on Altamirano, some of whom would remain there once the city was taken. As the battalion advanced, it would incorporate more compañeros, in order to reach Rancho Nuevo with about 500 troops. The Eighth Battalion was mainly composed of indigenous Tzeltal combatants.

Along the highway I stopped at one of the highest areas and I contacted via radio the Twenty-Fourth Battalion (also part of the Fifth Regiment), whose mission was to take the municipal seat of San Cristóbal de las Casas and participate in the joint attack (together with the Eighth Battalion) of the Rancho Nuevo military base. The Twenty-Fourth was also a reinforced battalion. It had almost 1,000 combatants, almost all of them indigenous Tzotzils from the region Los Altos.

When I arrived in San Cristóbal, I went around the city and headed to the place that housed the General Headquarters of the EZLN's High Command. From there I communicated via radio with the head of the First Regiment, Subcomandante Insurgente Pedro, Chief of the Zapatista General Staff and second in command of the EZLN. His mission was to take the municipal seat of Las Margaritas and then advance to attack the military base at Comitán. With 1,200 combatants, the First Regiment was composed mostly of indigenous Tojolabal men and women.

In addition, in the so-called second strategic reserve there was another battalion composed of indigenous Chol combatants, and deep in our home bases there were three battalions in the Tzeltal, Tojolabal, Tzotzil and Chol regions, making up the so-called "first strategic reserve."

Yes, the EZLN came to public light with more than 4,500 combatants in the first line of fire, the so-called Twenty-First Zapatista Infantry Division, and with around 2,000 combatants who remained as reserves.

On the early morning of December 31, 1993, I confirmed the order to attack, the date and the time. In sum: the EZLN would simultaneously attack four municipal seats and three others "on the way." It would defeat the police and military forces in those places, and it would then march to attack two large military bases of the Federal Army. The date: 31 December 1993. The time: 24:00.

The morning of December 31, 1993, was spent clearing the urban positions we held at several places. At around 14:00 the various regiments confirmed via radio to the General Command that they were ready. At 17:00 we started the countdown: That time was referred to as "minus 7." At that point, all communication was cut off with the regiments. The next radio contact was planned for "plus 7," at 07:00 on January 1, 1994. . . with those who survived.

What happened then, if you don't already know, you can read about in this book; if you do know, you can remember it. In this book the bottle-pot becomes a giant tapestry whose general outline has fortunately already been drawn by Gloria, and filled with those little pieces of mirrors and crystals that make up the various moments of the EZLN in the last ten years, that is, the period between January 1, 1994, and August 1, 2003. I'm sure that many will find the mirror and the crystal that belongs to them. It was precisely thinking about this that I wrote the following Introduction:

Introduction
or presentation
(or both)

ZAPATISTA ARMY OF NATIONAL LIBERATION MEXICO (EZLN)

To whom it may concern:

It was 1994 and the calendar read April. It was the dawn of the 18th, and in the same letter in which I wrote about the "Cinderella syndrome" (see the Thirteenth Estela, Part 2), appears the following:

"But then the other night a journalist interviewed me and among the questions about Zedillo, Salinas, etc. was one that made me understand everything: 'And what do you think about this romantic stage of the war?' I turned around to see if he was joking, but no, he was serious and checking to see if the tape on his tape recorder was running. 'Romantic?' I thought. This journalist, along with others, had been in one of the poorest villages of the jungle for several days, sleeping under the roof of an old

33

schoolhouse and eating. . . canned food. Just yards from where he slept, a family ate only beans and tortillas (and every morning a woman from the base community offered to wash clothes or make coffee for 'the compañeros from the city') and took turns on guard duty day and night, while we slept just yards away from them.

"If this is romantic for someone who is so close, I said, what does it seem like for those who are far away?

"Some hours after the 'romantic' question, and in the haze of a fever that laid me out for three days, we had to activate the defense plan because we found out about an armed attack on the military checkpoint in Tuxtla. The few journalists that were left we got out of the area. Nobody liked it. In fact, I can sense an obvious annoyance in all the journalists when they have to go through a red alert—it throws them off balance, they feel needlessly put out: 'Why if nothing's going on?' 'That damn Marcos just giving us shit and bothering us,' etc. So we were alone, and it looked like it would be like that for awhile. Even the apparently diligent ones left for a little bit despite the fact that I explained to them it would be better if someone always stayed because things came up that people should see, etc. But they get bored. Their sense of time is different, and I amuse myself thinking about who will leave first, in the midst of the impatience of just a few days 'with nothing to do so I should concern myself with other things at least as important if not more.'

"So what did you expect, little Marcos? John Reed? No, but I did expect the equivalent. Someone with enough patience to gain access to the internal workings after overcoming the giant first step of outright mistrust. Someone without so many ties to the outside, or willing to cut them for a while. No, not forever. Someone who, without ceasing to be a journalist, would live with the Zapatistas, with us. I know that if I say that, more than one would volunteer, but they have to pass a series of tests first that up to now no one has passed. I mean that we have to choose this someone. But nobody stays long enough to enter the contest. In short, as we say here, 'complain, complain, complain.'"

Three years after writing these lines, a woman journalist managed, not without difficulties, to jump over the complicated and heavy wall of Zapatista skepticism and stayed to live in the indigenous rebel communities. From then on, she shared with the compañeros dreams and sleeplessness, joys and sadnesses, food and its absence, persecutions and respite, deaths and births. Little by little, the compañeros and compañeras accepted her and made her part of their daily lives. I am not going to tell her story. Among other things because she prefers to tell the story of a movement, the Zapatista movement, and not her own.

The name of this person is Gloria Muñoz Ramírez. From 1994 to 1996, she worked for the Mexican newspaper *Punto*, for the German news agency DPA, for the U.S. newspaper *La Opinión* and for the Mexican daily *La Jornada*. On the morning of February 9, 1995, along with Hermann Bellinghausen, she interviewed for what could have been the last time Subcomandante Insurgente Marcos for *La Jornada*. In 1997, she left her work, her family, her friends (and other things only she knows) and came to live in the Zapatista communities. For seven years she didn't publish anything, but kept on writing, and her journalistic nose never abandoned her. Of course she was no longer the journalist, or no longer just the journalist. Gloria learned another perspective, one far from the glare of the spotlights, the roar of the podiums, the scramble for the story, the race for the scoop. The perspective you learn in the mountains of southeastern Mexico. With patience characteristic of women who embroider, she gathered together the fragments of reality inside and outside the Zapatista movement in these ten years of the public life of the EZLN.

We didn't know what was going on. It wasn't until the Caracoles and the Good Government Boards were announced that we received a letter from her, presenting this tapestry of words, dates and memories, and spread it out in front of the EZLN.

We read the book, well, it wasn't a book then, but an extensive and polychromatic tapestry that portrayed the complex fabric of Zapatista life from 1994 through 2003—the ten years of public life of the Zapatista Army of National Liberation. We liked it. We hadn't seen anything else published with this attention to detail and completeness.

We responded to Gloria like we always respond, that is, with a "Mmhh, so?" Gloria wrote back and talked about the double anniversary (twenty years of the EZLN and ten years since the beginning of the war against oblivion), and about the new stage that was beginning with the creation of the Caracoles and the Good Government Boards, something about a plan for anniversary events by the magazine *Rebeldía* and I can't remember what else. Among all this, one thing was clear: Gloria was proposing to publish the book so today's youth would know more about the Zapatista movement.

"Today's youth?" I thought and I asked Major Moisés, "Aren't we today's youth?" "Sure we are," he responded while saddling his horse, and while I continued to oil my wheelchair and curse the fact that the first aid kit didn't include Viagra. . .

Where was I? Oh yeah! In the book that wasn't a book yet. Gloria didn't wait for us to say "yes," or "who knows," or—in the purest Zapatista style—simply not respond. On the contrary, she tagged onto the tapestry, the draft of the book that wasn't a book, a request to carry out extensive interviews.

I went to the committee and, on the muddy floor of September, spread out the tapestry (the draft of the book).

They saw it. I mean, the compañeros saw themselves. That is, that apart from the tapestry, it was a mirror. They didn't say anything, but I understood that there were more people, many more, that maybe would also see it and see themselves.

We told Gloria "go ahead."

That was August or September of 2003, I don't remember so good, but it was after the party of the Caracoles. I remember, yes, that it was raining hard, that I was climbing a hill, repeating in each step the curse of Sisyphus, and that El Monarca was determined that Radio Insurgente play a remix of "La del Moño Colorado." When I turned around to tell him that he'd have to go over my dead body to do that, I fell for the umpteenth time, but this time I landed on a pile of sharp rocks and cut my leg. While I checked out the wounds, El Monarca, as if to prove a point, passed right over me. That afternoon we transmitted over Radio Insurgente a version of "La del Moño Colorado" that, judging by the calls the radio received, was a great success. I sighed. What else could I do?

The book that the reader now has in his or her hands is that tapestry-mirror, but disguised as a book. It can't be pegged to the wall or hung in your bedroom, but you can approach it and look for us and for yourself. I'm sure that you'll find us and yourself.

This book, written by Gloria Muñoz Ramírez, has been edited through the combined effort of the magazine *Rebeldía* and the Mexican newspaper *La Jornada*, directed by Carmen Lira. Mmh. Another woman. The book design is by Efraín Herrera and the illustrations are from Antonio Ramírez and Domi. Mmh. . . one more woman. The photos are from Adrian Mealand, Angeles Torrejón, Antonio Turok, Araceli Herrera, Arturo Fuentes, Carlos Cisneros, Carlos Ramos Mamahua, Eduardo Verdugo, Eniac Martínez, Francisco Olvera, Frida Hartz, Georges Bartoli, Heriberto Rodríguez, Jesús Ramírez, José Carlo González, José Nuñez, Marco Antonio Cruz, Patricia Aridjis, Pedro Valtierra, Simona Granati, Víctor Mendiola and Yuriria Pantoja. The photography and copyediting were done by Yuriria Pantoja and Priscila Pacheco, respectively. Mmh. . . again more women. If the reader notes that women are the majority, do what I do: scratch your head and say, "such is life."

As far as I can tell, (I'm writing from afar) the book has three parts. In one there are interviews with compañeros from the base communities, committees and insurgent soldiers. In them, the compañeros and compañeras talk a little about the ten years before the uprising. I should tell you that it's not a complete image but pieces of a collective memory that's still waiting to come together and present itself.

However, these pieces help a lot in understanding what happens later, that is, in the second part. This is a kind of record of the public actions of the Zapatistas, since the beginning of the war in the pre-dawn hours of January 1, 1994, to the birth of the Caracoles, and the creation of the Good Government Boards. It is, I think, the most complete version of the public activities of the EZLN. In this panorama, the reader will find many things, but one leaps out: the integrity of the movement. In the third part there is an interview with me. They sent it to me in written form and I had to answer into a tape recorder. I've always thought that the "rewind" of the tape recorder is "record," so in this part I try to look back on the ten years to evaluate them, as well as reflect on other things. When I responded into the tape recorder, it was raining outside and one of the Good Government Boards shouted the "cry of independence." It was the dawn of Mexico's Independence Day—September 16, 2003.

I think the three parts go well together. Not only because it's the same pen that writes them; also because they have a viewpoint that helps to see, to see us. I'm sure that, like Gloria, many people when they see us will see themselves. And I'm also sure that she, and with her many more, will know themselves better.

And that's what all this is about, to be better.

So. Cheers, and don't look for beetles in the tapestry, because you might find them and then—poor you.

From the mountains of Southeastern Mexico.
Subcomandante Insurgente Marcos
Mexico, October 2003

Prologue

ZAPATISTA ARMY OF NATIONAL LIBERATION, MEXICO

THE POSTSCRIPT, BEING REBELLIOUS, HAS TAKEN BY STORM THE PLACE OF THE PROLOGUE. EVERYONE KNOWS THAT POSTSCRIPTS GO AT THE END OF LETTERS AND NOT AT THE BEGINNING OF BOOKS, BUT HERE, IN THE MOUNTAINS OF SOUTHEAST MEXICO, WE HAVE A "NEW KIND" OF DISCIPLINE, THAT IS, THAT EVERYONE DOES WHATEVER THEY WANT. THE DEAD, FOR EXAMPLE, NEVER STAY STILL. END OF NOTE.

P.S. THAT EXPLAINS ITSELF. Ten years ago, on the dawn of January 1, 1994, we rose up in arms for democracy, freedom and justice for all Mexicans. In simultaneous actions, we took seven municipal seats in the southeastern state of Chiapas and declared war on the federal government, its army and police. From then on the world would know us as the "Zapatista Army of National Liberation."

41

But we already called ourselves that well before. On November 17, 1983, twenty years ago, the EZLN was founded and as the EZLN we began to walk the mountains of southeast Mexico, carrying a small flag with a black background and a five-pointed red star and the letters "EZLN," also in red, below the star. I still carry that flag. It's full of patches and beat up, but it still waves cheerfully in the General Command of the Zapatista Army of National Liberation.

We are also full of patches on the soul, wounds that we think have scarred over but that open up when we least expect it.

For ten years we prepared for the first few minutes of the year 1994. Now January 2004 is coming up. Soon it will be ten years of war. Soon it will be ten years of preparation and ten years of war, twenty years.

But I'm not going to talk about the first ten years or the next, or the twenty years all together. What's more, I'm not going to talk about years, dates, calendars. I'm going to talk about a man, an insurgent soldier, a Zapatista. I won't talk much. I can't. Not yet. His name was Pedro and he died fighting. He held the rank of subcomandante and was, at the time of his death, chief of the EZLN security force and my second in command. I won't say he hasn't died. He is dead and I wish he weren't. But, as all our dead, Pedro is walking around out there and every so often he shows up and talks and jokes and gets serious and asks for more coffee and lights the umpteenth cigarette. He is here now. It's October 26 and it's his birthday. I say "a toast to the birthday boy." He lifts his mug of coffee and says "cheers, Sup" or something like that. I don't know why I chose the name Marcos if nobody calls me that, everyone calls me "Sup" or the equivalent. Pedro calls me "Sup." We chat with Pedro. I tell him stories and he tells me some. We remember. We laugh. We get serious. Sometimes I scold him. I scold him for lacking discipline, because I didn't order him to die and he died. He did not obey. So I scold him. He just opens his eyes wide and says to me, "*ni modo*" (what can you do?). Yep, too bad. Then I show him a map. He always likes to look at maps. I show him where he fell. He smiles.

42

Josué comes up, says hi and congratulations. "Congratulations compañero Subcomandante Insurgente Pedro." Pedro laughs and says "Damn, by the time you get through saying all that I'm another year older." Pedro looks at Josué and at me. I agree in silence.

Suddenly we are no longer celebrating his birthday. We are all three of us climbing a hill. On a rest break Josué says, "We're about to complete ten years since the start of the war." Pedro doesn't say anything, just lights a cigarette. Josué adds, "And twenty years since the birth of the EZLN. We should have a big dance."

"Twenty and ten," I repeat slowly, and add, "and those to come. . ."

By now we are at the top of the hill. Josué puts his backpack down. I light my pipe and with my hand point to something far off. Pedro looks where I'm pointing, gets up and says, he says to us, "Yes, you can already see the horizon. . ."

Pedro leaves. Josué picks up his backpack and says that we have to follow.

And yes, that's how it is. We have to follow. . .

What was I saying? Oh yes! We were born twenty years ago and ten years ago we rose up in arms for democracy, freedom and justice. They know us by the name of "Zapatista Amy of National Liberation" and our soul, with all its patches and scars, still waves like that old flag that's there above, that one with the red five-pointed star on a black background and the letters "EZLN."

We are Zapatistas, the smallest of the small, those who cover their faces to be seen, the dead that die to live. And all this is because ten years ago, on January 1, and twenty years ago, on November 17, in the mountains of Southeast Mexico. . .

Subcomandante Insurgente Marcos
Mexico, October 26, 2003

43

1983–1993
Pieces of the puzzle

I

On November 17, 1983, a small group of indigenous people and mestizos set up camp in the Lacandón Jungle. Under cover of a black flag with a five-pointed red star, they formally founded the Zapatista Army of National Liberation. And they began an unlikely adventure.

Ten years later, on January 1, 1994, thousands of armed indigenous people took over seven municipal seats and declared war on the Mexican government. Their demands: employment, food, housing, health, education, independence, justice, liberty, democracy, peace, culture and the right to information.

What happened in Southeast Mexico between November 17, 1983, and January 1, 1994? It is still not possible to fully gauge the history. Not because it's clandestine, not because these people are ashamed of it, but because, as they put it, "it was a really big thing we did."

Twenty years after its founding, three indigenous members of the original villages that made up the Zapatista Army of National Liberation speak

47

out. Representing the thousands of indigenous people who made the dream possible, they talk about how they met the first guerrilla fighters, how they organized in the villages, how they prepared for war and how the organization spread. These testimonies help to imagine those first ten years—how the organizing capacity developed, and the determination and courage that made the 1994 armed uprising and moved the entire world.

Compañero Raúl
Regional representative of the Zapatista villages

The time to tell about our clandestine history has come. I am from a village called Chico and my name is Raúl. I was recruited by my brother. He said, "Do you want to go somewhere to listen to what they have to tell you," then I went to that place and they asked me if I had decided to listen to the politics of the organization. They just said this, and I said yes.

At that time, the only security we had was the night. We went to the meetings at ten and returned at midnight or one in the morning, so that no one would hear us getting home. Later they invited me to another place they knew of, where we met with the insurgents, and there I met a captain and a lieutenant. They were wearing Pemex uniforms, like oil workers, or dressed like teachers. When you met them along the road they said they were teachers, so no one figured they were doing political work for the organization.

Well, later they told me to go to the camp called "Fogón." I got there and there were only seven insurgent compañeros, among them Major Moisés. We stayed in the camp for seven days and they taught us what to do in the villages. When we were leaving the camp, they gave us instructions. We learned little by little. The compañeros gave us pamphlets and we began to understand the exploitation by the government. Later, when we understood what it was all about, we began recruiting in our villages, little by little, until the whole town was recruited and the work got much easier.

When we went to leave supplies at the camps, we had to leave at three in the morning so that by dawn we'd already be way up in the mountains. That's the way we did it. The most important thing was security. What you knew, you held in your heart. No one else knew. Just other compañeros, and anyone who wasn't, no.

When the whole village was already recruited and there were lots of villages like that, then some people decided to be recruits for insurgents. Many left, and so

Compañero Raúl

the guerrilla forces began to grow. While some went to the mountains, in the villages we were preparing the militia, first in squads, then platoons. Then the time came when we had five or six militia platoons in each village that received training and everything. That's how the organization developed.

When the insurgents arrived in a village, it was because the whole village had already been recruited, the whole village was *compa*.[1] Then we had to look for a local supervisor and then a regional supervisor, because there were already a lot of villages.

When we took supplies to the camp, we'd take tostadas, *pinole*,[2] sugar or *panela*, or if we had a little money we'd take cigarettes for the compas. When we arrived they were happy to see us and we'd have a little party there. If there was a guitar, well, we'd dance, since there were compañeras there we could dance with them. So they began to trust us and we them. We would stay ten or fifteen days in the camp.

At the very first, the war name of my village was "Fright," because when we didn't know anything about the organization, an insurgent compañero passed through and went into a field and we thought it was weird that he went into the field. We went to look for him but we never found

[1] *Compa* short for *compañero* or comrade, in this case member of the organization.
[2] Pinole is a typical drink prepared with a cornmeal base.

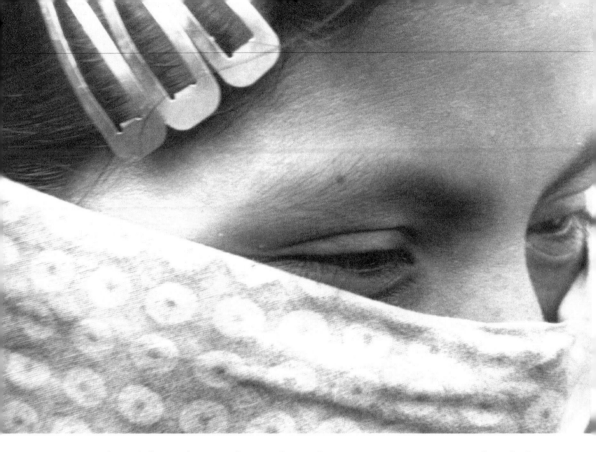

him. Then when we knew about the organization we remembered that and named the village "Fright."

In the camp called "Maleficio" in 1985, I met compañero Subcomandante Marcos. He was very young and very thin, I guess from walking so much. He would climb really difficult hillsides, they were really high and he would climb them. There we met him and also Subcomandante Pedro, who also arrived.

When the town is all compa then the insurgents visit the village. All the compañeros of the community meet them, and we organize a party and a dance. The village gives food, coffee, and we all socialize together. There is a lot of political talk that orients us about the situation. They tell us how to organize and how to prepare for the struggle.

That's what times were like when we began. . .

COMANDANTE ABRAHAM
Clandestine Revolutionary Indigenous Committee

Comandante Abraham

My name is Abraham, I'm from village "45."

When the Zapatista Army first came to our villages, around 1984, 1985, we had already taken part in peaceful struggles. The people were already protesting against the government. When the clandestine organization arrived, they talked to us about revolutionary struggle. We were among the first. The one who brought the idea to our village was a compa who is no longer alive, his name was Tomás. He talked to us about the struggle, but we didn't really believe him, because this compa was half drunk. But he explained to us and little by little we began to take him seriously, all his words, until an insurgent compa came and then he gave us a talk. The insurgent compa arrived with a pamphlet that had a political explanation of the national situation and there it said what exploitation is and all that.

We understood pretty much right away, because we had participated in other movements, not in the revolutionary sense, but in struggles where we negotiated with the government for land, for coffee, for a road in the Lacandón Jungle in Montes Azules. Since the repression that the compañeros told us about already existed, when the message of the EZLN arrived we were glad, and we felt happy that there was another struggle to defend the security of the small farmers and the poor.

We were just a handful, we were young, and little by little we passed the message on to other compañeros. We told them the explanation but told them not to tell anyone. If it was a young person, we told him not to say anything to his father or mother or even to the little brother.

Village "45" was called "Suicide" before. We had given it that name at first because Tomás wanted to commit suicide for a girl, but later we changed it and put "45," for other reasons.

When we had recruited a good group of compañeros in the village, we saw the need to go on to the next village. We went to Sinai and later we organized the entire region. I was 18 years old.

The compañeras were working to make the tostadas that we'd take to the mountains and the men also helped. We distributed bags to gather pinole to carry it in the night. When we moved around at night we had to invent a story in case we met anybody, because above all we had to be discreet to take the things. When you met somebody on the road you had to tell a story about where you were going. I could say I was visiting my family or something else. Everything was for security, to deliver the supplies. At this time there were still people who didn't know anything.

I saw Subcomandante Marcos and Subcomandante Pedro come through my village. They arrived at the house and then Tomás told us that we had to let these compas go through, guide them. So we went with them. The departure was at midnight. We had to go through the other villages at night and be in the mountains by daylight. When we got to where the camp was, we returned and left those two there.

The first camp I went to was called "Zapata" and then they took us to another camp called "Puma." Soon after we went to other camps with them, we arrived and lived there with the compas and then left to go back to our villages. Captain Marcos—he wasn't yet a Subcomandante—talked to us about how it is in the mountains and how the camps operate. When we visited him he told us where to get drinking water and how security was set up, how to respect others and where to go to the bathroom. All this was organized and Captain Marcos told us that if we wanted to live there, we could. He told us, "Here we're as happy as monkeys." After a while of being there, we had to go out and work in the villages.

As we progressed and began to grow, the forces began to get organized. More insurgents came down to the villages to live with the people and talk to them. We threw parties with them, organized cultural programs and all that. That's how we developed in a year. Between 1985 and

Comandante Gerardo

1986 the entire village joined the struggle. We no longer had to keep secrets among us, just from those outside that still weren't *compas*.

When we were new in the organization we searched for ways for the compas to travel safely. They would sometimes say that they were doctors, teachers, oil workers, all these things. When they were carrying cargo they said it was canned goods for the store in wherever.

The compas told us in class that someday we would have to use arms to end the system. We had already tried peaceful ways but nobody paid attention to us. Then we saw that there was no other option but to enter the armed struggle, so we organized to get stronger and stronger. When we went to the camp, when we arrived on a visit, we did exercises and trainings. The compañeros gave us talks on how to use the arms, what each one is called and what power it has. So the work developed and we got bigger and bigger. From one village it went to another, and from a few regions it went to other regions.

When we had formed the regions we started to do work there, for example, a clinic was built, a hospital, called "Posh." There I met a few compañeros, and that's when we realized that the organization was already big, that it had advanced a lot. By this time it was almost 1994 and that's when the villages were asked how they felt, if they felt good enough to screw the government. The people were fed up and said it was time. They began to make decisions and draw up documents, and the villages signed the documents and then we went to war.

COMPAÑERO GERARDO
Of the first Zapatista villages

My name is Gerardo, from the village of Israel. Some compañeros know me. We'll talk about what we know, about when this all began.

We saw the very beginning of the work of the organization of the Zapatista Army in the villages. In the first place, we learned security measures, because without security you can't do anything. Then with the measures we could advance and that's what we did. As we learned about the struggle and we grew more, we adopted more measures because the work was developing, getting big. We learned more or less where the camps were. I went to four camps during that time, from 1984. The first camp I went to was called "La Rosita." The other was "Agua Fría," the other I can't remember its name. . . that's what we learned during those years that we worked carrying tostadas, pinole, to the insurgents and helping them. We helped each other because what we didn't know, they knew. We needed to know things and so we started to do the tasks.

As the work grew, we had to have even more security. Our friend was the night, because only in the night could we walk around. In the day we couldn't, in the day we slept and at nine, ten, eleven at night you go out with your twenty-five kilos to walk for three or four days. We left the house at this hour to where the food had to be delivered.

On days when we went to the camps the insurgents helped us with some little chores that we didn't know how to do. We saw how the work was developing and how later our struggle was transformed as the villages gained force.

At first, twenty years ago, a militia member came out of a village, then two, and later they received some training and as more joined, the work advanced. If there were five militia members then maybe an insurgent would come out of the same village. I mean to say that it all took place step by step, not fast, keeping up the struggle, helping the struggle.

That's how everything grew. Before 1994, we saw that we were building up strength, we saw it and that we were a hell of a lot of people.

My brother recruited me. Once when he had to make a trip he began to talk to me. Then we started almost at the same time, like I didn't even give him time, after just one or two talks I said yes, I'll join, that if not now, when?

First we listened to the explanations of the struggle. We found out about simple things, because later they'd tell us there's this and that, because the recruiter also had security measures and couldn't say everything at once. Now, when you decide to do the work then you can travel and learn from that, but you have to do your part to begin to learn.

My village was one of the first that helped the organization. It was 1984 when we joined. We weren't everybody in the village at first, but later we organized everybody and so the insurgents came to our community and felt protected. That's how we prepared for war. . .

II
Subcomandante Insurgente PEDRO

On February 21, 2000, Subcomandante Insurgente Marcos wrote a letter to the recently deceased Mexican writer Fernando Benítez. The letter contained a story "to try to remember today those who aren't with us, but who were before and made possible what we are today." El Sup referred then to Subcomandante Insurgente Pedro, killed in combat the dawn of January 1, 1994.

In the story that the military chief of the EZLN told, Subcomandante Pedro appeared in the first person, telling his own story from the other side, from the dead:

"I remember that day. The sun wasn't moving straight, but a little sideways. I mean, it did go from here to there, but kind of on its side, without climbing to that point that I can't remember what it's called but El Sup told us once. The sun was cold. Well, this day everything was cold. Well, not everything. We were hot. As if the blood or whatever we have inside our body was fevered. I don't remember what El Sup called it—the 'zenith' or something like that, it's when the sun reaches the highest point. But not this day. It just seemed to fall over to the side. We were advancing. I was already dead, lying belly up and I could see perfectly well that

the sun wasn't moving upright but on its side. That day El Sup wrote 'Here we are, the dead of all times, dying once again, but now in order to live.' When exactly did we all die? Well, in truth, I don't remember, but that day when the sun moved on its side we were all already dead. All of us, men and women because there were women too. I think that that's why they couldn't kill us. It's really hard to kill a dead person and, well, dead people aren't afraid of dying because they're already dead. That day in the morning there was a stampede of people. I don't know if it happened because the war had started or because we saw so much death advancing around us, walking as always without a face, without a name. Well, first the people ran, then they didn't run. Then they stopped and came close to hear what we were saying. What nonsense! If I had been alive, no way would I come up to listen to a dead man! I'd figure that the dead had nothing more to say. I mean, they're dead. Like the work of the dead is to go around scaring people by not talking. I remember that where I was born they say that the dead still walk around because they have something pending and so they can't be still. That's where they say I was born. I think it's called Michoacán, but I can't remember well. I also don't remember very well but I think I'm called Pedro or Manuel or I don't know what. I think it doesn't matter now what a dead person is called because he's dead. Maybe when one is alive it's important what they call you, but dead—who cares?

"Well, the thing is that the people, after running, came up to see what all of us dead people were saying. And then we talked, just like the dead talk, like a little chat, not much noise, like if you were talking to someone who wasn't dead but alive. No, I don't remember what words we said. Well, I do remember a little. It had to do with the fact that we were dead and at war.

"At dawn we had taken the city. By noon we were preparing everything for the next one. I was already laid out by noon, that's why I saw so clearly that the sun wasn't moving in a straight line and I saw that it was cold. I saw but I didn't feel, because the dead don't feel but they do see. I saw that it was cold because the sun was kind of like turned off, very pale, as if it were cold. We all wandered around from one side to the other. Not me, I stayed lying belly up, watching the sun and trying to remember what El Sup said it was called when it's way up in the sky, when it stops climbing and starts to slide down the other side. Like the sun gets embarrassed and goes and hides behind that hill. When the sun had already gone to hide I didn't notice. The way I was, I couldn't turn my head; just look straight up and without turning see a little bit on one side and the other. That's why I saw that the sun wasn't moving straight, but that it was going sideways, embarrassed, like it was afraid to climb up to that place I can't remember what El Sup called it, but maybe I'll remember later.

"I remembered all this now because the stone gave way a little and a slit opened up like the wound of a knife and then I could see the sky and the sun moving again on its side like that day. I couldn't see anything else. Lying down like that, I could barely see the sky. There weren't many clouds and the sun was kind of pale. That is, it was cold. And then I remembered that day when the dead like us began this war to speak. Yes, to speak. Why else would the dead wage war?

"I was saying that through this slit I could see the sky. Helicopters and airplanes were flying across it. They would come and go, daily, sometimes well into the night. They did not know but I saw them, I saw them and watched them. I also laughed. Yes, because in the end, those airplanes and helicopters come here because they're afraid. Yes, I already know that the dead always cause fear, but these airplanes and helicopters are afraid that us dead are going to walk again. I don't know why they make so much fuss, since they can't do anything about it since we're already dead. They can't kill us. Maybe because they want to find out first and advise their commanders. I don't know. But I do know that fear can be smelled and the smell of fear of the powerful is like a machine, like gasoline and oil and metal and gunpowder and noise and. . . and. . . and fear. Yes, if fear smells like fear, then those airplanes and helicopters smell like fear. The air that comes from above smells like fear. Not the air below. The air below smells nice, like things that are changing, like everything is getting better and more beautiful. Like hope, that's what the air below smells like to me. We are from below. Us and many like us. Yes, that's the thing then: on this day the dead smell like hope.

"All this I see through the slit and all this I hear. I think, and my neighbors agree (I know because they told me so) that it's not OK for the sun to move sideways and that it has to straighten up. It can't go on moving sideways like this, all pale and chilly. After all, the sun's job is to give heat, not be cold.

"And if you push me, I'll even be a political analyst. Look, I say that the problem in this country is that it's full of contradictions. There you have it: a cold sun, people who are alive don't do anything as if they were dead, and the criminal is the judge, and the victim is in jail, and the liar is government, and the truth is persecuted like a sickness, and the students are locked up, and the thieves are free, and the ignorant give classes, and the wise are ignored, and the lazy are rich, and the workers have nothing, and the least rules and the greatest obeys, and he who has the most gets more, and he who has the least has nothing, and the evil are rewarded, and the good are punished.

"And not only that, but here the dead speak and walk and do weird things, like trying to straighten up a sun that's cold, and—just look at it— moves sideways, without getting up to the point that I can't remember what it's called but El Sup told us once. I think that I'll remember some day." (Letter from Subcomandante Insurgente Marcos, February 21, 2000)

In the mountains of Southeast Mexico Subcomandante Insurgente Pedro is not just a legend, he still lives, exists and remains in memory all the time. The insurgents talk about Subcomandante Pedro and get a knot in their throats. "I still can't talk about him, its really painful," says Major Insurgente Moisés, who took over the command of the zone minutes after the fall of Subcomandante Pedro.

He was a man who liked to walk at night, who smoked Alas, who always demanded his coffee, who danced to *El Caballo Blanco*, who recited the Tecún Umán, who took care of his troops, who was the consummate military man and very strict in questions of security, who joked around with Subcomandante Marcos and was his second in command. The insurgents who lived with him and saw him fall along with the rest who died in full combat on the first dawn of 1994 still talk about him. The people of the villages also testify as to how he lived with them for nearly ten years, how he taught them to struggle, how he prepared them for the day when they would rise up in arms in search of a better life.

Today, ten years since his death, it's clear that the path of the EZLN cannot be understood without the history of people like Subcomandante Insurgente Pedro.

Insurgent Infantry Major Moisés

Talking about Subcomandante Pedro. . . I worked with him, it's a little painful. I met him when I was an insurgent, I met him while I was just starting out too, and I saw him fall carrying out his duty. It left me in charge of his unit. Subcomandante Pedro was very concerned about doing his job well. He did everything he had to do.

When it was time to get ready he was very strict, like they said. Also, when we discussed work with him, we helped each other especially in the political part. He would ask me what the custom of the villages was, how the compas did things, why different organizations existed, who led them, he asked me all this to be able to plan the right way to do the work, to get to know the village people. . .

Subcomandante Pedro was very strict in security because we were clandestine and no one could know anything about our army. He was also strict in the handling of arms, and in the explorations that had to be done to get to know the terrain. He was always tough about that, and when there was a problem he got even more tough. But it's also true that he was very cheerful, there are lot of stories you can tell about him, anecdotes and that kind of thing. . .

I didn't meet him in the mountains; I met him in the city, in a safe house where I was taken. I'm talking about December of 1983, when they took me to the city. I didn't think they were going to take me to the city; I thought they were taking me to the mountains, because I really liked what I heard on Radio Venceremos, of the Frente Farabundo Martí in El Salvador. But before going to the mountains they took me to the city and there I met Subcomandante Pedro. He had already been in the mountains, with the founders of the EZLN, but he had to come down to the city because he had gotten Leishmaniasis, what we call *chicle* fly, and was recovering in the city and I got to met him there.

At the time I couldn't speak Spanish like I can now, back then it was difficult. The indigenous of Chiapas speak Spanish as a second language. Their primary language is one of many Mayan dialects in the region. I didn't want him to come near me, because he talked to me about things I didn't understand. . . One thing that happened to me at this time is that some of them there in the safe house, they didn't teach me things and they ordered me to prepare food for the compas' trip. I didn't even know how to use the stove or anything, and then Subcomandante Pedro (who didn't have that rank yet) saw me doing the work and asked me "What are you doing?" and I told him "I'm frying chicken." And he said to me, "but you're going to blow up the stove." I asked him why, and he explained that because I had covered it with oil. Then he got mad and went and woke up the person responsible and scolded him for not showing me how to do the work. And then I saw that he was strict, very tough in questions that had to do with teaching. He said that once someone

61

had been taught how to do it, then you could leave them to do the work, but not before.

In 1985 I went to the mountains and I met him again there, but he was already a sublieutenant. He was a very dedicated member, he didn't care if he didn't know the mountains, because no one from the city knows the mountains, just like when a person from the mountains goes to the city and doesn't know how to get around. But that didn't matter to him, he always made an effort and he prepared us. We worked a long time in preparation, you can do the calculation, we're talking about how I met him again in the mountains in 1985 and the training went on until the last days, practically to the morning of 1994.

We can say all the words of the revolutionary, rebel or militant, or whatever, like a lot of people from outside do, but he didn't just say the words—he did what he said, and took it to the ultimate consequences. When you organize, you orient, you lead, you have to go to carry it out to its consequences, even in a peaceful mobilization. If you say you have to struggle, you have to go through to the end.

And in this case, for us as the EZLN, Subcomandante Pedro showed us that it's not just saying it, you have to be willing to go where he showed us. I don't mean to say that peaceful struggles are no good, of course they are, but you have to understand that there too you can fall in many ways, whether they put you in jail, you "disappear," whether they kill you in torture and no one ever finds out where your body is. In this case, we know where Subcomandante Pedro is, we do know that.

What he showed us, his word, we keep before us every one of us, and every one of us now has the responsibility of showing that we too can carry out our duty like he did.

There will be another time to say more, I have a lot of stories about him. In the last months of 1993 he told me, "If something happens, you take charge, whatever happens, you take charge." I didn't believe him, I said, "It's up to you," and it turns out that when we were already fighting we lost communication and there was no communication with him. I sent a messenger to headquarters to find out how he was and there was no communication until we had to take the municipal building.

Mayor Moisés

When I received the sign that Subcomandante Pedro had fallen, then I said, "Darn, now it's what he told me, now!" And at that moment you forget that you too can be attacked. At that moment I didn't care, I had to go on to the next street and there was Subcomandante Pedro. I talked to him but there was no movement in him. So I ordered him taken to the where the health workers were. . . and that was something really hard for the compañeros, for some militia and some insurgents that saw him. . . Some started to say, "How is it possible that a commanding officer goes down, he's prepared," and all these things as if it weren't possible for a commanding officer to be killed. Then I had to assume the responsibility, I had to control this, well, fear, this demoralization. I told them, "Bullets show no respect, it doesn't matter who it is, but we have to go on."

I think that if we're going to be revolutionaries we have to be revolutionary to the last, because if one doesn't accept the full consequences or abandons the people and all that, it's no good. We who struggle, the other brothers and sisters of other states, of this same country Mexico and of the world, need to accept this.

One thing that's interesting is how Subcomandante Pedro and Subcomandante Marcos met. I met both subcomandantes together, when they met. I remember one time, and I think it was the last or one of the last times they met, in a community called Zacatal. I was there, we were seated all three of us in a triangle, and I listened to the instructions from Subcomandante Marcos to Subcomandante Pedro: "You have to take care of yourself." Subcomandante Marcos told him. "We have to take care of ourselves, because you're the first comandante," Subcomandante Pedro was saying. And then Subcomandante Marcos said "Yes, but I'm telling

63

you that as second in command you have to take care of yourself because you're my second and whatever happens to me you're next." Then Subcomandante Pedro said, "We have to take care of each other, but both of us." Both understood that both of them had to be careful, but both wanted to go out and fight. They understood each other. Subcomandante Pedro always respected it when they told him things very clearly.

As a relationship of comandante to comandante, I saw that they respected each other and loved each other. Sometimes they were talking and I listened to those serious voices, and a moment later they were joking around, teasing each other. That's the way that one understands, comprehends what needs to be corrected, or what should be learned.

On another occasion we'll talk more about Subcomandante Pedro. Now it's hard to go on because it hurts. . .

Insurgent First Infantry Captain FEDERICO

I met compañero Subcomandante Insurgente Pedro when I first joined the insurgent ranks. From the first I saw his qualities as a combatant. He was a good compañero in struggle and he was with us until his death.

When his time came I was with him in his unit, as subcomandante he was my commanding officer. He always undertook plans with strong conviction, you could tell, he was very tough in questions of security, we talked about the importance of security and in military questions we learned a lot from him.

He got very close to the people, he lived with them, shared what the people ate, whether it was *pozol*, beans or bitter coffee, he never put it down. You could tell he was a very committed compañero in the struggle of the people. Another thing about him is that he always supervised the work he gave us to do. I remember a day I went out with him and he told me: "Prepare yourself for tomorrow because we're going to reconnoiter the peak," and we walked and I said, "Subcomandante, we already walked

64

Capitán Federico

a lot and there isn't anything" and he told me, "We have to go on." And we walked and walked and kept on walking and I said again, "There isn't anything, we've already walked a lot" and we walked and walked and he told me, "Just a little more, there it is," and at last we arrived and he said that I was right, because I was just learning how to walk, to endure better physical conditions. And then I realized that he was in top physical condition, that he could walk for miles and endure all kinds of terrain and conditions.

The compañero really appreciated the insurgent compañeras and also the members of the base communities, the women, children and old people.

To get ready for 1994, he ordered me to advance to the front, and said that I had to take on more security with the tasks. The day we were going out to the place where we would carry out military operations on December 31, 1993, he still checked the vehicles and told me, "Lico, I'm going to try this vehicle because I'm out of practice." I laughed because I saw that he knew how to drive the vehicle. And we went out, we marched toward the staging grounds for the operation, and the last orders that he gave were that each one of us had to go to the place we were to cover. And for me these were the last instructions that he gave us.

I remember another thing. He really liked to recite poetry, the Tecún Umán, and it made me laugh a lot, and he said, "Why are you laughing?" "It's that it's a little strange." Then I listened to him and I realized the Tecún Umán was about Jacinto Canek, an indigenous leader.

Insurgent First Infantry Captain NOÉ

Our compañero Subcomandante Pedro. . . first of all, I have to say, all our respect for him. Although physically he isn't with us anymore as a member of this regiment, we still respect him. . . for me he isn't dead.

65

I also lived with him for a long time and I got to know his character and his way of living with us in the mountains. Like the other compañeros said, he was really happy when he was hanging out with the troops, he had a gift of commanding in a way that educates, he was the teacher of everyone, he oriented us about war, and he taught us well how to organize the war against the bad government.

For us he's like a father, because there are things that we can't do well and he helps us. He might say to you, "You didn't do this very well and that's why I called your attention to it, so you won't keep doing it badly," and so he gave us this experience of not making the same mistake that we usually made. This is how it was during the time we were with him.

I remember that he always walked at night, and he tested us to see how well we had learned to walk at night with arms, how well we could walk carefully. He was also strict about security, when there were serious things he told us, he always alerted us, so we would learn.

When we commemorated a fallen compañero or a birthday, I remember that he liked to dance a lot to music called, "El Caballo Blanco." He threw himself on the ground and started to dance. He always liked to dance, and to recite the poetry of Tecún Umán, that's what he did to make the troops happy.

When we went out in 1994, all the time he told us, "Now's the time, compañeros, this is the moment, we have to show the bad government that we are going to win the war because it's pushed us too far." So he advised us on things about war, how you have to prepare, we didn't know the exact date but he said "train, prepare, practice" and all that. We never thought that on that First of January he would fall, but we knew that some of us would. It's still was hard for us to understand, but we don't have a choice, we have to go on following in his footsteps, like he taught us. . . That is what I respect about him, because he fulfilled his duty, he loved his people, he loved us as his troops, he taught us, and that's why we go on learning from him, although he is no longer with us.

66

Insurgent First Infantry Captain LUCIO

Capitán Lucio

Well, speaking of Subcomandante Pedro, I met him in 1989. Before, in the other unit where I was, all the compañeros that came back from training with him said he was a cheerful guy, really friendly with the people. For that reason I wanted to meet him. I had met him in the commemorative acts we held, but I didn't know him personally, and from 1989 I started to get to know him and prepare with him, and that's when I realized that it's true, that he was a very good guy, very self-sacrificing, but also very strict. Self-sacrificing because he liked to walk at night, walking in the mountains, in the hills. One suffers in the night, the rain, the dark, the load, the equipment. . .

In military issues he was strict, because the insurgent has to learn what discipline is, what unity is, the fellowship. He didn't allow anyone to put themself above anyone else. Thanks to him we can now teach others. In military questions he taught us what we had to learn from him. In politics the same, we learned everything from him, when we went to the villages, we made plans to do the work in the communities. What I teach, he said, is what you should teach too, to others and what other communities should receive. He was also very strict about security, to go into a community first we had to ask what was there, to know what we had to confront. Subcomandante Pedro's teachings have served us well up to now.

Finally the moment arrived when we decided to start the war. That day, that afternoon, he asked me, at six or seven in the night, if I was ready, because at that time I carried a weapon called SKS, and he changed it right then and gave me a Sten, because he told me that I had to have a really good one. I said, "I think I'm ready, that's what I'm here for." From then on, as the others explained, we set out and got close to the place where we were to stage the military operation. Missions were distributed.

67

We got Major Moisés as commanding officer and under his command we covered the place where the police force was and we had to carry out our mission there. Many hours went by. The Major ordered us to see what had happened to the group where Subcomandante Pedro was. I offered to go and see where he was, and unfortunately I found him, but full of bullet wounds, and I didn't check to see if he was alive. I was given another task and so I only said he was wounded. I left him and others stayed with him.

The memory that we have of him is all the teaching he left us and that still serves us.

Insurgent First Infantry Captain CORNELIO

I trained in the unit run by Subcomandante Pedro, that's how I know him perfectly, because he was my commanding officer in the Sixth Battalion. In his military character he was very strict about security mea-

Capitán Cornelio

sures, about handling arms, about all things that were dangerous, but also as a friend that has a lot of patience to teach and correct mistakes.

Always, during all the time that I was with him in the unit, he seemed to me cheerful, happy around us. . . he shared a lot with us. When things were going well he was content because there are moments when there are problems with the villages, problems of security, and he would just concentrate on solving the problems.

Of course, I always spent more time with him because he named me his bodyguard. When he went to meetings in the villages he took me with him, at times another compañero went, but almost always it was me. He liked to walk at night, sometimes we walked all night, and there was rain, mud, all this suffering, hunger and everything happened to us. When we arrived at a village, he never showed fatigue; he always arrived content, cheerful—and even more so when he knew the people.

Subcomandante Pedro liked coffee and cigarettes, his Alas of course, and when we'd go to a village sometimes they already had his carton of cigarettes and his mug of coffee ready. Then he'd be really content, even more cheerful, the tiredness would drop away. . .

When the work wasn't going well, he would call our attention to it, correct us, swear at us sometimes. That is, he was strict about that but we analyzed it and saw that he was right, because we weren't doing the work well. And the good thing is that he would analyze it too and see that he overreacted, and then he'd come and apologize to us and say that swearing at us wasn't fair. That's how he recognized that fault.

Before the war had been set, he wanted and we wanted to kick some ass. . . He asked us what we wanted and we told him that we wanted it to start already. When he knew that the war was going to start, he was even more content, happier. . .

When the moment of the war arrived, we came out of the mountains, talking as always. . . we were the last ones to come down from the mountains, he and I, talking about combat, that the day had come, that the time had come that we were going to kick some ass. He gave me some things to hold and to this date I have a souvenir of him, a pen I have of his. . .

When we got to the point that we had to attack the enemy, he showed us his bravery, he showed that being a vanguard is to go and attack the enemy. So that's what I remember, the courage of a really committed person. That's how we went into attack, and because attacks are always done with plans, he was assigned to be in a different place. Later we found out that he was dead.

We got there. I arrived personally to where Subcomandante Insurgente Pedro was, I lifted him and carried him to a place where other compañeros were. That's how he died in battle, but for us he isn't dead. He's still alive, for my part, he'll always be with me—that's what I can say about our compañero Subcomandante Pedro.

Insurgent Lieutenant of Public Health GABRIELA

I met Subcomandante Pedro when I joined the ranks of the Zapatista Army. The compañero was very strict in his orders, in discipline, in fellowship, and any error that we made as troops he corrected us in a good way.

Subcomandante Pedro really loved the compañeros, compañeras, children and old people, everyone, in the base communities. He explained to them what the situation was, why we were struggling. He liked to walk at night, he didn't care if it was raining, and he took us with him, that's the way he taught us to walk at night, without light, he never used a flashlight.

I remember one day we had to go out, we went to a camp called "Tortuga" and the compañero Subcomandante Pedro dressed like a doctor, as a security measure in those days. And he told us that we had to wear civilian clothes. When we were walking we saw some animals and he

Teniente Gabriela

began to shoot and he told us that we had to hunt animals, because there were other compañeros who didn't have any food and he was worried about how to feed the troops.

Afterward, he told the medical troops that we had to prepare more, prepare the first aid kits for the war. I remember that in the last moments he spoke to us and asked us if we were ready. I answered yes. When we were already in the operations terrain he told me that if there were wounded I had to tell him, but afterward I didn't know what happened. When I began to look for him to tell him that there were wounded, they told me he wasn't there. . . Major Moisés arrived to tell me that Subcomandante Pedro had fallen. . . I checked him, he had several wounds, I gave him a shot of adrenaline but we couldn't do anything for him. That's how it was, but the important thing is that he fulfilled his duty, he died in front of his troops because he was a commanding officer that did not hang behind, and he taught us many things. . . That's why we remember him to today.

Comandante Abraham
Clandestine Revolutionary Indigenous Committee

That was the life of Subcomandante Pedro. I met him many times, but I didn't live with him much. I met him in 1985 in the insurgent camps, and also in the villages. When I first met him he didn't have a rank, later I learned that he had earned a rank in the guerrilla. . . The memory that he left me, when we made the decision to go to war, was that he clapped and danced because a majority voted to go to war. He knew that there was no other choice and he was glad that the decision of the villages was respected. That's the memory I have of him, it almost seems like I can see him now. . .

And also when he spoke, when he explained something, when he told you how to solve problems, how to do a task, he spoke to you with fondness, he explained to you well. On several occasions I talked with him, he joked around, it's funny how we'd joke around. On the day of the battle I didn't go out with him because he went out with other compañeros, and we were in a different place. We have him present in our minds, we follow his example, his struggle of the compañero who died with us.

Compañero Gerardo
Of the first Zapatista villages

In the case of Subcomandante Pedro, I surely knew him and worked with him and he helped with many things, he oriented us. He was a good person, I knew him as a good person.

Compañero Subcomandante Pedro was a conscientious person. Whenever we went to meetings he was the one who gave us talks in the regions because at that time there weren't townships like today. We worked together for a long time.

Then one day it came time for the war of 1994. Up to then he still gave us talks, he instructed us on some things, he told us how to run our villages as the ones responsible, that we always had to be conscious at all times when the village people needed us. I couldn't move up in rank because I wasn't much of a reader, but he still listened to what we said. He always guided us, he told us that we had to make an effort, be patient, that that way we could achieve something.

Changes came about that we see now. And he guided us, he told us the things we had to do. When the war started, we didn't talk to him again, but we still remember what he told us.

It's as if he was still alive, it's a little painful, but we remember him and we respect him.

COMPAÑERO RAÚL
Regional head of Zapatista villages

I met Subcomandante Pedro. He was very cheerful. I saw him in a village called Zulma. There all the insurgents were gathered, he felt right at home there, he made faces, really happy.

Subcomandante Pedro really helped in the war. When we held the meeting to decide whether to go to war, I could see that he was very happy, because the villages had made up their minds.

That's how I remember him, happy. . .

III
1983–2003
From the initial clandestine stage to the Good Government Boards

"Twenty years is very little—there's more to come," say the insurgents of the EZLN, the same ones who day after day stand guard in the mountains, who keep vigil, who marched out that first dawn of 1994 willing to die without imagining the road before them.

In this part of the testimonies, the insurgents and the representatives of the villages agree that after the First of January everything took them by surprise. "We didn't even know if were going to survive," they say, and their words make more sense after hearing them talk about Subcomandante Pedro.

Everyone agrees that they are proud of belonging to a struggle "where they don't tell us what we've gained—we see it, we live it, we make it." They never imagined the encounter with civil society, and much less that one day the villages would be organized in Good Government Boards, now a reality in rebel territory, where whoever rules, rules by obeying.

"Our way—they say—is that first we build the practice and then the theory," and that explains the organization of autonomy, the current phase of the struggle.

Regarding the government? "You can't expect anything, we know that," they all agree separately. What follows, they claim, is to resist, organize and keep on being rebels. "We'll always be that. . ."

Major Infantry Insurgent MOISÉS

An evaluation of these twenty and ten years? First I'm going to talk about the first ten years when we organized the villages and formed the insurgents and militias, from 1983 to 1993. The organization found the way of getting to know the people in those years. Our EZLN learned how to adapt itself to our indigenous peoples, that is, that the organization knew how to make the changes necessary to be able to grow. We recruited by becoming political commissaries. . . The compañeros had a way of life, and by understanding that, we could go much further in the work of organizing the villages.

When we began there were problems of land, for example, in the Lacandón area in Montes Azules, in the prices of the products, in marketing, and all these problems led the compañeros to understand a movement like the Zapatista Army. We talked to them about the struggles of Lucio Cabañas, of Zapata, of Genaro Vázquez.

Our organization began to organize itself better. When we explained why we were fighting back we began to make it more clear what we want in this struggle, and why. I always did the work of political commissary, that is, I was the one who had to explain our struggle to groups of families in each village. I explained why we struggled in the EZLN, I invited them to participate in the struggle and they were told how to be careful because everything was underground. They were told that we were against the government, that we struggled against the system that was screwing us. We explained each point of why we were fighting back. When we described our struggle the

74

problem was that, for example, when we told them about health, and they thought that right away there would be good health and good education. Then comes the explanation that the struggle is long, that one day there will have to be a war to bring about these ends, that the government doesn't understand any other way because the government isn't interested or concerned about indigenous peoples. We explained to them what they experience on a daily basis and they understand what their own situation is, and they ask us what they have to do. And we explain the struggles of Villa, of Zapata, of Hidalgo, and how things have been won; we explain to them that thanks to these movements we won some things but that it's not enough.

Then we explain our dream. And we tell them that we struggle for good education, good health, good housing and all the other things. With time, the organization began to show itself and grow. Battalions of insurgents and militias came first. Clinics were built in each region, these clinics were organized by insurgents and that's how the EZLN began to provide services to the people and to organize with them. All this was a big sacrifice, but in this way the villages began to participate more and they themselves helped to build their clinics.

As insurgents it was a big step forward when we got the support of the villages. The result of the political work was that the villages were now maintaining their army. Before it wasn't like that. Food for the insurgents in the mountains was brought from the city. As the political work advanced, the sustenance of the troops became the job of the communities. When they begin to form structures like an organization, the two began to feel that they were one. The villages named their representatives, their local individuals in charge, with tasks like control, vigilance and carrying information to their village. The local person responsible is the link between that village and the insurgents. Later the regions were formed where all the local representatives gathered. There in the meetings of local representatives, they elected a regional representative, someone to be in charge of several villages.

The organization grew so much that we had to create new mechanisms for communication. Earlier, it took several days to contact us because messages were carried on foot, but later the organization was so big that we began to use radios so there was communication between us and those in the mountains.

In the regional meetings the compañeros began to feel the strength of the organization, because each representative knew how many insurgents and how many militia there were, and there were a fucking lot of us. In addition to seeing the strength, they saw that the situation was more and more difficult, that we were getting more and more screwed over, and they started wanting to break out. They already knew that they could organize, they knew how many insurgents and militias there were, how many villages we controlled, and from there the idea was born that the people need autonomy.

The villages realized that the projects the government were giving the communities were never decided on by the people the government never asked the people what they wanted. The government doesn't want to address the needs of the villages; it only wants to maintain itself. And from there the idea was born that we have to be autonomous, that we have to impose our will, that we should be respected, and that we have to do something so that what the people want will be taken into account. The government treats us like we can't think.

Then, little by little, the decision took form that it was almost time to rise up in arms. That decision was reached in 1992.

There were already so many thousands of us that it was getting hard to control security. Can you imagine trying to keep everything underground with so many thousands of compañeros?

How were we going to get good health, good education, good housing for all of Mexico? It was too great a commitment. And that's how we saw it. In those first ten years we acquired many skills, experiences, ideas and ways of organizing. And we wondered how the Mexican people were going to

Comandante Abraham, Capitán Lucio, Mayor Moisés, Teniente Gabriela, Compañero Raúl, Capitán Federico, Capitán Noé, Compañero Gerardo y Capitán Cornelio

receive us (we didn't call it civil society at that time). And we thought they were going to receive us with joy because we would be fighting and dying for them, because we want freedom, democracy and justice for all. But at the same time, we thought, what will it be like? Will they really accept us?

During the last ten years—from the last hours of 1993 and the first minutes of 1994 to now—we have seen that the people have already known who we are, what we seek and for whom. After the first days of January 1994 what we saw was huge demonstrations of the Mexican people. They, the people, came out to defend us, they hit the streets to demand that the war end. . . I still ask myself how it was possible that thousands and thousands of people, without yet knowing who we were, came out to the streets to support us. I think that they saw that we were willing to die for what we seek, and that there was no other option.

After that the Mexican people obliged us to seek ways other than arms. After ten years of public struggle we realize that we were in another stage. We didn't know the people and the people didn't know us and then we got to recognize each other. It was a stage in which we needed to get to know each other.

As the Zapatista Army we accepted dialogue because that is what the people asked us. But now that's history, now the Mexican people, indigenous or non-indigenous, realize that you just can't do anything with the government. The government and the rich are not going to just stop exploiting us; they are going to defend their interests. They will put us in jail, kill us, torture us, disappear us—that's their way. They even try it with us, and we're an army.

The government and the parties have gone hack to disdaining indigenous peoples. Supposedly to dialogue is to resolve problems, and it didn't work at all with them, but it did work to get to know the people.

The question that arises then, when it becomes obvious that the government is no good, is what are we going to do if the government doesn't resolve anything and you can't do anything with them?

But dialogue did work with the people. We met the exploited, the poor, from all over. We began to learn from them, from their struggles, and we also explained to them how we were struggling.

We felt that with the Mexican people, both sides were reaching out a hand. The Mexican people take risks coming to meet us here and we are also take risks going to their places, all to get to know each other and listen to each other. That helped a lot to explain to our villages and peoples the support of other people through struggle. The people confirmed directly that they are with us, although they aren't willing to take up arms.

We already had territory under our control, and we created the autonomous townships in order to organize there.

The EZLN had lots of ideas of how a free and organized people should be. The problem is that there aren't any governments that obey, only ones that give orders and that don't listen and don't respect you, that believe that indigenous peoples don't know how to think. They want to treat us like broken Indians, but it all turned back on them and we showed them that we do know how to think, and we do know how to organize ourselves. Injustice and poverty make you think, they make you produce ideas, they make you think how to do things better even if the government doesn't listen.

The dialogue with the government didn't work but it enriched us, because we met more people and it gave us more ideas. After the "Color of the Earth March" we said that with or without a law we were going to build our government the way we wanted.

We already have a way of doing practice first and then developing the theory. And that's how it was, after the betrayal, when the political parties and the government refused to recognize Indian peoples; we began to see how we would do things ourselves.

In practice we formed the autonomous townships and afterward we started thinking about an association of Autonomous Townships that would be the forerunner to the Good Government Boards. That association was a practice, a rehearsal of how we have to go about organizing ourselves. From there the idea was born to improve it and the idea of the Good Government Boards came up.

We had the idea and we were carrying out the practice. We thought that theory can have good ideas but in practice we can see if there are problems, or how to go about solving the problems.

Each municipality has different problems to confront. There are some that progress more and others less, but when they got together and began to talk about how to solve each one of the problems, that led to forming a new structure—the Good Government Boards.

Now we're having meetings among the different Good Government Boards because we see that's the best way to solve the problems. They get together when they have problems with one Board or another, but also to help each other in their jobs and to advance in everything that each Board has to deal with.

We are showing the country and the world that to be able to develop a better life, you can do it without the participation of the bad government. The progress in health, education, trade, these are projects that we are carrying out with national and international civil society, because together we are building what we think will be good for the people.

Why do the Mexican people and people from other countries support us? We think it's because they see that we are not thinking only about ourselves. We simply say that the people can plan and decide how their economy and their government should be, and we are working in practice on this form of government.

All this work is a very big responsibility. It feels like the song "time passes and we are getting old" (*el tiempo pasa y nos vamos haciendo viejos*) and we don't want to become *caudillos* or leaders, that's why the people need to be organized.

This training takes place in the midst of patrols, of counterinsurgency efforts, of paramilitaries, and in the middle of many other problems. And so in the middle of all this, we keep preparing.

What isn't recognized by the people is the constitutional government, because if it were, why would the Boards have more work than the government does? The Boards are solving problems that used to be resolved in the Public Ministry before. Now the people, even the ones who aren't Zapatistas, look for justice in the Boards. So I say the others are the ones who aren't constitutional. We are the ones who are recognized.

What do I feel in this twentieth anniversary? These nineteen years that I have been here have been hard, but we've done something, and there's a lot more to do. But now the difference is that we know each other and we are with the Mexican people and with other brothers and sisters from other countries. I hope that it is in their hearts that we are not alone, as they say. Now we need to put it in practice. We hope that some day it won't be "them" and "us" but we will all be the same, Zapatistas. We are going to build together with them for the benefit of the people.

I really didn't think that we were going to see this. It turns out that we didn't all die and that we are here, and that there's more to come. Now it's the role of the Mexican people to say what's been accomplished and above all what needs to be done.

Twenty years is very little. There's so much more. . .

Insurgent First Infantry Captain FEDERICO

The way I see it, me neither the insurgents nor the villages thought that the struggle would come so soon, that we would arrive at this moment so soon, although much more remains to be done. . . As an insurgent, the idea and the thought was that we would prepare to wage the war against the government and then go on, as it says in the First Declaration of the Lacandón Jungle, to battle our way to the capital, and I was convinced of that.

And that's how we trained, that's the idea we had. And it turns out that it wasn't like that. The struggle, the war—nobody knew how it would be. The compañeros of the villages, for example, if they had animals or a little money, since you knew you were going to die you had to eat them or spend the money. That's how we were preparing. We're thinking that if they kill us for some reason in the struggle, we're not going to die just to die. The mentality in those days was more centered on the military question; we were thinking that the Mexican people were going to rise up in arms and all together we would defeat the government.

In the first ten years, from 1983 to 1993, a lot of good things happened. The organization knew how to grow, it knew how to solve internal problems and it knew how to protect itself from the enemy. Although the enemy discovered our presence as an armed revolutionary group, we knew how to go on and continue to grow. Our problems or our faults

were never so great as to ruin us, because we were very clear and convinced of the idea of our first compañeros, that whatever happened we would never turn back. It became clear when we were a lot of villages and militias and insurgents.

In these ten years of public struggle without using arms, although without setting them aside either, we've accomplished a lot. Such as, for example, the political question. From the first days of January 1994 we were very clear in our work, showing through deeds why we were fighting and the people could understand our cause. We told the people how we really live, the poverty, the situation of workers, the exploitation, that we aren't fighting for our own interest, but for all of Mexico, for all the people, and that's why the civil society supported us and still supports us.

The first accomplishment is that civil society understood us and not only that, but also began to make the same demands and confront the government with us.

There is another lesson, and that is that we see that there are other people fighting and resisting, because exploitation isn't only in Chiapas, but in all of Mexico. We have heard about the struggles of other indigenous peoples, who also have died making their own demands and resisting in their own ways.

I feel good that we have made it twenty years. We see that we have built something through peaceful struggle, but that doesn't mean that we are finished, more is left to do. It looks good and I feel good about it, but I think there's still a ton left to do. . .

Speaking internally, the biggest project is the formation of the Good Government Boards. Our own villages have learned and are still learning to govern themselves without the Mexican government. Our people actually know how to govern themselves. For example, our education is much different from the education given by the government. We have our health services and our hospital. We have our small storage facilities. And it's not some other guy who's telling us how to do things, we're the ones, even though many of us don't know how to read and write, we are carrying out the work.

I feel proud of all this work, because we see that we are going forward, because each day we advance and we can see it. We see that when we say something we achieve it, and that gives us much pride. And our people feel it, although nobody feels overconfident. We're convinced that we will continue to be rebels, we'll always be rebels.

Insurgent First Infantry Captain Noé

For me it's a great achievement to reach the twentieth anniversary of the formation of the EZLN. Reaching twenty is good. It's an achievement of

Capitán Noé

the dream of the first compañeros. When we prepared I thought that it was going to be pure shooting. After the first days of 1994, when we let people know who we were and why we struggled, everything changed, because civil society began to understand our struggle. And there I want to say thank you to Subcomandante Insurgente Marcos who helped the people to understand that our struggle is not just for us but for all of Mexico, to see that we all have been forgotten.

We didn't think that we would make it to twenty years like this. When we went to war we were wondering who will return and who will not. That's why Subcomandante Insurgente Pedro asked us if we were committed. We were.

In these ten years we've seen many accomplishments. First of all, civil society understood our objective of demanding our rights as indigenous peoples, our thirteen demands for all Mexicans. When people began to understand our struggle, they started to organize to find a way to organize with us. They came to meetings with the EZLN, like the National Democratic Convention, and our organization committed itself more to the peaceful struggle and we started to work together with them in these ten years. Even with the peaceful struggle with civil society, we have never laid down arms completely. We know that they are our security. If we don't accomplish our goals by peaceful means we are still ready. We do not call to organize an army, but that everyone organizes resistance. We, our peoples, are organized in Good Government Boards and that shows that we can do things without the government. We create measures without permission from them.

As the Zapatista Army that we are, we the insurgents are going to protect the villages. Now the Boards, for example, should rule through obeying. In other places they can also organize their autonomy. You don't have to wait for the government because it will never give anything. It

84

takes awareness and courage because you're going to confront the government and this government is going to prohibit it.

We have seen that in these ten public years our struggle has become combined, seeking alternatives so we can be less war-oriented, as we say. We give an opportunity to organize outside and we also organize within.

Yes, you can carry out a peaceful struggle, but we are willing to use our arms, as we did ten years ago. That's why we're the EZLN.

We want to respect how we organize ourselves. We are showing that we can start very small and get bigger, and we are sure that we will accomplish it. We never think that we are going to accomplish everything, but we'll see.

I never imagined that so many people would join. Before 1994 we weren't afraid. We thought that the people would rise up with us in arms, but we didn't think that civil society would stop us in order to get to know us. We've gotten to know each other a lot and now we know who they are. In these ten years we've learned things. In politics we learned that the government should rule by obeying, and we knew that but we also learned it. In military questions we also learned a lot in ten years. We learned to resist faced with 75,000 soldiers that they sent to fight us. We learned to get around fences and fool their military intelligence. We learned what strategies they applied to us, and we fooled them with and without arms. We never fell in the traps that they set, we always discovered them in time. In economics, we kept on resisting. We use what the people give us. In ideology we've learned that we're going to go as far as our people tell us.

Insurgent First Infantry Captain LUCIO

The first ten years of the struggle was a time of political and military preparation for us, the insurgents, and for our communities. It was a lot of training for everyone. What I see now is that those ten years, from 1983 to 1993, helped a lot and still help, because we learned so much and that is what you see now. Our organization—for us and for many people—brought something that didn't exist before. Now what we're seeing are the results of what we went through before, during those ten years of preparation.

We had to go to war and we did. We had to struggle with arms and so we did. We were clear that we had to take up arms. We were convinced, and so we prepared for that.

Now what I see is that after ten years, we are still clear that we just had to declare the war in 1994 and that it could still last longer because the road is long, but we see that we have not let the people down.

What we've learned in all this time, well, it's that we know well where the enemy is, but also where our allies are.

We orginally had the idea that we were going to struggle for a long time, but in armed struggle. It turns out that we have to do other things and that we have to learn and that the people support us, but not with arms.

I'm proud of that time. There are a lot of things that I can see now and that our people still live out since the war. What I see is that we not only say things, we do them.

The people didn't come out to support us with arms, but they did support the causes and they are against the government. That doesn't mean that arms don't ever work. The arms are there. But we also fight back peacefully with the people and with people from other parts of Mexico and the world.

From 1994 to now we have had the opportunity to meet a lot of people and we've learned. We've also learned a lot from the war, how to defend ourselves and struggle, to trick the enemy. Because before, in the first ten years, it was pure preparation and now in the next ten years we used that political-military preparation to defend ourselves. We've taken some heavy blows, but that's taught us how to resist and to resolve problems that we face.

I think that because of the way we've struggled, we've had the opportunity to meet other people from Mexico and from all over the world. Maybe we would have never met them another way. That is, if we kept shooting all the time, then who knows if we would have had time to meet these people.

I am very clear that we are now fighting back according to the needs and the growth of our peoples. That's what we're doing now, and we think that other people of Mexico are probably going to say or are going to see that you can organize the people, although they may do it in another way.

I didn't know if we were going to ever have Good Government Boards and now we already have them, because we needed them and that is very good for the villages. And it's moving forward because we have many plans and it's growing a lot.

I see a lot of differences between this time and other times. Our children are being born with a school and a clinic, with their own system of education and health. Still it's hard in areas of production and marketing, but they're already searching for ways to solve it and to have projects, and that's really good, because it's not the same as before.

We still maintain our troops and we are still growing. Our work is to protect the work of the Good Government Boards and in this regard we are always on guard. We are waiting for orders for something else but now this is our job, our task and our duty as insurgents.

Insurgent First Infantry Captain CORNELIO

During these twenty years many things have happened, but it's all for the best. Before we had a different idea of working underground. We prepared ourselves for war. We had goals that we had to reach. We dedicated ourselves a lot to military preparations and we were clear that we had to fight with arms until victory, we were not thinking about anything else or about doing it in any other way.

We were soldiers and the time came for us to go into combat. Before we left the camps to go to war, I said goodbye to the mountains. I knew that the combat would go on and that I was either going to live or die, but it turns out that afterwards we started to see new things, and that confused us a little, but now after ten years, we're very clear. We know that the struggle can be carried out in many ways. After ten years we are clear that all that we've achieved is because we went to war. The popular support, the confidence that they have in us, is another arm and with that we can achieve many things, although with the government we already saw that you can't get anywhere.

Now I see what the development of our struggle is really like, how it's a war, how it follows its path, the movements that we made with our struggle, to go out and talk to other peoples of Mexico, to go out in masks and uniforms, we did all that, and I never thought we would be able to.

We even made it to the capital itself but before we thought that we would do it with arms. The government and the political parties do not hear us, but that doesn't matter because we made it, we were with the people and that is a great gain.

We keep on resisting and we keep on organizing. We, as insurgents, keep on taking care and preparing ourselves militarily and politically. We keep on preparing, keep on training and keep on doing what we have to as a military organization. The people have to work to make the autonomous municipalities a success. Rule by obeying, this is how an authority really should govern. Now we're putting everything into practice because that is our role.

During the past ten years the insurgents learned how to reject the different wars that the government waged on us, such as the psychological war, the dirty war, the provocations, the paramilitaries. . . we already knew how to reject those wars and we learned to resist in questions of life. We see how our villages go on improving and how we continue to learn to resist. For that reason, we say that we insurgents have learned from our people.

I feel content because we're living our advances. Nobody tells us about it, we see it ourselves. We didn't even feel these ten years pass. How can you feel the years go by when there is so much work?

Insurgent Lieutenant of Public Health GABRIELA

As insurgents we explained to the villages that the struggle is going to take many years. We talked to the women, the youth, and that is how we began forming battalions and regiments. And we started to grow a lot and our organization became very big. It was growing and growing those first ten years and more and more insurgent compañeros kept joining.

After 1994, when we went to war, we were determined to face whatever happened. It turns out that here we continue to exist, we see our advances and we feel that we live to keep on working. What I see is that each year there's more participation and more growth. For example, before the compañeras hardly participated, but after 1994 the path opened up for them, the compañeras of the villages saw how the women insurgents went to war too, how they used arms, and how they went

89

along with the compañeros. That's where we saw how the women weren't only good for cooking and taking care of kids, but also how they can participate in the ranks of insurgents.

That was how more women started to arrive after the war. Now, twenty years later, women insurgents continue to join. That is, more are still joining and we are showing that we are really growing. We're also growing in the villages. There are more women as local and regional coordinators, members of the Committee, also joining in tasks of health, education, and other jobs that are necessary to the struggle.

And there's been a change in the men's way of thinking in the villages. Now they let the women participate. Earlier, they did not permit it. The men's way of thinking has changed, and although we have a way to go, it's not the same as before. The women have had to fight for these changes in the men, because they are aware of their rights and they force the men to make these changes.

These ten years have gone by quickly. I think it seems like that because of all the work we have and the participation. Although we have problems, the people don't quit participating, and we already have our governments of the people. The Good Government Boards are already taking care of resolving problems, but it's little by little. The people run the Boards, it's not like the Boards can do whatever they want. Here it's the people that run things.

As part of health services I see that we have grown a lot. At the beginning we built some clinics that attended to small needs but they were very small. Since 1994 the service has grown a lot, but little by little. Now there are health promoters in every village, first aid kits, and explanations of health. The people feel like their health workers understand them because they're from there too, not from the government. Now we even have hospitals and there we train health workers to work at the microclinics. We still have a lot of needs, but the less serious illnesses we can treat in our own villages.

In our territories we have decreased respiratory infections, parasites and intestinal infections. All this has been achieved just by our work and by the organization, and by the people of civil society who have helped out. The health workers give talks on hygiene and that's why disease has gone down.

In the hospitals, little by little, we've started to treat emergencies. I always thought we would someday because even though they told us our struggle was going to be long and it would be a lot of work, I also thought that we would see changes. Subcomandante Insurgente Pedro told us, "If we die, prepare yourselves because there will be more work, because more people will arrive."

I did think that more people would come from Mexico and other places, because that's what our comandantes said. They told us that workers, teachers, students, would be with us someday and it was true—they have come. Doctors have come even from other countries to see how we're organized, to participate with our health workers. There's a lot of difference between us and the government hospitals because we don't charge. Our health workers work for the people for free.

I'm proud of our struggle because you can really see the improvements in our villages. There are people from other countries helping us, because we are showing that we aren't looking for power but that we're fighting for all poor people. Other revolutionaries say that they are going to take power but they don't do anything, but we say that we are not going to take power and we organize. That's why I'm proud.

We are like a bridge that other friends can pass over, like our compañero Subcomandante Insurgente Marcos says.

COMPAÑERO RAÚL
Representative of the Zapatista villages

We spent ten years preparing ourselves collectively for a long war. We sowed beans, sugar cane, bananas, yucca because we thought it would help when the enemy attacked our villages.

So we as villages began to organize ourselves for the war. We signed our act of war because we just didn't see any other way. And we thought that our fight would make it to Mexico City, but then came the war and things happened in other ways.

Now we've seen many changes in our villages. The compañeros told us we had to prepare politically and militarily, that it would all be necessary later. And we saw that it was true, that everything was necessary. . .

We trust Subcomandante Marcos a lot because he does what he says for the people. It's not like others who do whatever they want. Not him, he is with us and we trust him and he trusts us. . .

We are organized now in the autonomous townships and we have more and more tasks. With the Good Government Boards even more work came and it just never ends.

At the beginning we thought that education and health and everything would be won through arms, but we saw that we can organize ourselves in other ways without setting aside our weapons, through our organization and our work. Not with the government. We don't expect anything from the government. We only expect things when we organize with the people.

I feel content because I never imagined that we were going to achieve so much, little by little, with our work. For this we have confidence in our organization.

Where I live there is no road, but we have education, the children are learning. We have health workers and they are taking care of our needs although we still lack a lot.

The government never gave us anything, so we have always resisted. We're not taking anything from the government, but then they never gave us anything anyway. Resistance is the most important thing for the future of the villages. Resistance and organization.

I've been part of this struggle for nineteen years. My village was one of the first. I'm not discouraged after nineteen years of struggle, because I've understood. What they compañeros originally told us has been carried out, so it's true.

COMPAÑERO GERARDO
From the first Zapatista villages

When we started in 1983 we didn't think about what it would be like. Little by little we learned, but we always put security first.

In the first years, almost twenty years ago, when the insurgent compañeros arrived in the village, the main part of the villagers' work was to assure security for the insurgents in the mountains. That was the task of the villages, to take care of them.

Also to sustain them. We took what we could get—tostadas, pinolito, sugar cane, or whatever we found. We realized that where they were there wasn't anything to eat and we gave them what we could.

Another task was to keep growing as villages and educating about the struggle. First to our families and then to the whole village. We had many jobs in those years. To take care of the security of the insurgents, to feed them little by little with what we could, and also to explain our struggle and bring more and more families and villages in.

Afterwards we decided on war. We decided that it had to begin. And then we had other jobs. So we know now that we have to organize ourselves to get what we want because no one is coming to give us things. Not the government or anybody else.

In my village there wasn't a school before, there wasn't anything.

Now the boys and girls are taking courses as education workers, and we are building a school, because we all have different jobs.

The resistance means that we have to make a real effort to be better off. The people aren't thinking about crumbs, they're eating from what they get from their own sweat. We're not leaving the resistance, that's all we have.

The struggle is long and hard, prolonged. At times we are happy, we throw a dance party, and other times it is work and we have to get down to it. So we go on, we're encouraged.

COMANDANTE ABRAHAM
Revolutionary Indigenous Clandestine Committee

One the first of January 1994, I never imagined what it would be like now. We imagined that we were going to take the cities with arms. We didn't think that we were going to live; we thought that most likely we would fall and that others would continue the struggle. We didn't think that there would be people to help us. We thought it would only be a few that would understand the struggle.

It was a big change, because we saw that many people started to talk about us. They started to say that the war should stop and we should look for other ways, political ways. We heard what the force of the people was saying—that we should look somewhere else. The people said *no* to violence and we listened.

We've seen that the society is mobilized with us.

We got excited on the road with the March.

In our territory we don't see other people. But thanks to the Consultation and the March we could meet other people. When we went out on the March we met a lot of people. . . They all yelled that we were not alone and it was very exciting.

It doesn't worry us that the government does not listen to the people. It doesn't worry us because we've seen the strength of the people. That's why it doesn't concern us about the government and the political parties. They just let us sit down in their chairs in their Chamber, that is, they just showed up to tell us to sit down but they didn't take us seriously, they just took it as a show.

We saw that we'd had enough with the government and that we had to continue to struggle. Time was running out and there were a lot of things we had to organize in the villages.

The organization now exists not because the government allows it, but because we struggle and organize. The government never gives us anything good. It's the people who decide. We exist because we are. They could not disappear us.

The politicians thought it wasn't important but that's not surprising because they never do anything. But the people decided that with or without a law [for indigenous rights] we're going to work.

It's like the war of 1994, the government didn't allow it but we did

95

it. That's how the Good Government Boards are going to be, whether the government likes it or not we're going to go on with this work.

Now I feel really proud. For one thing, because we're alive, and we're seeing the organization. The other thing is that there have been a lot of changes and we know that these twenty years aren't much. The struggle is long. They told us that in 1984, they told us it was long and hard, and we're clear on that.

Twenty years, then, and we're just beginning.

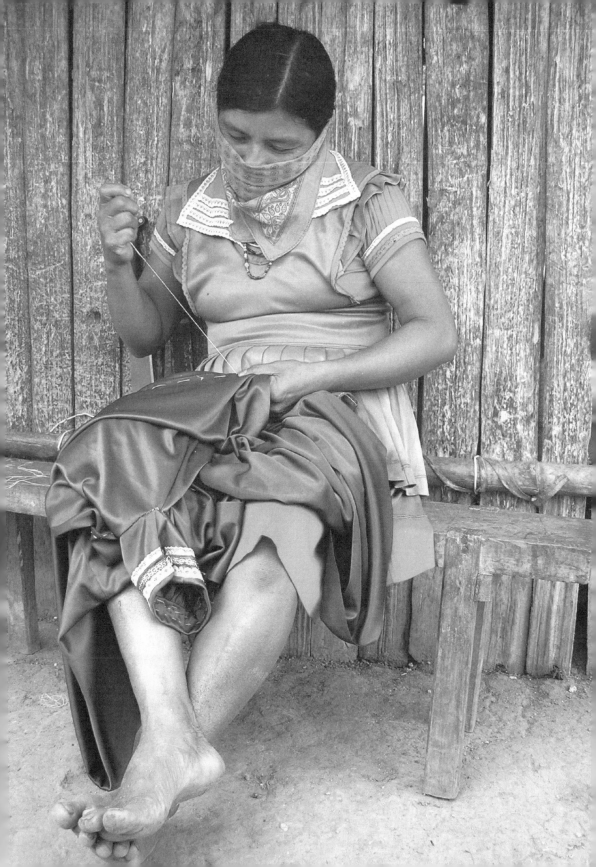

Ten Years of Zapatista Struggle and Resistance

On January 1, 1994 the EZLN arrived on the scene to stay. That dawn their troops surprised not only the country, but the whole world, with the military takeover of seven municipal seats in the state of Chiapas. These were the first days of a war decided on as "a last resort but just," as stated in the First Declaration of the Lacandón Jungle. A last resort against poverty, exploitation and racism, but above all, a last resort against oblivion. The demands: housing, land, work, health, education, food, freedom, independence, justice, democracy and peace.

November 17, 2003, marked the twentieth anniversary of the formation of an army made up mostly of indigenous people from the state of Chiapas. A regular army that also commemorated, on January 1, 2004, its tenth year since declaring war on the federal government. An army poor in arms but rich in words and rebellion, dignity and resistance, proposals and paradoxes.

Ten years of clandestine life and ten years of public life have gone by. It's easily said, but who would have imagined that on a November day in 1983 a small group of indigenous and mestizo people, hidden away somewhere in the Lacandón Jungle, would formally constitute a regular army that one day would declare war on the government of Mexico and claim their most basic rights? And who would have imagined that that day would arrive exactly when the Free Trade Agreement became the law of the land on January 1, 1994? And who would have thought, as well, that ten years after that warrior dawn and twenty years after its formal founding, the indigenous insurgent army would survive both the government's military power and a major political offensive carried out not only from the seat of power but on more than one occasion by groups that in other circumstances could have been considered allies?

The present text evokes mainly those ten years and tries to place the Zapatista political initiatives, their insistence on a political solution to the war, and the resistance and rebellion of thousands of Chols, Zoques, Tojolabals, Tzotzils, Mams and Tzeltals within that period. It also seeks to place the long list of meetings with national and international civil society that the EZLN held throughout the decade within a strategy that was developed along the way, based on what they call "walking and asking."

The major part of the EZLN's first decade was dedicated to the political struggle, placing priority on building the resistance and organization of thousands of rebel indigenous villages. However, this remarkable political path cannot erase the memory of those first armed combats that took place in San Cristóbal de las Casas, Las Margaritas, Altamirano, Oxchuc, Huixtán, Chanal and Ocosingo. They cannot and should not be forgotten because it wasn't a war of paper, as then–Secretary of Foreign Relations José Angel Gurria would later say, but a war with dead on both sides, an uneven war in which, on the one hand, there were Tzotzils, Tzeltals, Tojolabals, Chols, Mams and Zoques, united for the first time in an insurrection, and on the other, a fully equipped army with high-power rifles, aided by helicopters, tanks and land vehicles; an army—the institutional one—that was caught unaware by an upstart indigenous army that demanded "democracy, freedom and justice" for all Mexicans.

Nor should it be forgotten that the Zapatistas' political path emerged in the context of military, paramilitary and police offensives that to this day continue to confront hundreds of towns in the Selva, Altos, Norte and Costa regions of Chiapas. Their crime: to continue to think that a better world is possible, one world in which many worlds fit.

1994

The armed uprising of the Zapatista Army of
National Liberation: The War

The EZLN achieved a military and political triumph by occupying seven cities in Chiapas during the offensive of January 1, 1994. Their intent, as the Zapatistas later described it, was to deal a very hard initial blow to get people's attention. And it worked. From there on, history would take another turn, and soon the rifles quieted to give way to the word, the main weapon of the Zapatistas.

At dawn on January 1, the EZLN declared war on the "supreme government," headed by Carlos Salinas de Gortari, and the federal army. That same day the Zapatistas announced a political program of ten demands and announced, with the armed takeover of several municipal presidential palaces, their struggle for democracy, liberty and justice for all Mexicans.

In the First Declaration of the Lacandón Jungle, read on January 1, 1994 from the main balcony of each of the municipal buildings taken and distributed through a small and legendary newspaper called *El*

Despertador Mexicano, the EZLN addressed the people of Mexico: "We, free men and women of integrity, are conscious that the war we declared is a measure of last resort, but just. The dictators have been carrying out an undeclared dirty war against our peoples for many years, so we ask your committed participation to support this plan of the Mexican people who struggle for work, land, housing, food, health, education, independence, freedom, democracy, justice and peace. We declare that we will not quit fighting until we achieve fulfillment of these basic demands of our people, forming a free and democratic government of our country." (First Declaration of the Lacandón Jungle, January 1, 1994)

In an editorial in *El Despertador Mexicano*, the Zapatistas explained the motives of the armed uprising: "We have lived hundreds of years asking and believing in promises that never were fulfilled, they always told us to be patient and that we should wait for better times. They recommended prudence; they promised that the future would be different. And we have seen that it's not, everything is the same or worse than when our

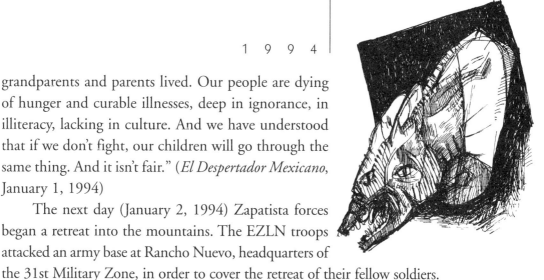

grandparents and parents lived. Our people are dying of hunger and curable illnesses, deep in ignorance, in illiteracy, lacking in culture. And we have understood that if we don't fight, our children will go through the same thing. And it isn't fair." (*El Despertador Mexicano*, January 1, 1994)

The next day (January 2, 1994) Zapatista forces began a retreat into the mountains. The EZLN troops attacked an army base at Rancho Nuevo, headquarters of the 31st Military Zone, in order to cover the retreat of their fellow soldiers.

The worst battles were in the township of Ocosingo, where the indigenous rebels were surrounded for two days by a contingent of 1,000 soldiers that was reinforced by another 2,400 the next day. In the municipal marketplace a group of Zapatistas and civilians was trapped. Shooting was intermittent. "Yes, I was a little scared at first, but then, when you shoot you stop feeling. Yes, it's scary, but it's scarier to go on letting them kill you with hunger and sickness. That's why we fight, to avoid dying," stated Zapatista Lieutenant Amalia, a Tzeltal insurgent who spoke to the press in the rebel community of Prado Payacal.

War, with its quota of horror and death, had set up shop in Mexico. The Mexican Federal Army began establishing roadblocks and shot at a bus filled with Zapatista health workers. Government troops also shot two ambulances of the International Red Cross, leaving two rescue workers wounded. The federal army arrived in San Cristóbal de las Casas, the most important of the seven townships taken, on the afternoon of January 2, 1994, when it became known that General Absalón Castellanos Domínguez—a former governor of Chiapas known for his despotism, corruption and constant repression of the opposition—had been taken as a prisoner of war by the rebels.

Between January 3 and 4, 1994, the soldiers took control of the Ocosingo marketplace. After that day and during the next hours, reporters

from hundreds of communications media arrived and began to count the dead. There were dozens. All the journalists came up with different numbers, but they agreed that the majority were civilians. In the market, photographers and cameramen from the large international news agencies captured the image of five Zapatistas shot at point-blank range with their hands tied behind their backs.

In those same moments, in the township of Altamirano, the Zapatistas carried their wounded to the local hospital, and in San Cristóbal de las Casas more than 3,000 soldiers from the 75th Infantry Battalion regained control of the city.

News of the military aggression soon reached the journalists, and vehicles belonging to reporters working for the Mexican newspaper *La Jornada*, the France Press news agency and the daily paper *El Financiero,* were shot at by the federal army.

Military convoys patrolled the highways, followed by caravans of journalists, and not long after, carloads of representatives from non-governmental organizations. Entry into the zone of conflict was barred, but the press got in by alternative routes. News of the indigenous uprising had spread throughout the world by now and covered the front pages of the main newspapers.

The federal government, which had held its tongue so far, made its first declaration in the voice of a second-level official—Undersecretary of the Interior Socorro Díaz—who read a document famous for its insensitivity and despotism. From that moment on, the Salinas adminstration's communications policy, which up to then had functioned surprisingly well, suffered its first defeats. From there on it would begin to rapidly lose the battle for credibility and legitimacy.

The document from the Secretary of Interior's office deliberately downplayed the magnitude of the conflict: "A delicate situation has presented itself in just four of the 110 municipalities of Chiapas; in the remaining 106 conditions are normal." It also tried to delegitimize it: "The violent groups present a mixture of interests, both national and foreign, and show affinities with other violent Central American factions." And, as so often in the past, it revealed deep prejudices against indigenous people: "Some indigenous peoples have been recruited and without doubt manipulated."

While the battles continued on the outskirts of Ocosingo, Samuel Ruiz García, Bishop of San Cristóbal de las Casas and a key figure in understanding the situation in Chiapas, called for a truce and suspension of hostilities. That same day, planes and helicopters of the Mexican Air Force started bombing the hills south of San Cristóbal de las Casas and in the mountains of the Selva region. The next day, the government's military power was taken by surprise by the scantily equipped Zapatista Army, which shot seven aircraft.

The EZLN's military evaluation of the first five days of the fighting showed the following results: nine Zapatistas dead and twenty badly wounded (not counting the indigenous men executed in Ocosingo). For the federal army, according to the Zapatista report, there were twenty-seven dead, forty wounded and 180 prisoners who surrendered and were later freed. (EZLN communiqué, January 6, 1994)

Likewise, on January 1 and 2, 1994, Zapatista forces freed 230 prisoners who were found in the four military headquarters of the state (two in San Cristóbal de las Casas, one in Ocosingo and one in Las Margaritas.)

The Day of Kings (January 5, 1994) President Salinas gave his first message to the nation. In it, he denied that this was an indigenous uprising and offered pardon to those who laid down their arms. Simultaneously, civil society began to organize with the goal of ending the war and overseeing the actions of the Mexican Federal Army, and more than fifteen civic organizations formed the Association of Civil Organizations for Peace (Conpaz).

So, with widespread civilian support, the EZLN proposed its conditions to establish dialogue with the federal government. In the first of what would be a long series of communiqués as part of a communications strategy with society that would end up being its principal weapon, the EZLN laid out its terms: recognition as a belligerent force, ceasefire on both sides, withdrawal of federal troops, a halt to the bombing, and the formation of a National Commission of Intermediation. (EZLN communiqué, January 6, 1994)

While this was taking place, national and international solidarity with the insurgent movement grew. The most critical questioned the method, but no one, either in the government or in the most reactionary

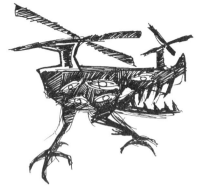

---

sectors, could disqualify the causes. The League of Sovereign Indigenous Nations of the Western Hemisphere, the International Indian Treaty Council and the Washington Center for Peace marched in the capital of the United States, in front of the Mexican embassy, to demand suspension of the "military persecution of the EZLN," and the Spanish party Izquierda Unida demanded an end to repression and the search for a political solution.

Likewise the Canada Action Network carried out a vigil at the Mexican Embassy in Ottawa, while the Mexican Spartacist group, the Independent Democratic Movement, the Popular Defense Committees and the Labor Party demanded an end to the war, respect for human rights, creation of conditions for dialogue and solutions to social demands. In Madrid, the solidarity committee with the Mexican indigenous people held a march to demand an end to hostilities.

The bombings in the Selva and Los Altos continued when Manuel Camacho Solís was named Commissioner for Peace and Reconciliation in Chiapas and the war led to the removal of the first high-level official—the Secretary of Interior and ex-governor of Chiapas, Patrocinio González Garrido, resigned and was replaced by Jorge Carpizo.

From London, Amnesty International condemned the bombings by the federal army against indigenous communities. In Spain, a group of intellectuals, artists and writers emphasized the need to find a political solution to the conflict. The Center for Constitutional Rights, based in Manhattan, denounced the executions and bombings of indigenous peoples.

Not even two weeks had gone by from the start of the uprising when the EZLN began the difficult task of trying to explain its struggle, a struggle being built along the way based on the surprising encounter with civil society, but one that was based on basic principles conceived of before the outbreak of war. In one of the first communiqués, the Zapatistas

111

explained their position on power and electoral processes, the same position they have maintained (and have been explaining) for all these years:
"The EZLN does not seek the victory of one party or another. The
EZLN seeks justice, freedom and democracy so that the people can
choose whoever seems best to them and so that their choice, whatever it
is, receives the respect and understanding of all Mexicans and of people
in other countries. The Zapatista Army of National Liberation asks that
the government, of whatever party it is, be a legitimate government and
the result of a truly free and democratic election, and that it resolve the
most pressing needs of our Mexican people, especially of our indigenous
peoples." (EZLN communiqué, January 11, 1994)

Twelve days after the indigenous insurrection began, a mass demonstration was announced to demand that the president call a ceasefire and
open up dialogue with the indigenous insurgents. National civil society
raised its voice and was heard. Under pressure from the Mexican people,
who demanded a political solution, Salinas took the first step and
decreed a ceasefire hours before the demonstration. "The army will only
attack if attacked," he said, The march was held anyway and more than
100,000 people filled the Zócalo (central plaza) of Mexico City to protest
against the war in southeast Mexico.

However, twenty-four hours after the ceasefire was decreed, military
troops backed up by artillery helicopters attacked a Zapatista unit in
Ocosingo. The war moved to the mountains and the ceasefire only held
in the cities. In spite of this, the EZLN accepted the proposal to end
hostilities.

The EZLN burst onto the national scene that January First, started
the war and found, as its leaders later explained, a different world, a sce-
nario they hadn't contemplated, an unimagined panorama; a world that
understood their causes but that marched and mobilized to quiet the
rifles on both sides. It was a decisive moment in the history of the EZLN.
When the organization faced the decision to listen to civil society, stop

and confront an unknown world for which it was obviously unprepared or, on the other hand, to continue with the armed struggle for which it had prepared for ten long years, it opted for the first and dedicated itself from that moment on to the use of the word as its principal weapon, to listen, to ask, and to try to understand the demands of this civil society that supported it, but that did not follow with a rifle on its shoulder.

February–December

1994

Dialogue in the Cathedral of San Cristóbal de las Casas, the Zapatista delegation returns to the mountains, the National Democratic Convention (NDC), federal and state elections, and breaking out of the military enclosure.

After the ceasefire, events happened one on top of the other. From January 13 to 24, 1994, the EZLN recognized Manuel Camacho Solís as the representative of the federal government. The interim governor of Chiapas resigned and was replaced. Many changes occurred in very few days, but none, as Subcomandante Marcos would explain later, were of great significance.

The Zapatista spokesperson replied to the pardon offered by President Salinas de Gortari with a text titled "What Will We Be Pardoned For?" deemed by intellectuals a magnificent and unanswerable statement of the reasons for the Zapatista movement. "What do we have to ask pardon for? What will they pardon us for? For not dying of hunger? For not remaining silent in our misery? For not having accepted humbly the gigantic historic load of hatred and abandonment? For having risen up in arms when we found that all other roads closed off? For not having followed the Penal Code of Chiapas, the most absurd and repressive of our times? For having demonstrated to the rest of the country and the world that human dignity still lives and is present in its poorest inhabitants? For having prepared willfully and consciously before setting forth? For having taken rifles to combat instead of bows and arrows? For having learned to fight before we did it? For being Mexicans, all of us? For being mostly indigenous? For calling the Mexican people to fight, in all possible ways, for what belongs to them? For struggling for freedom, democracy, and justice? For not following the patterns of previous guerrilla wars? For not giving up? For not selling out? For not betraying the cause? . . . Who needs to ask for pardon and who can give it? . . ." (EZLN communiqué, January 18, 1994)

One of the first actions of the commissioner Manuel Camacho was the establishment of "two open zones": San Miguel in Ocosingo and Guadalupe Tepeyac in Las Margaritas. But none of these actions prevented the social effervescence in Chiapas, as thousands of peasants mobilized to demand the removal from office of several town mayors and the delivery of lands. In this context, the State Council of Peasant and Indigenous Organizations was formed (CEOIC, by its Spanish initials), which united 280 organizations in Chiapas.

They were days in which the Zapatistas, in the middle of a war that wasn't over (even with the ceasefire decreed), established positions, defined strategies and broadened contacts. So on January 20, 1994, they addressed for the first time the indigenous organizations of the country in a communiqué that ten years later continued to define their relationship with the national Indian movement: "We, the Zapatistas, have always respected and will continue to respect the different independent and honest organizations. We have not obliged them to join our struggle; when they have, it has always been of their own free will. . . If we had not risen up with our guns, the government would never have cared anything about the indigenous people of our lands. . . We will continue to respect you and respect your forms of struggle. We invite you, each one in his or

116

her organization with their different ways of fighting back, to join our hearts with the same hope of freedom, democracy, and justice." (EZLN communiqué, January 20, 1994)

The dialogue was drawing near and an indication that the pre-negotiations were going well was the liberation of General Absalón Castellanos Domínguez in exchange for the federal government liberating hundreds of indigenous Zapatistas detained and tortured in state jails. The ceremony of delivery of the retired military man served to mark the first public presentation of an entire rebel village: Guadalupe Tepeyac, the same one that over the years would become a symbol of indigenous resistance.

The act of freeing the former governor of Chiapas was not only the exchange of a cruel and heartless prisoner of war for hundreds of jailed indigenous Zapatistas. It was also the ethical debut of an insurgent movement that instead of sacrificing the ex-governor accused of various assassinations, condemned him to carry the forgiveness of those whom he had despised, humiliated and exploited over so many years.

With the participation of the Bishop Samuel Ruiz García as mediator, it was agreed that the dialogue between the rebels and the governmental commissioner would begin on February 20, 1994. So nineteen delegates of the EZLN arrived in San Cristóbal de las Casas on board an International Red Cross ambulance to participate in the dialogue. They were eighteen indigenous people and one mestizo who directed them militarily but took political orders from the indigenous command, a man who caught the attention of the press to explain the reasons for the struggle and who introduced himself with the name of Subcomandante Insurgente Marcos. The dialogue of San Cristóbal was a key moment in the Zapatista struggle. It was an encounter directly with the press, with national and international civil society, and with the political class that it rose up in arms to fight.

Comandante Tacho of the Clandestine Revolutionary Indigenous

Committee (CCRI) explained later that the dialogue "served to let people get to know us and for us to get to know many people. It served to explain to them who we were and why we were fighting." The EZLN took advantage of the occasion to do interviews with hundreds of accredited journalists from all over the world and to make contact with representatives of NGOs, the church, political parties, rural organizations and with regular people from civil society. It was the beginning of the political learning process of the armed movement, the beginning of a series of encounters and mis-encounters, the beginning of the construction of a movement that would be characterized by knowing (and learning) how to listen, to have its say, to ask and to walk together.

On March 2, 1994, the peace conversations concluded with the presentation of a document containing thirty-four governmental commitments that the EZLN agreed to take to consultation. When the round of negotiations ended, the Zapatistas returned to the mountains and continued their meetings with representatives of civil society and with a broad spectrum of political forces in the country. Media representatives entered rebel territory at the invitation of the Zapatista leadership, and reports on the Zapatista indigenous communities were sent around the world.

The consultations in the villages on the government's proposals began in the Lacandón Jungle, but the process was interrupted on March 23, 1994, with the assassination of the presidential candidate of the Institutional Revolutionary Party, Luis Donaldo Colosio.

On April 10, 1994, the Zapatistas commemorated the anniversary of the death of the revolutionary Emiliano Zapata. All month long, aid caravans from all over arrived in rebel territory, while cattle ranchers and plantation owners intensified hostilities against indigenous communities.

A month later, the first meeting between the EZLN and Cuauhtémoc Cárdenas, then–presidential candidate of the Party of the Democratic Revolution (PRD), took place. Cárdenas was a major political figure with whom the Zapatistas would have a relationship of constant

agreements and differences. At the time, the rebels were in a process of reassessing the national political panorama by holding countless meetings with representatives of nearly every position on the left political spectrum.

Just six months after the uprising, the Zapatistas had already formed a movement not only around the demands of indigenous peoples, but against governmental authoritarianism and its social and economic policies. In this context, they responded with a "NO" to the government's proposals, while deciding to maintain the ceasefire and open up dialogue with civil society. The strategy of opening up alternative dialogues and meetings with civil society, to listen and ask, independently of the negotiation process with the federal government, would come to characterize its political strategy over the following years. To learn to talk and listen, to walk asking questions, would be the key.

At the same time as the negotiations with the government were breaking off, the Zapatistas published the Second Declaration of the Lacandón Jungle, in which they called on society to bring about a peaceful transition to democracy through the organization of the National Democratic

Convention (NDC). The objective, they explained, was "to organize civil expression and defense of the people's voice. . . and demand that free and democratic elections be held, and to struggle tirelessly for the respect of the popular will." (Second Declaration of the Lacandón Jungle, June 12, 1994.)

While the meeting was being organized in a village in the Lacandón Jungle, Manuel Camacho resigned as Peace Commissioner in Chiapas, leaving his place to Jorge Madrazo, a man who left no mark in his passage through the state, did not achieve a single agreement with the rebels and left as he arrived—with empty hands.

The National Democratic Convention was held from August 5 to 9, 1994, in the midst of the presidential electoral campaign. It was held in the first political and cultural meeting place designed by the EZLN, named "Aguascalientes" in reference to the place where the convention of the revolutionary forces of Mexico was held in 1914, the town of Guadalupe Tepeyac. There were close to 7,000 Mexicans, among them representatives of grassroots organizations, artists, intellectuals, indigenous people from all over the country, workers, homosexuals, peasants and Zapatistas, who called on civil society to defeat the armed option, to defeat themselves as a military force, and to open up the possibility of continuing to fight but not with weapons and with their faces uncovered. The National Democratic Convention was the first large-scale political action after the war, in which the EZLN could measure its capacity to call people together with results that they later confessed exceeded their own expectations.

The indigenous rebels took only twenty-seven days to build the first "Aguascalientes." They were days of collective work and hope, days in which from the other side of the jungle, thousands of people organized to participate in the first voyage of a boat, the *Fitzcarraldo*, replete with paradoxes. "The paradoxical anachronism, the sweet insanity of the faceless, the crazy purpose of a civil movement in dialogue with an armed movement." (Inaugural speech to the NDC, August 8, 1994)

Days after the National Democratic Convention, the EZLN declared

that it would not interfere in federal or state elections, and would allow the installation of polling places and the free transit of personnel from the Federal Electoral Institute, the State Electoral Commission and representatives of political parties. In this way, and for the first time in the modern history of the country, elections were held in territory declared openly to be in rebellion.

On August 21, 1994, federal and state elections in Chiapas were held. An election marked by fraud declared the ruling party candidate, Ernesto Zedillo, the winner, while the PRI candidate for governor, Eduardo Robledo Rincón, was proclaimed winner in the midst of protests and accusations of fraud. One month after the elections, the PRD candidate for governor of Chiapas, Amado Avendaño Figueroa, survived an assassination attempt against him.

During the following weeks various acts of civil resistance and post-electoral conflict occurred in the state, adding tension to the military scene. In this atmosphere, the National Democratic Convention was convened a second time without reaching concrete proposals.

In this context, the EZLN announced its interpretation of the electoral process: "It is not possible to end the ruling party system with the same arms that sustain it and support it in public opinion. As long as the organization of elections remains in the hands of the State party, any attempt to challenge it will end in frustration and political paralysis or cynical defeat. A government of transition, on the other hand is necessary for democracy. For this, calls for the formation of a broad opposition front that unites all the millions of Mexicans who are against the system of the State party are viewed with hope." (EZLN essay, "The Long Road from Pain to Hope," September 22, 1994)

In late September another assassination occurred within the upper echelons of Mexican power. The victim was the secretary general of the Institutional Revolutionary Party, José Francisco Ruiz Massieu.

Afterward in the context of the twenty-sixth anniversary of the student massacres of October 2, the Zapatistas continued their discussion with civil society through a message sent to the demonstration to commemorate the event held in Mexico City: "You brothers and sisters, the students, workers, urban movement, peasants, housewives, employees, honest artists and intellectuals, men and women who twenty-six years ago participated in one of the most important movements of this painful century, know what it is to fight against lies and calumnies, your children know, the men and women who after 1968 struggled and struggle against the system of injustice. Today, as twenty-six years ago, the Mexican who does not accept handouts, who does not accept oppression, who has dignity, who rebels, who struggles, is suspected of not being a Mexican and is called a foreigner." (EZLN communiqué, October 2, 1994)

Six days later, on October 8, the EZLN officially broke off dialogue with the federal government, so as "to avoid being an accomplice to the deceit of the Salinas de Gortari government, to not endorse the culture of political crime that now characterizes the current adminstration, to reaffirm its commitment with the struggle against fraud and imposition. . ." (EZLN communiqué, October 8, 1994.)

On November 18, in the "Aguascalientes" of Guadalupe Tepeyac, the Zapatistas celebrated their anniversary in public for the first time. The press and civil society attended the festivities of the eleventh birthday of the EZLN. Through Subcomandante Marcos, they spoke publicly for the first time about the mistakes they had made: "For our part as the Zapatista Army of National Liberation we can say that we have made many mistakes. Some of them are the product of our political clumsiness, our ignorance, and the limitations of our armed struggle, faceless and besieged. . . Our word has not been, many times, the most correct or timely."

And so in the midst of the insurgents' dances, poems and plays, the EZLN announced its plan: "Today, as in 1993, when we prepared to go to war, as in 1992 when we decided to do it, as in 1984 when we cele-

122

brated our first year, as in 1983 when we began to wake up to hope, the Zapatista plan is the same: to change the world, to make it better, more fair, freer, more democratic, that is, more human." (EZLN communiqué, November 17, 1994)

On the First of December, Ernesto Zedillo took office as the president of the republic. The EZLN issued a communiqué titled "Welcome to the nightmare." "You all should disappear, not only for representing a historical aberration, a human negation and a cynical cruelty; you should disappear also because you are an insult to the intelligence. You made us possible, you made us grow. We are your other, your Siamese opposite. To make us disappear, you must disappear." (EZLN communiqué, December 1, 1994)

Amado Avendaño assumed his post as governor-in-rebellion of the state of Chiapas, and the Zapatistas recognized him in a ceremony full of indigenous rites in which, in the plaza of the governmental palace in Tuxtla Gutiérrez, they gave him the ruling staff—the symbol of indigenous government.

To finalize the year, on December 19, 1994, one day after the huge devaluation of the Mexican peso (a result of the economic ineptness of the new government and capital flight that led to an unprecedented economic crisis), the indigenous rebels, without firing a single shot, launched a new political offensive to break out of the military blockade around them. They appeared in thirty townships of the state, and declared them autonomous and rebel municipalities. Thus began a long process for recognition of autonomy. In this atmosphere, and faced with the imminent renewal of hostilities, Bishop Samuel Ruiz initiated a fast, and several days later the government recognized the National Mediation Commission (Conai) as the mediating body for the dialogue.

123

1995

The third Declaration of the Lacandón Jungle.
The government offensive of February 9.
The dialogue of San Andrés Sacamch'en de los
Pobres and the national and international
Zapatista mobilization.

Thousands of Zapatista base communities, accompanied by hundreds of journalists and people from civil society, ushered in the new year of 1995 in the "Aguascalientes" of Guadalupe Tepeyac. There, amid songs, poems and dances, EZLN support communities and the insurgents celebrated the first year of the insurrection that announced their struggle to the world. At the "happiness" (the term indigenous people use for their parties) the EZLN released the Third Declaration of the Lacandón Jungle, in which it proposed to civil society the creation of the National Liberation Movement (MLN, by its Spanish initials).

This new attempt to unite diverse social and political forces in a broad oppositional front put forth the objective of struggling "by all means and at all levels, for the establishment of a government of transition, a new constituent assembly, a new Magna Carta and the destruction of the ruling party system."(Third Declaration the Lacandón Jungle, January 1, 1995) They extended the call to join the front to the

National Democratic Convention and to Cuauhtémoc Cárdenas Solórzano.

In mid-January 1995 a meeting was held that would mark the events of the following months. Subcomandante Marcos and members of the CCRI met with then-Secretary of the Interior Esteban Moctezuma Barragán, in the Aguascalientes of Guadalupe Tepeyac. Moctezuma and Undersecretary Beatriz Paredes arrived on board an enormous helicopter. Everything looked like it was going well since, as a result of the meeting, the EZLN declared an indefinite ceasefire of all offensive and unilateral actions. Days later the rebel leadership met for the third time with Cuauhtémoc Cárdenas Solórzano.

The days that followed were uncertain. On February 2–4, 1995, the National Democratic Convention held session in the state of Querétaro, to follow up on the Third Declaration of the Lacandón Jungle and build the Movement for National Liberation, an objective that looked difficult given the clear differences between the different factions and organizations on the left. The meeting received veiled threats from President Zedillo, who was in Querétaro to celebrate another anniversary of the Constitution.

On February 9, 1995, the government betrayed the peace process. In the middle of negotiations to reinitiate dialogue, President Zedillo announced on national television the supposed identification of Zapatista leaders and ordered their arrest. The Mexican Federal Army stationed in Chiapas initiated a military offensive against the insurgent base communities.

That morning, two journalists held a meeting with Subcomandante Marcos, who, visibly worried, already suspected the government's plans. "Tell them that we are going to win," were the words of farewell. The atmosphere was charged, but the Zapatista leader still did not imagine that by this time the Federal Attorney General's Office had already detained the activist Elisa Benavides in Mexico City, accusing her of being "Comandante

126

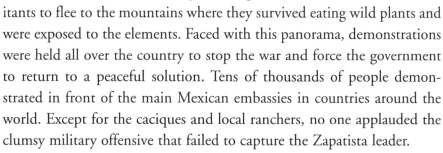

Elisa"; the army was preparing to invade the communities in resistance, and hours later, the government would detain the historian and activist Javier Elorriaga and Jorge Santiago, accusing them of being EZLN leaders.

During the following days the federal army advanced into the rebel territory in the Selva and Los Altos regions. On its way through the communities it destroyed rudimentary houses, stole work tools, broke water hoses into pieces, burned clothing and made off with livestock, causing the indigenous inhabitants to flee to the mountains where they survived eating wild plants and were exposed to the elements. Faced with this panorama, demonstrations were held all over the country to stop the war and force the government to return to a peaceful solution. Tens of thousands of people demonstrated in front of the main Mexican embassies in countries around the world. Except for the caciques and local ranchers, no one applauded the clumsy military offensive that failed to capture the Zapatista leader.

The imposed governor, Eduardo Robledo, resigned from his post, while the Conai issued an urgent call to all involved to resume dialogue. The Zapatistas conditioned a return to negotiations on the withdrawal of the Mexican Army from indigenous communities and the cancellation of arrest orders. Detentions, skirmishes, assassinations, rapes, looting of whole villages, presumed Zapatistas detained and tortured in Toluca, Mexico State and Yanga, Veracruz, and more than 30,000 people displaced—all of this occurred as a result of the offensive.

Dozens of reporters arrived in the mountains where hundreds of women and children survived under the cover of trees, eating plants and without water, but determined and furious at the betrayal, with no intention of surrendering or accepting the government's conditions. "It's sad but that's how the struggle is and we're going to keep right on. . . We don't want anything from the government, just that they get their armies [the indigenous expression for soldiers] out of our villages because we don't want them, nobody wants them," said Verónica, a young Tojolabal who, along with her sisters, was ripping plants from the ground in order to eat.

On March 11, 1995, the Mexican Congress discussed and approved the Law for Dialogue, Conciliation and Dignified Peace in Chiapas and created the Commission for Concordance and Pacification (Cocopa) made up of deputies and senators from across the political spectrum. In the following days, the EZLN publicized the situation in the Zapatista communities, thanked civil society for mobilizing and reiterated its commitment to move toward a negotiated settlement.

Shortly thereafter, it was announced that following an exchange of letters, the government and the EZLN had agreed that the seat of the first meeting would be in the rebel village of San Miguel in Ocosingo. Two days later, the EZLN and the government signed the Joint Declaration of San Miguel and the Protocol for the Basis of the Dialogue, and agreed to meet in the township of San Andrés Sacamch'en de los Pobres, named from that moment on as the permanent seat of dialogue and negotiation.

On March 20, 1995, the day scheduled for the resumption of the negotiations, the meeting was suspended between Zapatistas and government officials due to the presence of thousands of indigenous supporters of the EZLN, who showed up to accompany their delegates. The government orchestrated a media campaign to argue that the dialogue could not begin because the indigenous supporters were armed. Although nobody detected any weapons, the next day the Zapatistas thanked the mobilization and as a sign of good faith, asked the members of their base communities to return home. But the demonstration of strength was not lost on the hundreds of journalists who testified to the endless parade of thousands of Tzotzil men, women and children who showed up to support their representatives.

The new dialogue began formally and in it they discussed as the first point the measures for relaxing the military tension. There were three rounds

128

of negotiations in which the same point was discussed without arriving at any agreements, but meanwhile the EZLN prepared another political move: national and international consultations with the purpose of gauging society's opinion on the Zapatista demands and whether or not to create an opposition front.

In the midst of the consultation and the government's persecution of foreign priests committed to the cause of the indigenous peoples (three foreign priests were expelled from the San Cristóbal diocese), the fifth phase of the San Andrés dialogue began in which no agreements were reached on the issue of military stand-down.

On August 27, 1995, the National Consultation for Peace and Democracy was held throughout the country and more than 5,000 promoters helped organize and install more than 10,000 polling tables. The vast majority of the 1,088,000 Mexicans who participated responded affirmatively to the question of whether the EZLN should become a new kind of political force. Moreover, in the international consultation some 100,000 foreigners from fifty countries participated. This was the first mobilization called by the Zapatistas, and it gathered thousands of people from Mexico and other parts of the world. It was, moreover, the beginning of a series of international relations that would sustain the indigenous rebels.

Five months after the renewal of talks, during the sixth round of negotiations in September, finally the working groups and procedures were agreed on: 1. Indigenous Rights and Culture; 2. Democracy and Justice; 3. Well-being and Development; 4. Conciliation in Chiapas; 5. Women's Rights in Chiapas; and 6. End of Hostilities.

From there on in, the Zapatistas' agenda broadened. They respond to the results of the consultation with a proposal to organize a dialogue without the government, and so they issued an international call to hold what they called the First Intercontinental Encounter for Humanity and against Neoliberalism. In the process of negotiations with the government, they agreed to organize a Special Forum on the Rights of Indigenous Peoples, another on Reform of the State, and one more on women's issues. The message of the Zapatistas was clear. Comandante David explained it this way: "We do not want only our word to be heard in the dialogue. We want the voices of all the men and women who struggle like us to be heard."

And so the Zapatista strategy of dialogue included the participation of all possible voices. The Clandestine Revolutionary Indigenous Committee (CCRI) dealt another political blow by announcing that it would invite more than 100 advisers—among them indigenous leaders, anthropologists, historians, intellectuals and representatives of diverse social and political organizations—to participate with them in the San Andrés negotiations. Thus was inaugurated a new form of negotiating with power, an inclusive form that replaced the "give and take" and the model of "customer service window" in which a group presents a list of demands to negotiate and power says yes or no.

The atmosphere of calm didn't last long since with the dialogue apparently on track, the government struck again at the Zapatistas with the detention on October 23, 1995, of Fernando Yáñez Muñoz, accused of being the EZLN's "Comandante Germán." This would be a recurring theme of the negotiations: when it looked like everything was going well, some new blow by the government would interrupt the process. Faced with this situation, the rebels declared a red alert, until two days later when the architect Yáñez—a committed, longtime activist—was freed by the Attorney General's Office of the Republic.

The talks started up again in November and the following month the atmosphere got tense again with the Zapatista announcement to build four new "Aguascalientes" (political and cultural meeting places) in the Selva, Norte and Los Altos regions of Chiapas to celebrate the second anniversary of the uprising, The government took these measures as armed actions and threatened to occupy the meetings places. Once gain, open hostilities came close to breaking out since the Zapatistas refused to destroy the Aguascalientes and their base communities, unarmed, defended the centers. On December 14, 1995, after suspending a meeting between the Conai and the EZLN due to the military patrols, the Cocopa and the EZLN signed the call to hold the Special Forum on Indigenous rights. The atmosphere relaxed some and they arrived at an agreement to celebrate the second anniversary. And so the Zapatistas celebrated   the second year of the armed uprising with festivities and dancing.

1996

The Fourth Declaration of the Lacandón Jungle and the call to found the FZLN. First accords on Indigenous Rights and Culture. Paramilitary offensives. Noncompliance with the accords, suspension of dialogue, and the first Zapatista trip from the jungle to Mexico City.

On January 1, 1996, the Zapatista Army of National Liberation released the Fourth Declaration of the Lacandón Jungle. The Declaration was released simultaneously from the five Aguascalientes, which, having survived intensive military attempts to destroy them, were inaugurated this same day. The Declaration reaffirmed the EZLN's commitment to a peaceful solution and proposed the construction of the Zapatista Front for National Liberation (FZLN), a new kind of nonpartisan political force that did not seek to take power but was an independent, autonomous, civic and nonviolent organization, based in the EZLN. The Zapatistas announced their intention to join the FZLN after negotiations.

"We invite national civil society without party affiliations, social and citizen movements, all Mexicans, to build a new political force. . . A new political force whose members do not hold or aspire to hold public office or government posts at any level. A political force that does not seek to take power. A political force that is not a political party. . . A new political force

133

that can organize the demands and protests of the citizens so that the rulers rule by obeying. A political force that can find solutions to collective problems without the intervention of political parties or the government. We do not need to ask permission to be free. The function of government is the prerogative of the society and it is its right to exercise that function. . ." (Fourth Declaration of the Lacandón Jungle, January 1, 1996.)

In spite of the recent military assaults, in the five EZLN Aguascalientes members of civil society and the Zapatista base communities listened to the taped announcement of the Fourth Declaration in a festive atmosphere. A broad debate ensued. Columnists and editorialists from all the newspapers poured out criticism or praise for the new rebel initiative. The questioning of political parties, the decision not to try to take power, the construction of a new kind of political force based on "ruling by obeying" were, among others, the points most heatedly discussed by the political class and at the same time the most understood by a civil society disenchanted with the political parties and elections.

As this new political force entered the early stages of construction, during the first days of January 1996 the EZLN began work on the Special National Forum on Indigenous Rights and Culture, in which more than 500 representatives from at least thirty-five Indian peoples discussed and arrived at consensus on their demands. Indigenous autonomy, they agreed, would be the guiding principle of their efforts to build a new relationship between indigenous peoples and the state. On January 7, 1996, Subcomandante Marcos arrived unexpectedly in San Cristóbal de las Casas to participate in the forum. At the end of this first meeting of the Zapatistas with a wide range of national indigenous organizations, the participants agreed to call for the founding of the National Indigenous Congress (CNI, by its Spanish initials).

"This National Indigenous Forum can be an example that we don't have to ask for permission to think of ourselves as free, just and democratic. We are not asking them to forget their differences and debates; we

134

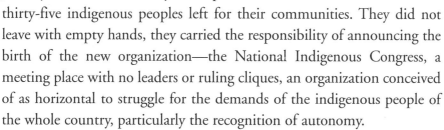

are not asking that they adhere to another way of thinking. We ask that they have respect and tolerance for those who think differently along the way but have the same desire for life. . . We ask that together, we give this country and this world that offer us only death or humiliation as a future, a lesson: the lesson of human dignity that saves the world from stupidity and crime." (Speech at the inauguration of the National Indigenous Forum. January 4, 1996)

Subcomandante Marcos concluded the forum on January 8 and the next day the representatives of the thirty-five indigenous peoples left for their communities. They did not leave with empty hands, they carried the responsibility of announcing the birth of the new organization—the National Indigenous Congress, a meeting place with no leaders or ruling cliques, an organization conceived of as horizontal to struggle for the demands of the indigenous people of the whole country, particularly the recognition of autonomy.

The Zapatista strategy of building spaces for participating and meeting not only among indigenous organizations but also on the international level, had now been outlined but not yet filled in. During the following days this strategy advanced considerably. On January 30, 1996, the EZLN announced the First Declaration of La Realidad against Neoliberalism and for Humanity, in which it called for Continental Encounters and later the First Intercontinental Encounter for Humanity and against Neoliberalism.

Based on the outpouring of international support they received after the war began on January 1, 1994, the Zapatistas began to organize solidarity with their movement during the First Consultation held in August of 1995. The event corroborated the major influence and scope of their message with people in other parts of the world. In January of 1996 they launched the second international initiative for a cause that was at once specific and global: "Against the internationalization of terror that neoliberal-

ism represents we should develop an internationalization of hope. Unity that transcends borders, languages, colors, cultures, sexes, strategies and thoughts; of all those who want humanity to live." (First Declaration of La Realidad against Neoliberalism and for Humanity, January 30, 1996)

The Zapatistas called for "all individuals, groups, collectives, movements, social organizations, citizens and politicians, unions, neighborhood associations, cooperatives, all the left that has been and will be, nongovernmental organizations, solidarity groups, bands, tribes, intellectuals, indigenous peoples, students, musicians, workers, artists, farmers, cultural groups, youth movements, alternative media, ecologists, popular urban movements, lesbians, homosexuals, pacifists, feminists. . . all human beings who are homeless, landless, out of a job, hungry, sick, without education, without liberty, without justice, without independence, without democracy, without peace, without a homeland, without a tomorrow. . . to participate in the First Intercontinental Encounter for Humanity and against Neoliberalism."

So they entered the long process of struggle against globalization and the formation of an international movement that would produce some big surprises in the years to come.

On February 10, 1996, the Zapatista base communities held a march to mark the first anniversary of the military occupation of their communities, the first anniversary of the expulsion of the indigenous inhabitants of Guadalupe Tepeyac, and of the arrest of the political prisoners accused of being Zapatistas. The march of thousands of men, women and children with their faces covered, started off in the old village of Guadalupe Tepeyac, now occupied by the army, and ended in La Realidad with a cultural celebration in the Aguascalientes. The reason for the celebration? "It's just that we're alive," said the men and women between dances and songs. Freedom for the political prisoners and a halt to military harassment constituted the major demands, and the indigenous people of Chiapas called, once again, for Mexicans to come out and demonstrate.

Meanwhile in the dialogue with the government, on February 15, 1996, the General Command of the EZLN presented a document written in collaboration with a broad group of advisers, "The Dialogue of San Andrés on Indigenous Rights and Culture: The end of one phase and the beginning of another," in which they announced the end of the first phase of the negotiations while making it clear that the fundamental demands of the indigenous peoples had not been completely fulfilled, and therefore the fight for meeting the demands would continue.

The document warned that the accords did not cover the serious nationwide problem of agrarian reform, nor the reform of Article 27 of the Mexican Constitution. They noted that the minimum commitments between the EZLN and the federal government left out municipal and regional autonomies and that, among other omissions, was the need for a sweeping transformation of the judicial system to guarantee not only individual rights but also the collective rights of indigenous peoples. The document listed issues still pending: a real solution to the problems of indigenous

137

women, access of indigenous people to the media and the full exercise of self-government. (Document of the EZLN and advisers, "The Dialogue of San Andrés and Indigenous Rights and Culture," February 15, 1996)

Finally, on February 16, 1996, after ten months of work and a long series of meetings and conflicts, of tensions and pressures, of persecutions and harassment, the EZLN and the federal government signed the first peace accords, on the first round of negotiations on Indigenous Rights and Culture. In these agreements the government promised to recognize the right to autonomy of Indian peoples in the Constitution, to broaden their political representation, to guarantee full access to the justice system, and to build a new legal framework that guaranteed political rights, legal rights and cultural rights. The government promised also to recognize indigenous people as subjects of public rights. It seemed like things were going well—the Zapatistas stated that although the accords represented just a part of the rights of Indian peoples, they had decided to sign them and promised to fight for full compliance.

There was no formal signing ceremony for the first accords since the Zapatista delegation headed by Comandantes Tacho, David and Zebedeo noted that, for the time being, they were just paper and the important thing would be compliance. Time would tell. So each delegation signed separately.

The negotiations on the second issue, Democracy and Justice, began under a dark cloud. Just as the EZLN presented their list of advisers and guests made up of more than 300 people from diverse political affiliations, prospects dimmed when the paramilitary group "Peace and Justice" destroyed a Catholic temple in the township of Tila.

In spite of this, the Zapatistas continued to attend to other areas, the forums where real dialogue was going on. On March 3, 1996, they held the Second National Meeting of Civil Committees for National Dialogue in Poza Rica, Veracruz. The Special Organizing Commission of the Zapatista Front for National Liberation (FZLN) was formed and spearheaded the formation of civic committees for dialogue as a basic structure for citizen participation in the new Zapatista political force—the FZLN.

Simultaneously, the rebels continued their work on indigenous issues, sending a proposal to form an Organizing Commission of the Permanent National Indigenous Forum charged with organizing the National Indigenous Congress. The guiding principles of the Organizing Commission that would later be adopted by the CNI were: to serve and be served, to represent and not supplant, to build and not destroy, to obey and not rule, to propose and not impose, to convince and not overcome, and to lower oneself not strive to be on top.

The Zapatistas promoted the organization of the FZLN, of the CNI and of the international meetings against neoliberalism while at the same time they continued the dialogue with the government, as well as attending to their own internal organization and mobilization. On March 8, 1996, women members of the Zapatista base communities took the city of San Cristóbal de las Casas in a unprecedented demonstration in which the voices of insurgent indigenous women were again heard. The streets filled with thousands of women wearing face masks and multicolored dresses, many carrying children on their backs or in their arms, with signs and slogans, cries, songs and dances. That's how the rebel women commemorated International Women's Day.

"Zapatista women, the combatants and the noncombatants, struggle for their own rights as women. They face a macho culture that Zapatista men manifest in many ways. Women Zapatistas are not free just by being Zapatista, they still have to fight for more and have much more to gain," said the indigenous women, as they greeted women in struggle from all over the world. (EZLN speech, March 8, 1996)

In addition to organizing the women's march, in March the rebels gave their economic support to buy petrochemicals, held a dialogue with cartoonists, endorsed the protest of the citizens of Tepoztlán, Morelos, who were opposing the construction of a golf course in their town, and

asked the United States and Europe to cease selling arms to Mexico.

Despite the increase in repression and forced relocation by the government, negotiations continued with the federal government, and in the middle of them, police carried out another raid this time in the township of Nicolás Ruiz, in which four peasants were killed. The new massacre of indigenous inhabitants created tension in the atmosphere of the recently installed negotiations round and the dialogue entered into crisis again.

As if that weren't enough, in the negotiations the government representatives remained totally silent. It turned out that they did not go to engage in real dialogue or to listen, but only to be present. Not only the Zapatistas but all the participants noted that their attitude showed a lack of commitment to the peace process.

However, keeping to the strategy of opening up various channels for dialogue, on April 4–8, 1996, the First Continental Encounter for Humanity and Against Neoliberalism was held in La Realidad, in the township of San Pedro de Michoacán. For the first time, thousands of participants from throughout the Americas gathered to discuss proposals to confront neoliberal polices imposed throughout the world.

Men and women from Canada, the United States, Mexico, Guatemala, Costa Rica, Venezuela, Puerto Rico, Brazil, Peru, Chile, Uruguay and Argentina, along with observers from France, Germany and Spain, met in the Tojolabal community of La Realidad to prepare what would be in August the First Intercontinental Encounter for Humanity and against Neoliberalism, better know as "the Intergalactic."

"The powers that be will try to stop other meetings like the one in La Realidad. And we should defend this dream, carry it carefully in our pants pockets and take it out once in a while to stroke it and encourage it," were the prophetic words of the closing speech. (EZLN speech, April 7, 1996)

On the next two commemorative dates—April 10, the anniversary of the death of General Emiliano Zapata, and May 1, International Workers' Day—the EZLN sent messages of support to the demonstrations that took place in Mexico City.

The dialogue with the federal government continued without advancing. Then on May 3, 1996 a judge in Tuxtla Gutiérrez, the capital of the state of Chiapas, sentenced activists Javier Elorriaga and Sebastián Entzin to thirteen and six years in prison respectively on charges of conspiracy, rebellion and terrorism. The EZLN immediately declared that the sentence signified that for the government, the Zapatista were terrorists and dangerous delinquents that should be behind bars or killed. The judge's decision, they said, was a direct provocation to peace and a violation of the law for the dialogue. They decided to suspend their participation in negotiations in which they were the only ones talking and making proposals.

"The dialogue between the EZLN and the federal government has been dealt a decisive blow with this decision. . . The only future the government is offering us at the end of the dialogue and negotiations process is prison and death. All the efforts at dialogue and peaceful struggle that the EZLN has undertaken since its public appearance in January of 1994 and that we have repeatedly called on the Mexican people to uphold have been condemned along with the alleged Zapatistas," declared the EZLN General Command in a communiqué dated May 5, 1996.

In a long letter to the legislators of the Commission on Concordance and Pacification (Cocopa) dated May 18, 1996, the EZLN was firm: "Whether the alleged Zapatistas are free or in prison, the dialogue of San Andrés is impossible if the EZLN is defined as a terrorist organization by any state, federal or local authority."

The atmosphere grew tense again and to make matters worse the paramilitary group "Los Chinchulines" from the township of Chilón committed an armed attack on a group of peasants from Bachajón and lit several houses on fire. The National Human Rights Commission asked the governor of Chiapas to investigate but there was no response. Days later, another attack was carried out, this time by the paramilitary group "Paz y Justicia" in the community of Usipá in the township of Tila.

Paramilitary forces, trained by the federal army, burned down houses, temples, schools and assassinated men and women members of EZLN base communities with complete impunity. That was the atmosphere when the Court appealed the judge's decision and, under intense national and international pressure, Javier Elorriaga and Sebastián Entzin were released. The EZLN responded by lifting the state of alert, and days later Elorriaga, a historian and social activist, joined the FZLN.

By early June the Cocopa had reestablished direct contact with the rebels, in the view of resuming the dialogue. However, right when negotiations between the EZLN and the federal government were about to start up again, the Popular Revolutionary Army (EPR, by its Spanish initials) made its appearance in the state of Guerrero. The EPR, an armed guerrilla group that had formed out of a coalition of several revolutionary forces, appeared on June 23, 1996—a year after the massacre of seventeen farmers in Aguas Blancas, Guerrero. Its emergence complicated the scene in the country.

In an atmosphere of tension, the Zapatistas declared that they were not associated with the new movement and they were able to hold the Special Forum on Reform of the State, the second of the meetings agreed on in the negotiations. More than 1,300 persons participated, among them representatives of political, social, labor and citizen organizations, as well as intellectuals and figures from the political and cultural arenas.

The Special Forum on Reform of the State was held on June 30, 1996, in San Cristóbal de las Casas and formed part of the tasks surrounding the second round of negotiations on Democracy and Justice. An EZLN delegation made up of a group of commanders from all the rebel regions and Subcomandante Marcos participated. The forum was a success, since it brought together a broad and diverse group across the political spectrum that proposed designing a new national project.

In the forum, again the Zapatistas offered more questions than answers: "How many guerrilla groups have to appear, and where, to get society and the government to recognize that there are states in the country that are being run as if we were still back in the plantation age of the dictator Porfirio Díaz? How much political and economic instability is necessary to remember that the closed-door politics of power represented by Porfirio Díaz led to the bloodiest war Mexicans have had in their history? How many deaths, how much destruction, how many jails, how much impotence, how many political assassinations, how many criminals allowed to take refuge in Ireland or Manhattan, how much economic security? How many drug-dealing governors? How much of the country destroyed? How much is needed to recognize that something is not working, that something is rotten, and that something is definitely dying in the Mexican political system?" (ELZN speech, June 30, 1996)

During the weeks that followed, the federal government decided to take advantage of the Zapatista clarification that it wasn't associated with

143

the EPR by carrying out a campaign to distinguish between the "good guerrilla" (the EZLN) and the "bad guerrilla" (the EPR). The rebels in Chiapas denounced this strategy and without falling into the trap, continued their political meetings and dialogue with civil society.

In July, the Zapatistas increased their meetings with civil society, but this time on the international level. From July 27 to August 3, 1996, they held the First Intercontinental Encounter for Humanity and against Neoliberalism. The gathering represented a new phase in the struggle against neoliberalism throughout the world, and close to 5,000 people from forty-two countries participated in discussions in five Zapatista "Aguascalientes" in the communities of Oventik, La Realidad, La Garrucha, Morelia and Roberto Barrios.

The inauguration of the event was held in the Aguascalientes of Oventik, in the township of San Andrés Sacamch'en de los Pobres. Men and women from all the continents gathered there. Delegations from Italy, Brazil, Great Britain, Paraguay, Chile, Philippines, Germany, Peru, Argentina, Austria, Uruguay, Guatemala, Belgium, Venezuela, Colombia, Iran, Haiti, Denmark, Nicaragua, Zaire, France, Ecuador, Greece, Japan, Kurdistan, Ireland, Costa Rica, Cuba, Sweden, Norway, Holland, South Africa, Switzerland, Spain, United States, Portugal, Basque Country, Catalonia, Canary Islands, Turkey, Canada, Puerto Rico, Bolivia, Australia, Mauritania and all over Mexico met in the highlands of Chiapas to then disperse among the different Aguascalientes holding the event.

In the fog of Oventik, in front of thousands of people of different colors, the Zapatistas made use of the word: "Behind us are you. Behind our face masks is the face of all women excluded. Of all indigenous people forgotten. Of all homosexuals persecuted. Of all young people belittled. Of all migrants beaten. Of all people imprisoned for their thought or word. Of all workers humiliated. Of all who have died in oblivion. Of all the simple and ordinary men and women who don't count, who are not seen, who are not named, who have no tomorrow. . . Today, thou-

144

sands of human beings from all continents cry "Ya Basta!" [Enough's enough!] to conformity, to apathy, to cynicism, to the modern god of egotism. Today thousands of little worlds in the continents practice a principle here, in the mountains of Southeastern Mexico: the principle of building a new and good world, one world in which many worlds fit. (EZLN speech, July 27, 1996)

The Intergalactic Encounter ended on August 3, 1996, with the reading of the Second Declaration of La Realidad for Humanity and against Neoliberalism, a document born of the agreement to make up a collective network of opposition to neoliberalism. The declaration recognized the differences and noted the similarities. This intercontinental network of resistance, it was proposed, would not have an organizational structure or a defining center or a centralized leadership or hierarchies. It was the articulation of a network that, in time, would become the anti-globalization movement.

When the Encounter was over, after consulting its base communities, on September 3, 1996, the EZLN announced that it was suspending its participation in the San Andrés negotiations. The time immediately after the announcement was one of great tension; the government escalated military harassment of the indigenous rebel communities.

In a communiqué from that time, the rebels set forth minimum conditions for reinitiating the dialogue: freedom for all alleged Zapatistas; a governmental commission with decision-making capacity and respect for the Zapatista delegation; installation of the commission on Follow-up and Verification; serious and concrete proposals for the round on democracy and justice; and an end to the climate of military and police persecution against indigenous communities. (EZLN communiqué, July 29, 1996)

The government of Ernesto Zedillo ignored these conditions and instead intensified paramilitary violence in the area.

At the same time that the negotiations were suspended the EZLN sent a letter to the combatants and leadership of the Revolutionary Popular Army in which it not only rejected military help offered by that armed organization but also explained again, and in no uncertain terms, its own struggle and its status as an armed movement, as well as its enormous differences with respect to traditional guerrilla armies: "The difference is not, as you insist on seeing it, that you will not engage in dialogue with the government, that you do fight to take power, and that you have not declared war, whereas we do engage in dialogue (note: not only with the government, but also, and especially in much greater proportion with national and international civil society), we do not fight to take power, and we did declare war on the Mexican Federal Army (a challenge that they never forgave us for). The difference is that our political proposals are diametrically opposed, and this is evident in the discourse and the practice of the two organizations. Thanks to your appearance, now many people can understand that what makes us different from existing

political organizations is neither the weapons we wield nor the ski masks we wear, but our political proposal. We have carved a path, new and radical. So new and radical that every political faction has criticized us and looks on us with disgust, including you. We make them uncomfortable. Too bad, that's just the Zapatista way. . ." (Letter from the EZLN, August 30, 1996)

The Zapatistas continued organizing with indigenous peoples from all over the country, and answered affirmatively to the invitation to send a rebel representative to the National Indigenous Congress to be held in Mexico City. The federal government and the business community dreaded the possibility of a Zapatista coming to the Federal District. Once again, tensions and hostilities escalated. The government insisted that the law of dialogue did not allow the Zapatistas to move freely within the country. The rebels, on the other hand, defended their decision to break out of the isolation imposed on them by the military enclosure in Chiapas and to head out for the nation's capital. The Cocopa, in these moments, was key in bringing the negotiations to fruition. Comandanta Ramona, an indigenous woman, ill but determined, was the rebel representative charged with challenging not only governmental military power but also the political and business elites.

On October 12, 1996, after a demonstration of tens of thousands of indigenous people, Comandanta Ramona gave a speech for the first time in Mexico City's central plaza, the Zócalo. Her speech culminated with the slogan that had accompanied the struggle for the recognition of indigenous rights and culture: "Never again a Mexico without us."

The presence of Comandanta Ramona in the First National Indigenous Congress gave the event international relevance. Hundreds of indigenous people from all over the country discussed and reflected on the issues of their respective communities, agreed to strengthen their fight

for compliance with the San Andrés Accords and decided to unite for recognition of their autonomy.

The indigenous people returned to their villages and a short while afterward, on November 7, 1996, the Zapatistas established the Commission on Follow-up and Verification (Conai, by its Spanish initials). On the EZLN side, distinguished figures participated including Rodolfo Stavenhagen, Amalia Solórzano (widow of ex-president Lázaro Cárdenas), and Bishop Bartolomé Carrasco.

Between November 24 and 29, 1996, the EZLN, the Cocopa and the Conai met to draw up the initiative on constitutional reforms on indigenous rights and culture. The government and the EZLN agreed that the legislators of the Cocopa draft the legislative proposal that would then be accepted or rejected without modifications.

At the end of the meeting, the Cocopa presented its final proposal and the EZLN accepted it as a show of good faith but made it clear that it had left out several important aspects of the San Andrés Accords. Secretary of the Interior Emilio Chuayffet verbally gave his approval but asked to wait until President Ernesto Zedillo returned from a trip to formalize the agreement.

That was one of the crucial moments of the negotiations, since the Secretary of the Interior then went back on his original decision and the negotiating process suffered a blow from which it still has not recovered. Chuayffet met with the Cocopa to inform it of the government's objections to the legislative proposal on indigenous rights and culture. He retracted his promise to accept the proposal as it was and made observations for in-depth changes. Never before had the commission of legislators had such an opportunity to exercise its autonomy and act with dignity. The deputies of the lower house and the senators met then with President Zedilllo to demand approval of the legislative proposal and he asked them for fifteen days to give his response. The response was "no," and since then compliance with the San Andrés Accords as approved on February 16, 1996, has been the central demand of Zapatista indigenous peoples from throughout the country and important sectors of national and international civil society.

The third year of the war ended with bad omens. Faced with the uncertainty of the Zapatista response to the presidential counterproposal, the government increased the military presence in the indigenous rebel communities.

In spite of threatening airplanes, helicopters and tanks the indigenous rebels proclaimed, "Whether this fourth year will be one of war or peace will depend on whether the supreme power accepts history and recognizes that people who are different deserve room to speak and walk. This fourth year will be, as all the past years and all that will come, one of. . . living for the country or dying for freedom!" (Message from the EZLN, January 1, 1997)

un Méx
sin Nos

EZLN

1997

Mobilizations to demand compliance with the San Andrés Accords. Increase in paramilitary actions in the Northern zone. Beginning of Zapatista silence as a weapon. March of the 1,111 members of base communities to Mexico City. Climax of paramilitary violence in Los Altos, refugees and the massacre of indigenous inhabitants of Acteal.

The year began with bad omens. In the first days of 1997 the EZLN had to respond as to whether or not it accepted the major modifications that the Zedillo administration made to the legislative proposal presented by the Commission on Concordance and Pacification. The original proposal, in spite of leaving out some important aspects of the accords signed in February 1996, had already been accepted by the rebels.

On January 11, 1997, in the community of La Realidad, in the context of a meeting with the legislators of the Cocopa and members of the National Intermediation Commission, the Zapatistas firmly rejected Zedillo's counterproposal for legal reforms and noted that they would not return to the negotiating table until the government complied with the San Andrés Accords. The day after the announcement, the government intensified military presence and harassment of indigenous communities and hostilities toward the Zapatistas.

"Mr. Zedillo refuses to comply with what was signed in San Andrés

151

by his own representatives. This is unacceptable. If today he refuses to recognize the commitments made on indigenous rights, you can expect that tomorrow will just bring noncompliance with the still-distant peace accords. . . The federal government's counterproposal puts the whole peace process in crisis in Mexico, it fundamentally questions the possibility of a quick and peaceful solution to the conflict, and casts the shadow of war again on the Indian peoples of Mexico," the EZLN denounced before the increasingly powerless legislators.

A month later, in February 1997, coinciding with the anniversary of the signing of the accords, more than 10,000 indigenous Zapatistas marched on San Cristóbal de las Casas, demanding that the government keep its word and accept the Cocopa's legislative proposal.

"Although it signed the first peace accords the federal government was always preparing and then executing its noncompliance with what was agreed upon in San Andrés. As it broke its word, tens of thousands of soldiers continued to surround us, harassing and persecuting the indigenous communities. That's how the government kept its promise to follow the path of dialogue and negotiations to resolve the just war of the Zapatistas," the indigenous rebels remarked during the large and colorful gathering.

In the event they denounced government attacks on the official organisms charged with assisting the dialogue: "Blind, the bad government not only dealt a blow to the indigenous rebels, but also to those who supported peace and who, like the Cocopa and the Conai, assisted and mediated to avoid war. The indigenous law initiative elaborated by the Commission on Concordance and Pacification, a body of the federal legislative branch, has been attacked time and time again by the executive branch. Now the legislators are accused of being 'false redeemers' and the legislative proposal is criticized for seeking 'the fragmentation of the Mexican nation. . .' Shielding themselves uselessly in legal technicalities, the federal government tries to hide the essential fact: it is not willing to comply with its word, it does not recognize the authentic demands of the Mexican indigenous

152

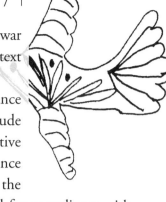

people, and it does not want to resolve the Zapatista war through dialogue and negotiation," explained a text signed by Subcomandante Marcos.

On March 4, 1997 the Cocopa gave up its chance to demonstrate a dignified and autonomous attitude and abandoned, de facto, the defense of its legislative proposal. The federal government's response was, once again, repression and harassment, not only against the Zapatistas, but also against all those who struggled for compliance with the accords. An example was the violent expulsion of sixty-five families of the indigenous organization Xi'Nich and on March 8 state Public Security forces violently detained two Jesuit priests, one of whom was an adviser to the EZLN in the dialogue, and two leaders of Xi'Nich.

In this context, the EZLN responded to the Cocopa's communiqué warning them that their position would worsen the political and military situation in the zone. In a letter dated March 9, 1997, the Zapatistas recounted all that the government had done to erode the peace process and reminded the Cocopa of the various steps and commitments along the way. Due to the document's importance, it is worthwhile to quote it at length:

First is the history: "In late August of 1996 (eight months after the accords were signed and not complied with) the EZLN base communities ordered the CCRI–General Command to suspend its participation in the San Andrés dialogue. The lack of compliance with the agreed-on accords, the political prisoners, the military and paramilitary harassment, the presence of a racist and inept negotiating team, and the lack of serious proposals on the issue of Democracy and Justice are just a few examples of how the government played and still plays with the war against the indigenous Mexicans. Our five demands were then presented in order to restart the dialogue. (By the way, the EZLN demanded and demands a government counterpart with decision-making capacity, political will and respect for the Zapatista delegation, and not the 'strengthening of the governmental counterpart' as you say in your letter.) The fact that Mr. Zedillo does not uphold the accords that his delegation signed confirms that the negotiators, Mr. [Marco Antonio] Bernal and Mr. [Jorge] Del Valle, did not have, and do not have, any decision-making capacity. On their lack of political will and lack of respect, history will decide.

"The Cocopa then proposed a series of initiatives to restart the dialogue. They agreed on the so-called 'tripartite meetings' between the Conai, the Cocopa and the EZLN to discuss and agree on options that not only resolve this crisis, but redefine the framework of the dialogue and make it more expeditious. In practice, the governmental delegation had been replaced by a new actor, the Cocopa. Mr. Bernal and Mr. Del Valle had led the process from crisis to crisis and the failure of their method was already clear.

"After establishing the Commission on Follow-up and Verification (not without first having to overcome various obstacles created by the gentlemen from the Interior Ministry), the Cocopa turned to resolving the point of compliance with the accords signed by the government and the EZLN in the round on Indigenous Rights and Culture. The EZLN accepted the proposal that the Cocopa draft the legislation for constitutional reforms, a task that gave the commission a concrete role in assisting the peaces process. Then, to build this initiative, the Cocopa took on the job of serving as a conduit during this phase (in spite of our warning that this would not work) and presented the proposals of each party to the other. After this method failed (as it failed before in the San Andrés talks) the two parties agreed that the Cocopa draw up a document on the accords and both the EZLN and the federal government would decide to accept or reject it.

"You will remember that having obtained this agreement between the parties for the Cocopa to draft a single document ('to avoid an endless exchange of proposals,' quoting your words) and having agreed that

154

respective positions would be defined based on this document, you worked on a legislative proposal. You presented your document on November 29, 1996, advising us that this was the Cocopa's last effort and that you would only accept a yes or no response to the document and that, in case of a negative response from either party, the Cocopa would consider that it had failed in its task of assistance and would dissolve. At that time, you told us that you had given the same warning to the federal government. We recognized that the efforts of the Cocopa were useful and that, in spite of not incorporating all of the San Andrés Accords on this issue, the proposal represented progress.

"Later (we're trying to remember here) you will recall that the Secretary of the Interior (I think it's still Emilio Chuayffet Chemor) accepted the document and just asked that you wait until Mr. Zedillo returned (he was on a trip then) to make public the acceptance. This was followed by cowardice and lack of honesty on the part of Mr. Chuayffet, when he denied having accepted the text, alleging that he hadn't even read it and that his response had been affirmative because he was under the influence of a well-known (to him) alcoholic drink called *chinchón* (or something like that). Then, Mr. Zedillo talked to you and asked us for some time to give his response (or maybe to allow Mr. Chuayffet to recover from

the *chinchones*). Two weeks later, the government responded with an authentic counterproposal that not only ignored the Cocopa's proposal, but also tried to renegotiate the whole round on Indigenous Rights and Culture. We read the government's document and of course we rejected it. Then, two months ago, we asked the Cocopa to establish a position on the government's actions.

"The Zapatista 'No' to Zedillo's counterproposal unleashed a heated and diverse debate, both nationally and internationally, on the issue of Indian rights. Particularly, the points on autonomy, legal norms and the political participation of indigenous peoples provoked interesting and insightful opinions and comments. Mr. Zedillo found he had no intelligent support for his weak arguments against the recognition of the historic rights of indigenous peoples.

"In less than two weeks, the government lost the national debate and could no longer sustain any logical reason for rejecting the Cocopa proposal. Then came the silence and attempts to minimize the final crisis of the dialogue between the government and the EZLN. Soon it became clear that the government did not have, nor does it have now, any argument to justify rejecting the Cocopa proposal and failing to comply with its word. The real reason—that the administration never had any intention of complying with the accords and resolving the conflict through peaceful means—was revealed clearly and fully. The authoritarianism, arrogance and blindness that are intrinsic to a presidentialist system took the crisis to its most extreme point, which is now, as a result of your response, legislators." (EZLN letter to the Cocopa, March 9, 1997)

The dialogue came to an impasse that was very difficult to break through, and national and international mobilizations began. Just as the EZLN had noted in the letter to the Solidarity Committees, the government's lack of compliance with the accords served in a positive sense since the protests that ensued made it clear that the Zapatista indigenous

156

demands were not just in Chiapas but responded to the aspirations of all indigenous peoples of the nation and reflected, taking into account specific conditions, the desires of all indigenous peoples on the continent. Moreover, once again, the demonstrations were a mirror of the international support for the indigenous cause.

The government, of course, did not understand what was happening, and for the umpteenth time the demands of indigenous peoples were met with violence. Several days later police entered the Zapatista community of San Pedro Nixtalucum, in the township of San Juan de la Libertad. The outcome was four Zapatista farmers dead, twenty-nine wounded and eighty families uprooted.

In April, the federal government named a new representative to replace Marco Antonio Bernal in the negotiations: Pedro Joaquín Coldwell, former secretary of tourism and ex-governor of Chiapas. Just a change in names.

The following months were characterized by an increase in the militarization of the state, accompanied by the extreme violence of the paramilitary groups against the civilian Zapatistas. The assassinations, expulsions and burning of entire villages—acts committed by the paramilitaries and supported by the federal army and local government—became a fact of life while lavishly expensive midterm election campaigns were being carried out in Chiapas and throughout the country.

The EZLN inaugurated the act of silence as a weapon and response. The Zapatistas reacted to provocations by the government with the absence of noise, and to the din of the electoral process by being quiet.

In this context, just three days before the federal elections, on July 3, 1997, the EZLN announced its decision to call on the rebel villages not to participate in elections held in the midst of military and paramilitary harassment and, in the same document, explained their silence: "In these past days we have remained quiet. To look inside ourselves, to re-sow ourselves, to make ourselves stronger, so that the heart and the word will find new places to grow. This is why our silence resounds."

In the middle of elections in which the partisan left had possibilities to win the nation's capital, the Zapatistas stated that some "progressive" groups had asked them to remain quiet and not cause disturbances. They asked them for "humility from the humble, silence from those who are always mute."

Then once again, they explained their political proposal: "At election time or at any other time, our political position is and has been clear. It is not partisan but not anti-party; it is not electoral or anti-elections. It is against the party system of the State, against presidentialism and for democracy, freedom, justice, the left; it is inclusive and it is anti-neoliberal."

Despite the criticisms received from the politicians—or precisely because of them—to build the "other" politics, the EZLN insisted on explaining, "The 'other' politics does not seek to occupy posts in partisan politics, it is born of the crisis of that system and tends to occupy the space that is not covered by party politics. The 'other' politics seeks to organize itself so to turn the logic of party politics on its head; it seeks to build a new relationship between the Nation and its parts: citizens with

158

the right to full-time, differentiated and specific citizenship, united by a history and to be creators of that history. This new relationship involves the government and the political parties, as well as media, churches, army, private sector, police, justice system and Congress."

Their position, warned that politics is a matter of elites, and that democratizing it did not mean broadening the elite base or supplanting one elite for another, but "liberating" politics that had been kidnapped by politicians and "taking it back down" to those who should rule and in whom real sovereignty resides—the citizens. The "rule by obeying" of the Zapatistas, they emphasized, implies this change in politics, and it is a process not a decree. In the turbulent year of 1997, they explained that it meant "a revolution that makes the revolution possible."

In this same communiqué the rebels refined their positions on presidentialism, the electoral sphere, democracy, the vote as a possible form of rebellion and the vote as legitimating authoritarianism, among other things.

The federal elections were held and the Institutional Revolutionary Party lost its absolute majority in the Chamber of Deputies, while Cuauhtémoc Cárdenas of the Party of the Democratic Revolution won as head of the Mexico City government.

In the midst of a "democracy" installed by decree and with the communities under siege and harassed by the army, on July 27, 1997, the EZLN—faithful to its strategy of opening channels of communication with civil society—left the country for the first time. Represented by a man and a woman from the insurgent base communities, the organization traveled to Spain to participate in the Second Intercontinental Encounter for Humanity and against Neoliberalism.

Once again the Zapatista Army of National Liberation decided to continue on its path of inquiry, of "walking and asking." The objective was no longer just to meet up with civil society in rebel territory, but to break the military containment and reach Mexico City. After the period of elections, they announced the march of 1,111 members of the base communities with the destination of Mexico City.

On September 8, 1997, the group of more than a thousand rebels departed from the state of Chiapas. The huge mobilization pursued several objectives: a) to mobilize national and international civil society during the post-election period when the government was dictating by decree that since there was a member of the opposition PRD heading the Mexico City government, democratic conditions now existed in the country to incorporate the EZLN into institutional life; b) to explain along the march the causes of the uprising, the conditions of militarization and paramilitarization and the process of autonomy; c) to publicize the San Andrés Accords, protest the failure to comply, and collect endorsements for approval of the law on Indigenous Rights and Culture drafted by the Cocopa in the context of a new Congress; d) to break through the military and paramilitary wall of containment extended around the communities in resistance; e) to establish direct contacts with civil society, nonpartisan political organizations, nongovernmental organizations, ecclesiastic base organizations, university members, workers and farmers and indigenous peoples from all over the country; f) to explain their struggle and find out about others'; g) to walk and ask questions. . .

The Zapatista base communities left Chiapas on September 8, 1997, amid a large farewell gathering, and on the way through the states of Oaxaca, Puebla and Morelos planted their word and found support for their cause. Indigenous and nonindigenous people discovered in the march a place for action and protest, not only against the government's failure to comply with the San Andrés Accords but also for the innumerable grievances that neoliberalism left in its wake.

Mexico City residents received the march on September 12, 1997, in a huge and enthusiastic way. In Mexico City the Zapatista delegates participated in the Congress of the Founding of the Zapatista Front for National Liberation, where they explained the reasons why they couldn't

160

join the recently formed front at that time. Sub-comandante Marcos sent a greeting and noted that as long as the government did not keep its word in the negotiating process, the Zapatistas could not form part of a civil political force.

The Zapatista Front for National Liberation was born, then, as a sister organization to the EZLN.

In its message, the EZLN made its position clear: "But there are not only Zapatistas in the EZLN. Not only armed and clandestine Zapatistas. There are also civilian and peaceful Zapatistas. There are also Zapatistas in the FZLN and in other places. . . But we can't go on holding them back or asking them to wait for us, not to go on, not to grow, not to get big, not to organize until there's a just and dignified peace so the EZLN can share with you the present and the future."

The 1,111 Zapatistas participated also in the Second Assembly of the National Indigenous Congress, where representatives of almost all the indigenous peoples of the country reaffirmed their commitment to fight for compliance with the San Andrés Accords, which included recognition of their autonomy, among other aspects of their rights and culture.

The members of the base communities returned to their villages after making their position on the military aggression known: "We will continue to do everything possible so that it is these kinds of civilian, peaceful actions, and not acts of war, that build peace for Mexicans," they said in a farewell speech in Mexico City on September 17, 1997.

During the next months the federal and state governments responded to the mass mobilization by intensifying the dirty war against the indigenous rebels. On November 4, 1997, bishop Samuel Ruiz and his coadjutor Raúl Vera survived an assassination attempt against them by the paramilitary group "Peace and Justice" in the township of Tila that resulted in several people wounded. Two days later, in San Cristóbal de las Casas, María de la Luz Ruiz García, Bishop Ruiz's sister, suffered an attempt on her life.

"The recent attacks attempt to send the EZLN a clear message: no mediation, no dialogue, no peace," declared the Zapatistas in a communiqué issued three days later.

Then came weeks of extreme violence by paramilitary groups. Thousands of indigenous peoples suffered aggressions in the township of Chenalhó, in the region Los Altos. The impasse in the dialogue generated a dangerous situation and violence, abetted by the government and its army. With the protection of police and soldiers, the paramilitary groups recruited by force, demanded taxes and burned down the houses of indigenous people who opposed the local and federal governments. In this situation, thousands of indigenous families fled from the violence and took refuge in the Zapatista community of Polhó, where they survived in subhuman conditions.

Along with the aggression came the protests. On November 29, 1997, members of the Zapatista base communities from the zones of Los Altos, Norte, Selva, Sierra, Frontera and Costa marched peacefully in San Cristóbal de las Casas and joined their protests to the simultaneous march in Mexico City that went from the Angel of Independence to the Zócalo. "Against violence and impunity" was the main slogan of the mobilization.

The first days of December 1997 saw the displacement of thousands of indigenous rebels in Los Altos. The situation turned critical and the EZLN denounced on December 12, "More than 6,000 displaced by the war are the result of the attacks of paramilitary bands and state police, both directed by the state government, with the blessing of the federal government. In the community of Xcumumal alone, there are more than 3,500 indigenous refugees. They are completely isolated, since they remain under siege by the white guards [as the paramilitaries were called] and state public security police."

"The Zapatistas of Chenalhó live out in the open and—in addition to a lack of housing, clothes and food—suffer illnesses that have already reached epidemic proportions," the rebel group informed.

While the state government pretended to negotiate the return of the

displaced persons, the PRI in Chiapas looted houses and destroyed the belongings of those expelled from their communities. Coffee, cattle, food and domestic utensils were distributed among the paramilitary aggressors.

Then came the reports in the press and television about the dramatic situation of thousands of indigenous families living in the township of Chenalhó. A television report by Ricardo Rocha, among others that stood out in the print media, showed society, "a small sample of the gigantic display of intolerance and crime in which the Institutional Revolutionary Party and the state and federal governments are trying to destroy the Zapatista rebellion."

In this extremely serious context, the Cocopa took its time. They announced that during the second week of January its members would travel to Chiapas. They admitted that the situation in the state was worse than in the first days of the uprising, since, they said, "it did not produce the number of deaths we are seeing now."

For its part, the National Commission for Intermediation (Conai) and the Fray Bartolomé de las Casas Center for Human Rights warned that the negotiations had run into serious problems due to "the mix of state interests and a counterinsurgency strategy." The same day of this warning a group of fifty indigenous PRI members shot guns and set up a roadblock in the zone of Chimix. All day the armed PRI members from paramilitary groups patrolled the highways that led between the villages of Acteal and La Esperanza.

That was the scene when on December 22, 2007, one of the most atrocious and sadly predictable massacres in the history of the nation occurred. In the community of Acteal, located in the township of Chenalhó in Los Altos of Chiapas, forty-five indigenous people, most children and women belonging to the civilian group "Las Abejas," were massacred with firearms and machetes by sixty armed men from a paramilitary band made up of indigenous from the PRI and the Cardenist Front (PFCRN). In the attack another twenty-five persons were wounded, including several children. The shooting lasted over six hours, while dozens of Public Security police remained 200 meters away from where the killings took pace, listening to the shots and screams without lifting a finger.

In the months after, 125 people were detained, including the PRI mayor and several police chiefs, but no higher level official was accused or investigated. Nearly six years later, the crime of Acteal still goes unpunished.

The EZLN named Ernesto Zedillo and his Secretary of the Interior Emilio Chuayffet, who two years earlier had approved the counterinsurgency strategy of the federal government, as directly reasonable. By then it was obvious that the government had followed a dual strategy of pre-

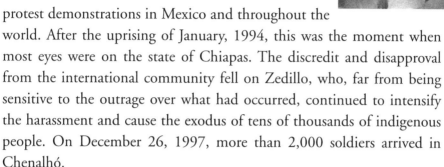

tending to engage in dialogue without any intention of complying with its terms, while gaining time to prepare the death squads.

The massacre at Acteal caused hundreds of protest demonstrations in Mexico and throughout the world. After the uprising of January, 1994, this was the moment when most eyes were on the state of Chiapas. The discredit and disapproval from the international community fell on Zedillo, who, far from being sensitive to the outrage over what had occurred, continued to intensify the harassment and cause the exodus of tens of thousands of indigenous people. On December 26, 1997, more than 2,000 soldiers arrived in Chenalhó.

This time the international repudiation came not only from groups sympathetic to the movement, but included the government of the Untied States, the prime minister of France Lionel Jospin, Pope John Paul II, the European Union, the secretary of the Organization of American States, the United Nations, and hundreds of famous cultural figures, journalists and politicians in Spain, France, Italy, Uruguay, Brazil and the United States, among others.

The year ended, again, with the increase of military elements in the region. The pretext: the commemoration of the fourth anniversary of the uprising which, according to the administration, the Zapatistas would take advantage of to occupy townships. Military surveillance was reinforced in the townships of Las Margaritas, Comitán, Ocosingo, Altamirano, Chilón, Citalá, Oxchuc, Palenque, Tila, Sabanilla, Tumbalá, Salto de Agua, Simojovel, Huitiupán, Jototol, El Bosque and San Cristóbal de las Casas. However, as always, the Zapatista still danced in the New Year.

1998

Increase in military, paramilitary and police violence. Zapatista silence as a response. National and international mobilizations. Call to the referendum on the Recognition of Indigenous Rights and Culture and for the End of the War of Extermination.

This year began with more of the extreme violence that characterized the preceding year. During the first days of 1998, still in mourning for the atrocious massacre of the forty-five Tzotzils in Acteal, the rebel indigenous communities suffered new military, paramilitary and police strikes.

The government's response to the massacre was to send thousands of soldiers into the communities. From the first hours of 1998, they stepped up persecution of EZLN members and sympathizers in an attempt to provoke armed confrontations. They dismantled the autonomous townships and raided the base communities of the insurgency.

On January 1, 1998, the army attacked the Tzeltal community of Yaltchilpic in the township of Altamirano, where it destroyed and robbed belongings of the village's indigenous inhabitants with the excuse that supposedly there was an insurgent arsenal there. That same day, the Tzeltal inhabitants of San Caralampio in Ocosingo were attacked by federal troops who detained the local EZLN leader on the ejido[3] and accused him of having a pistol that they never found.

On January 3, 1998 federal army troops staged a siege on the Tojolobal community of La Realidad for nearly seventeen hours. During the operation the army threatened the indigenous villagers and interrogated them, using physical force and threats, on the whereabouts of the Zapatista General Command. Simultaneously, army soldiers took the Tzeltal community of Morelia in Altamirano by assault. They searched houses and threatened the residents. Hours later, four people from the ejido were detained and tortured along the road that leads to the county seat.

On January 5, 1998 the community called "10 de Abril," also in Altamirano, was besieged by the federal army. While the government denied the offensive, assault troops tried to take the Tzotzil community of Aldama, in the autonomous township of San Andrés Sacamch'en de los Pobres, on the same day.

National and international protests following the Acteal massacre finally forced Secretary of the Interior Emilio Chuayffet to resign. He was replaced by Francisco Labastida. The interim governor of Chiapas, Julio César Ruiz Ferro also resigned and in his place Zedillo appointed Roberto Albores Guillén. All these were changes in names but did not represent a change in strategy; on the contrary, the government stepped up the harassment of indigenous communities.

At the same time that the military was making incursions into Zapatista territory, Zedillo presented a legal initiative on indigenous rights and culture to Congress that obviously violated the main points of the Cocopa proposal and the San Andrés Accords.

On January 12, 1998, the Zapatista base communities and civil society marched in protest against the governmental violence in Chiapas,

---

[3] An ejido is a socially held farm. Ejidos were a result of land reform following the 1910 Mexican Revolution.

Mexico City and other parts of the country. Members of the base communities that mobilized for peace were repressed in the municipal seat of Ocosingo. There they were attacked by the state Public Security police, who killed Guadalupe Méndez López, a Zapatista woman from the community of La Garrucha.

The death and repression prompted the EZLN to send a letter to the National Commission on Intermediation. The Zapatistas reminded the commission of the many ways in which the EZLN had demonstrated its commitment to a just and dignified peace throughout the four years since January 12, 1994. Examples of these peaceful initiatives, they noted, were the Cathedral Dialogue and the National Democratic Convention in 1994; the Dialogue of San Andrés and the National and International Consultation for Peace in 1995; the call to form the FZLN, the National Indigenous Forum, the signing of the first accords with the federal government (that were still not complied with), the Continental Meeting, the National Forum for Reform of the State, the Intercontinental Encounter

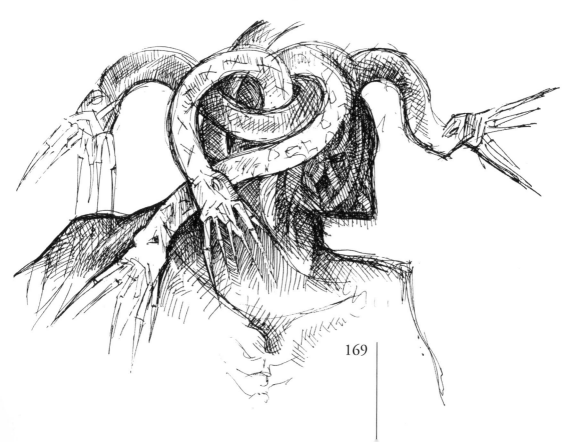

for Humanity and Against Neoliberalism; the meetings between the Cocopa-EZLN-Conai in 1996; and the march of the 1,111 members of the Zapatista base communities to Mexico City in 1997. (Letter from the EZLN, January 14, 1998)

The government's response to the EZLN's peaceful initiatives and mobilizations was to refuse to comply with the first accords signed, to activate paramilitary groups, to assassinate members of base communities, to persecute the rebel leadership and to saturate the state of Chiapas with military units. An example of the growing military presence could be found then in the permanent harassment of the community of La Realidad, where the federal army doubled the number of artillery and military vehicles and patrols. Four times a day, up to thirty-eight motorized units patrolled the Tojolabal community. Military planes flew daily and nightly flights at different hours and executed dive maneuvers (used in aerial combat to intimidate populations and bomb fixed positions).

The EZLN once again appealed to national and international civil society, which responded with permanent protests. From December 22, 1997 (the day of the Acteal massacre), to January 13, 1998 (the day after the assassination of Guadalupe Méndez), there were mobilizations in 130 cities in twenty-seven countries on five continents. On January 12, dozens of actions, big and small, were carried out in Mexico and other parts of the world, all with the same demand: stop the war of extermination, punish those responsible for the Acteal murders and comply with the San Andrés Accords.

Parallel to the repression, the pro-Zapatista movement in Mexico and around the world grew. Civil society's response was as large as the offensive, and besides marching and protesting, they were organizing new forms of mobilization without chiefs or leaders or protagonists, without anyone to tell them what to do or how. Dances, songs, poetry, marches,

170

graffiti, slogans and much indignation flourished within a cultural and social spectrum that was ever broader and more diverse: indigenous people, youth, women, housewives, students, feminists, homosexuals, unions, peasant farmers, workers, solidarity committees, intellectuals, artists, undocumented workers, etc., the named and the nameless. "People like those who say Enough Is Enough! and write the history that's worth writing and telling. People who talk to us, people who listen, the people we are writing to now. People like you, like us." (Letter from ELZN, January 20, 1998)

In this period, the government again changed its peace commissioner. The place occupied by the gray and mediocre Pedro Joaquín Coldwell was filled with someone with similar characteristics, Emilio Rabasa,[4] who took his new post as coordinator of a nonexistent dialogue, under orders from the also recently named Secretary of the Interior Francisco Labastida.

The government's strategy on the one hand was to strike the indigenous communities and, on the other, to offer a show to the communications media of reinitiating the dialogue. Labastida sent the Zapatistas an "offer" of "revision of the positions of the army in exchange for renegotiating the indigenous issue." The insurgents called this a mere trick to confuse the public. "So the government increases its military presence and persecution in order to negotiate a return to its former levels in exchange for the EZLN giving in on its demand for government compliance with the San Andrés Accords; it raids the autonomous townships and offers to redraw municipalities in exchange for 'getting rid' of their indigenous essence; it proposes that the commanders of the CCRI-CG of the EZLN directly receive the money of the government to administer it; and offers 'to forget' the rebellion that shook up Mexico and ruined its New Year's Eve dinner at the end of the century and the millennium."

---

[4] Pedro Joaquín Coldwell, former Secretary of Tourism, was the federal government–appointed Peace and Reconciliation Commissioner in Chiapas. He was replaced by Emilio Rabasa Gamboa in January of 1998.

"Sit down under my conditions or I'll kill you," was how the Zapatistas read the government's messages and proposals. They were an attempt, they warned, to make renegotiation acceptable in public opinion through threats of extermination. "And behind the renegotiation of the indigenous issue that the government wants," they denounced, "is the negation of San Andrés, the negation of the 'other politics,' of the politics that was spread and deepened when the San Andrés dialogues ceased to be a boxing ring and became a broad and profound forum for encounter and birth. . ."

It was just the second month of 1998 and there was already talk of the presidential succession for the year 2000. The federal government, meanwhile, tried to obtain advantages in the electoral process. Its wager was to try to "de-Chiapanize" the national agenda, to take a break to recompose its international image and relieve the wear and tear on its military. But for this it needed, with or without legislative endorsement, to retract the law of dialogue of March 11, 1995, to reactivate apprehension orders, and to resume persecution.

Before submerging itself for the second time in a loud and strategic silence, the EZLN announced its decision to continue to resist and stand firm in the struggle for recognition of the rights of indigenous peoples. The Zapatistas committed themselves to continue to "try to find the way or ways to build new bridges to national and international civil society and the political and social organizations of Mexico." (EZLN essay, February 27, 1998)

They asked civil society to continue on the road laid out: to continue with the construction of a table for dialogue "where all of us can sit down; a very different table, broad and deep like the one we built together in San Andrés two years ago; a table that has yesterday as its legs, the present as its surface and the future as its food; a table that lasts a long time and does not break; a table made of stones, of many little pebbles, that is, of many facets of resistances (that is how hope looks when times are hard). . ."

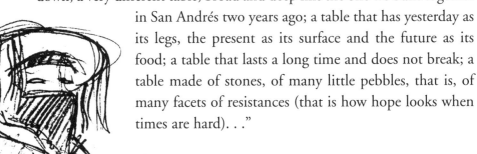

172

Meanwhile, the federal and state governments waged an open campaign against the autonomous townships. On April 8, 1998, an impressive police and military operation led to the detention of evangelical indigenous leaders in the La Hormiga neighborhood in San Cristóbal de las Casas. Three days later, in Taniperla, seat of the autonomous township of Ricardo Flores Magón, more than a thousand soldiers, police and immigration agents carried out a joint operation to capture and imprison civilian Zapatistas and a group of observers. In total, sixteen people were arrested and jailed, among them Sergio Valdez, a university professor, and Luis Menéndez, a student. Twelve foreigners were also expelled from the country.

The Zapatista Army decided then not to talk. It responded to the military provocations with acts of peaceful resistance. To the government's counterproposal rejecting what had already been agreed to, they responded with silence as a weapon.

173

On May 1, another police and military operation tried to dismantle the autonomous township of Tierra y Libertad. Hundreds of soldiers and police clashed with residents of the community Amparo Aguatinta, seat of the rebel township. The police burned and looted the new municipal offices and beat up several women. In the raid, thirty-three persons were detained from the Zapatista base communities, eight of whom were booked and jailed.

On May 5, 1998, a new operation was launched against the township of Nicolás Ruiz, dominated by the opposition. Thousands of military and police members broke up an act of protest and raided houses to arrest 150 community members of the PRD.

The operations to "restore the rule of law" included serious violations of human rights and there was more to come. The climax of the violence against the Zapatista townships and villages came on June 13, 1998, with a major raid in the community of El Bosque, where the combined military and police forces attacked three villages. In Chavajebal, military elements shot firearms and bazookas, and three farmers and a policeman

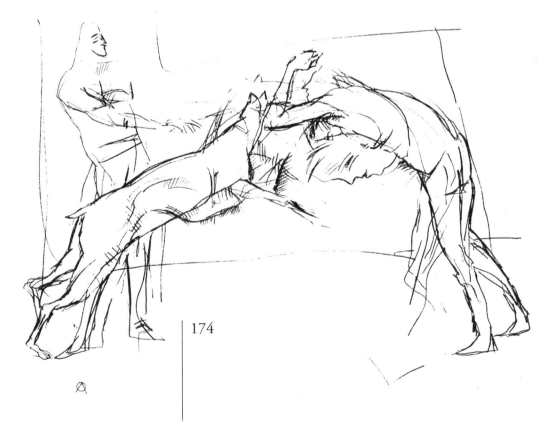

174

lost their lives. In Unión Progresso, where no one resisted according to residents' testimony, seven young Zapatista supporters were executed by police. Dozens of indigenous people were detained.

The dialogue, or the possibility of one, suffered a new blow on June 7, 1998, the day that Samuel Ruiz García resigned from the National Commission for Intermediation. The Conai was dissolved, leaving the negotiations process without a mediating body but still not officially dismantled. The Conai made it clear that its dissolution was owing to the lack of political will for dialogue on the part of the federal government.

On July 17, 1998, the EZLN broke its silence with an analysis of the national situation. Two days later it released the Fifth Declaration of the Lacandón Jungle, in which it called for a National Referendum on the Recognition of Indian Peoples and for an End to War of Extermination.

Assassinations, intimidations, dozens of arrested, tortured and jailed, military and paramilitary harassment, thousands displaced, and the burning of autonomous townships were the norm during these seven months of the year 1998. The rebels' response, once again, was to move forward asking questions along the way and to call for a new broad mobilization to confront to violence of the government with initiatives for peace.

The EZLN identified civil society as its only interlocutor. Under these conditions, no dialogue was possible with the government. There was no longer a mediating body, and the Cocopa had been weakened and made ridiculous by its decision not to defend its own legislative proposal.

The government's strategy to annihilate the Zapatista base communities and dismantle the autonomous townships failed, in spite of the extreme violence with which it was carried out. The EZLN survived one of the most ferocious offensives that had ever been unleashed against it. What's more, it managed to retain its military capacity, expand its grassroots base, and grow stronger politically by showing the justness of its demands.

The politics of walking-asking continued even with the repression. The Zapatistas built bridges with other political and social organizations and with thousands of persons not in political parties. Along with others, they kept building bridges around the world, contributing to the creation of a network to fight against neoliberalism through peaceful means. At the same time, they contributed to the birth of a new and fresh cultural movement based on one central humanist demand: "one world in which many worlds fit."

In the Fifth Declaration of the Lacandón Jungle, the EZLN explained its silence and the costs of it: "Silence, dignity and resistance were our strengths and our best weapons. With them we fought and defeated an enemy that was very powerful but lacked reason and justice in its cause. . . Despite the fact that in the time that our silence lasted, we did not participate directly in the main national problems by giving our position and proposals; despite that our silence permitted the powerful to spread rumors and lies about divisions and internal ruptures among the Zapatistas and make us out to be intolerant, intransigent, weak and obsolete; despite that some became discouraged by our lack of word and others took advantage of our absence to pretend to be our spokespersons; despite the pain and also because of it, we took some giant steps forward." (Fifth Declaration of the Lacandón Jungle, June 17, 1998)

The Fifth Declaration made clear what social and political organizations, intellectuals, academics, cultural figures and people from important sectors of civil society had noted at various times and places. "There will not be a transition to democracy or reform of the State, or a real solution to the principal problems on the national agenda, without indigenous people. A new and better country is necessary and only possible with indigenous peoples. Without them there is no future whatsoever as a nation," the Zapatistas warned. At the same time, they called on indigenous people throughout the country, Mexican civil society, and independent social and political organizations to hold a national referendum on the proposal for the indigenous law drawn up by the Commission on Concordance and Pacification, and for the end of the war of extermination.

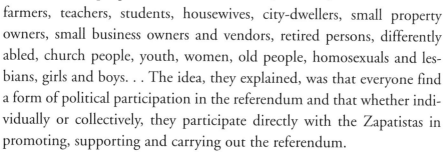

The mobilization revealed once again the creative and audacious nature of Zapatista initiatives. The EZLN would send its own delegation to every township in the country to explain the contents of the Cocopa proposal and to participate in carrying out the referendum.

The social spectrum called upon to participate was, as in all the Zapatista initiatives, broad and diverse: Indian peoples from all over Mexico, workers, farmers, teachers, students, housewives, city-dwellers, small property owners, small business owners and vendors, retired persons, differently abled, church people, youth, women, old people, homosexuals and lesbians, girls and boys. . . The idea, they explained, was that everyone find a form of political participation in the referendum and that whether individually or collectively, they participate directly with the Zapatistas in promoting, supporting and carrying out the referendum.

The scientific, artistic and intellectual communities were also invited, as well as independent social and political organizations and political parties that are "honest and committed to popular causes." The Congress of the Union was also called on, and of course there was a call to the Commission on Concordance and Pacification to comply with its labor of assistance in the peace process by smoothing the path for carrying out the referendum.

As in all Zapatista initiatives, organizing the referendum became a broad mobilization of important sectors of civil society around a concrete task. In other words, the organization was part of the mobilization itself, independent of the results.

To design the best way to hold the referendum, the Zapatistas held the "Meeting between the EZLN and Civil Society" in San Cristóbal de las Casas, November 20–22, 1998. Thirty-two Zapatista delegates (among them Insurgent Major Moisés, who appeared in public for the

first time since the 1994 war) and more than 3,000 Mexicans from all over the country attended.

The gathering also served as a framework for a meeting between Zapatista leaders and the Cocopa legislators. It was an unsuccessful meeting in many ways. There wasn't much to talk about with the deputies and senators who had been made irrelevant by the turn toward violence, with no room for initiative, no decision-making power and no willingness to defend the legislative proposal that they themselves had written.

However, the results of the other meeting reflected the enthusiasm of a society ready to participate in peaceful initiatives of the EZLN. The Zapatistas, again, surprised civil society with the announcement that 5,000 women and men from the base communities would be leaving their communities to promote the referendum. Moreover, among the resolutions agreed upon was for the EZLN to draft the final call to participate in the referendum, taking into account participants' presentations and proposals.

The invitation was presented on December 11, 1998. The date selected was March 21, 1999, and the questions were the following:

Question 1: Do you agree that indigenous peoples should be included with all their strength and wealth in the national project and take active part in the construction of a new Mexico?

Question 2: Do you agree that indigenous rights should be recognized in the Mexican Constitution in the terms laid out in the San Andrés Accords and the corresponding proposal of the Commission on Concordance and Pacification of the Congress of the Union?

Question 3: Do you agree that we should achieve real peace through dialogue, demilitarizing the country by returning the soldiers to their bases, as stipulated in the Constitution and laws?

Question 4: Do you agree that the people should organize and demand that the government "rule by obeying" in all aspects of national life?

The organization of the referendum-mobilization included, in the first stage, forming brigades for promotion and publicity and registering them in the Contact Office for the Referendum, which would be the direct responsibility of the Zapatistas. Again, the initiative had multiple objectives: 1) to demand the rights of indigenous peoples, 2) to make it clear that peace was only possible with the recognition of those rights and with the end of the war of extermination, 3) to encourage a new way of doing politics (walking-asking), a politics built "by all, with all, and for all," making it possible that everyone "make their voice heard and their strength felt in the big national decisions," 4) to promote the popular referendum as a form of free and voluntary participation, with the goal of demanding solutions to the problems that affect the nation, and 5) to promote the referendum as part of a process of mobilizing the people of Mexico in its struggle for democracy, freedom and justice.

This turbulent year ended for the Zapatista communities with the celebration of their fifth year since the uprising. They used the occasion to present a new analysis-evaluation of the situation: "The year 1998 was a year of government war against the indigenous communities of Mexico.

This year the war began December 22, 1997, with the massacre of Acteal. . . The brutal act meant the beginning of a long military and police offensive against the Indian peoples of Chiapas. . . Those directly responsible for masterminding the massacre of Acteal have names. At the top of the list is Ernesto Zedillo, followed by Emilio Chuayffet, Francisco Labastida, General Enrique Cervantes, Julio César Ruiz Ferro and Adolfo Orive. Along with them, others joined in covering the crime: Rosario Green, Emilio Rabasa Gamboa, Roberto Albores Guillén and Jorge Madrazo Cuellar. These criminals occupy or occupied different government offices at the federal and state levels and sooner or later will have to come before the courts for their involvement in this brutal and bloody act that definitively marked the Mexican end of the century. . .

"The activation of paramilitary groups constitutes the backbone of the Zedillo administration's dirty war against indigenous Mexicans. Since February 1995, when the military offensive launched by the government betrayal failed, Ernesto Zedillo knew, approved and applied the paramilitary strategy to resolve the Zapatista movement through the use of force. While the Institutional Revolutionary Party (PRI) supplied the labor force for this business of death and the federal army supplied the arms, ammunition, equipment, advising and training, the Zedillo administration initiated the simulation of a dialogue and negotiation that did not seek and does not seek a peaceful solution to the conflict. . . Esteban Moctezuma, Marco Antonio Bernal, Jorge Del Valle, Gustavo Iruegas and Emilio Rabasa Gamboa are different names for the same governmental hypocrisy. None of them has had the courage, knowing they are being used for war, to refuse to be accomplices to the assassinations that are the only action of the government in the conflict in southeast Mexico. . ."

The document in which the Zapatistas bade farewell to 1998 listed a chain of violent acts in the fifth year of the war: 1) attacks on autonomous townships, 2) attacks on the Conai and Cocopa, and 3) attacks on international observers. The offensive included the massacre of

indigenous peoples, attacks on the autonomous townships, revival of combat, destruction of the Conai, immobility of the Cocopa, noncompliance with the San Andrés Accords, lack of respect for Congress and expulsion of international observers.

However, the Zapatistas did not end the year with grievances, but with a call to action: the mobilization for March 21 around the referendum on the four questions—two on indigenous rights, one on the war and one on the relationship between government and the governed. They reiterated their main demand, which was—and is—recognition of the rights of Indian peoples, and reaffirmed that five years since the initiation of the uprising, the Zapatista Army for National Liberation would continue to fight for democracy, freedom and justice for all Mexicans. "Our objective," they repeated, "is not to take power, or to hold public office, or to convert ourselves into a political party. We did not rise up for handouts or credits. We don't want control of a territory or to separate from Mexico. We are not proposing destruction or buying time." (EZLN essay, dawn of January 1, 2000)

1999

The pre-electoral atmosphere, five thousand Zapatista spread throughout Mexico, the National and International Referendum for the Recognition of Indigenous Rights and Culture and the End to the War of Extermination. Meetings between the EZLN and civil society. Paramilitary violence, resistance in Amador Hernández. The strike at UNAM and its relationship to the Zapatistas.

The sixth year of the war against oblivion, 1999, began in the middle of a pre-electoral political whirlwind. The Mexican political class was already preparing for the selection of their presidential candidates. Without paying any attention to the electorate, the political parties were duking it out in internal battles that, as in every electoral process, had nothing to do with the demands of the people.

In this context that bordered on absurdity, the EZLN opened up a space for trying out a new way of doing politics, one that was inclusive and tolerant, one that listened all the time, one that moved out to the sides and looked up with dignity, and also had the tools necessary to force those above to continually look down below. This new way of doing politics was called "The Referendum for the Recognition of the Rights of Indian Peoples and for the End to the War of Extermination," to be held on March 21, 1998.

In January of 1999, while the Zapatistas were organizing the referendum, the federal army entered the community of Aldama in the town-

183

ship of Chenalhó with the excuse of destroying marijuana plants. Land and air patrols increased in the Zapatista zone and the communities lived with the menace of the dirty war.

In a second stage of the referendum, the EZLN called on the promotion brigades to organize in statewide associations, with the aim of allowing members of the Zapatista Front for National Liberation, other organizations and above all, unorganized civil society, to find a diverse, open, tolerant and inclusive form of political participation.

Simultaneously, it called for holding an international referendum in which all Mexicans over twelve years old who lived abroad would organize and participate in the event from their respective countries of residence. The Zapatistas also called to organize the "International Campaign for the Excluded of the World" to be held the same day on all the continents.

In this way, the Zapatistas widened the social and political range of people participating in the referendum. In the cultural area, writers, actors, painters, sculptors and musicians, among other art workers, saw in the Zapatista movement a new arena for political and cultural manifestation. Rock groups from Mexico and other parts of the world joined in, not only to show their solidarity with the cause of the indigenous peoples following the 1994 uprising, but also to express their own nonconformity with the neoliberal model.

On March 8, 1999, International Women's Day, the EZLN announced the plan of how the 5,000 delegates would cover the country to facilitate the referendum:

Members of the base communities from the Oventik "Aguascalientes" would go to the state of Oaxaca; from the Morelia "Aguascalientes" to the states of Nayarit, Jalisco, Colima, Michoacán, Guerrero, Guanajuato, Querétaro and Hidalgo; from the Roberto Barrios "Aguascalientes" to Yucatán, Quintana Roo, Campeche, Tabasco, Veracruz and Chiapas; from La Garrucha "Aguascalientes" to Baja California, Baja California Sur, Sonora, Sinaloa, Chihuahua, Coahuila, Nuevo León, Tamaulipas,

Durango, Zacatecas, the state of Aguascalientes and San Luis Potosí; and from La Realidad "Aguascalientes" the Zapatistas would leave for the states of Puebla, Morelos, Tlaxcala, Mexico State and the Federal District of Mexico City.

Each state coordinator, they announced, would send representatives to the corresponding "Aguascalientes" to pick up the Zapatista delegation slated to visit the townships of their state.

By March 12, 1999, the Zapatistas were already gathering in the "Aguascalientes" centers and getting ready to start the journey on the fourteenth of the month. That day saw the rare sight of 5,000 Zapatistas leaving their communities to travel to all corners of the country.

Civil society pitched in in a big way. They helped the Zapatistas cover national territory in trucks, trains, airplanes, burros, horses and on foot, and to link many struggles and acts of resistance throughout the country. Finally, on March 21, 1999, the referendum was held. In all of Mexico 2,800,000 people took part, as well as 48,000 Mexicans abroad, most from the United States.

The 5,000 Zapatistas returned to their communities and told of what they found: poverty, pain, anguish from the lack of employment, houses destroyed, lack of health and education, and in general, a desolate panorama of how millions of Mexicans were living. But they also discovered struggles and resistance, dignity and the will to organize. They found support for their demands and a willingness on the part of the people to keep progressing together.

The Referendum's success bothered the federal and state governments. They staged a farce in which supposed Zapatista rebels surrendered to the federal army and gave up their arms and uniforms. Soon it was revealed that the fake Zapatistas were really members of the paramilitary group MIRA and that they were paid for their alleged desertion both with livestock and with cash.

On April 7, 1999, just fifteen days after the referendum, armed forces of the Public Security Police of the State of Chiapas took over the municipal palace of San Andrés Sacamch'en de los Pobres by assault. The site housed the municipal council of the township (democratically elected according to traditional practices of the indigenous communities) and had been the seat of the San Andrés dialogue between the federal government and the EZLN.

The federal and state governments imposed an illegitimate municipal government made up of members of the Institutional Revolutionary Party in Chiapas, mounted guard with armed police and unleashed a propaganda campaign to herald having "dismantled" another autonomous Zapatista township.

However, the day after the occupation some 3,000 members of Zapatista base communities, all Tzotzils, peacefully retook the municipal palace of San Andrés Sacamch'en de los Pobres and remained to guard their government.

With this action, the Zapatistas noted, the seat of the peace dialogues was recuperated, indigenous rights and culture were defended, and above all, "the will of millions of citizens expressed in the referendum of March 21, 1999, when they voted yes to recognition of indigenous rights and no to war was respected."

Afterward, the federal and state governments initiated a series of troop and federal and state police movements with the objective of retaking the installations, but finally gave up.

The results of the Referendum were announced nearly two months later. May 7–10, 1999, in the Tojolabal village of La Realidad approximately 2,000 persons arrived to hold the Second Meeting between Civil Society and the ELZN, to analyze the results and plan together new strategies for demanding that the government comply with the San

186

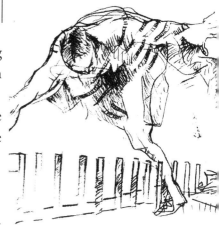

Andrés Accords. The major objective of the meeting was to continue their exchange and the link between their respective struggles.

The vote count also formed part of the huge mobilization and the final quantitative results of the referendum were:

Number of brigades formed in Mexico: 2,358.

Number of brigade members: 27,859.

Other countries where the referendum was carried out: 29.

Brigades in other countries: 265.

Zapatista delegates in Mexico: 4,996.

Number of Mexican townships visited: 1,299.

Population with which they came in contact in Mexico: 64,598,409.

Number of political and social organizations contacted in Mexico: 1,141.

Persons involved in organizing in Mexico not counting Chiapas: 120,000.

Panels and assemblies: 14,893.

Votes in Mexico: 2,854,737.

Votes in other countries: 58,378.

Based on these results, the Zapatistas asked:

"What does it mean when an organization that is surrounded, persecuted, harassed and attacked by military, political ideological, social and economic means can prepare 5,000 of its members to break through the fence and cover thirty-two Mexican states?

"What political, social and citizen force is needed to pick up these 5,000 law-breakers in the mountains of Southeast Mexico and take them to the farthest corners of Mexico?

"How was it possible to carry out the largest exercise in dialogue known in the history of the nation?

"What do these men, women, children and old people have in their hearts that enabled them to challenge threats, lies and risks to find themselves face to face with the Zapatistas, travel with them, eat with them, sleep with them, talk to them, ask with them, respond to them, walk with them?

"What happened to the fear of committing oneself, participating, being an actor and not just a spectator?

"What moved tens of thousands of Mexicans in national territory and abroad to raise the flag of the referendum not only without receiving payment of any kind but also having to pay out of their own pockets?

"How can we measure the dignity, duty, memory and commitment of all these workers, peasants, indigenous people, students, punks, *chavos banda*, political and social activists, members of non-governmental organizations, artists and intellectuals, gays and lesbians, ecclesiastical base communities, priests, nuns, old people and youth?" (Message from the EZLN, May 10, 1999)

But not everything was rosy. The Zedillo administration, along with the state government led by Albores Guillén, was determined to intensify the counterinsurgency campaign. During the National Encounter in Defense of Our Patrimonial Culture held in La Realidad, the army entered the Zapatista community of Amador Hernández in the Montes Azules bioreserve in the Lacandón Jungle. Its inhabitants were actively opposing construction of a highway that would only serve to open the way to the army and counterinsurgency efforts and to loot the area of timber and uranium and oil reserves. The rebels blocked the passage of heavy machinery and soldiers, and from that moment on began a resistance movement that would last over a year. During this time they kept up a permanent protest in front of the new military camp. On this occasion, as in all of the mobilizations, they were not alone—hundreds of people from national and international civil society arrived to accompany the protest at different times, even under direct threat from the governor, Roberto Albores Guillén.

The atmosphere against the foreign and national observers got worse throughout rebel territory. Roadblocks of military and immigration agents multiplied, and the campaign of harassment and persecution continued through the media against anyone who participated in solidarity with any Zapatista indigenous community.

However, the Zapatistas did not interrupt or diminish their contact with the national and international communities. Instead they increased links and in the following months sponsored a series of meetings with different groups of civil society. The General Command of the EZLN held meetings in the Tojolabal community of La Realidad with the Zapatista Front for National Liberation, professors from the National Pedagogical University, members of the movement in defense of patrimonial culture, the Mexican Electricians Union (SME) and striking students from the National Autonomous University of Mexico (UNAM, by its Spanish initials).

Then came a flurry of letters between Subcomandante Marcos and sectors of the national intellectual community about the different posi-

tions adopted toward the largest student strike in the history of the National Autonomous University of Mexico.

In the context of the university strike led by the general Strike Council, hundreds of students traveled to the Lacandón Jungle to exchange experiences with the CCRI. The Zapatista position on the strike was summed up in a letter to the students from Subcomandante Marcos and the writer Carlos Monsiváis: "Your cause is just, it's reasonable, we support it, we admire it, we love you, you are going to win. Furthermore, you are the symptom of 'something' that we are also a symptom of: the political crisis or the crisis in how to do politics. . ."

Once again, there were encounters and frictions with students in the movement who had legitimate demands but whose methods were questioned by broad sectors of society (sectarianism, intolerance, hierarchical decision-making, etc.). Here it is important to point out that only a part of the movement behaved this way, since many groups of students fought permanently to find a dignified solution to the conflict, without giving up on their legitimate demands.[5]

The UNAM strike went on and at the same time the Tzotzil or Tojolabal rebels continued to fight back—accompanied by groups of students on strike, students from the National School of Anthropology and History, and people from different organizations, mainly the FZLN—in a protest in front of the military camp in Amador Hernández. The Clandestine Revolutionary Indigenous Committee sent them a message of encouragement: "The example of dignity and bravery that you are providing now reaches not only us, your compañeros in the EZLN, but also

---

[5] The principal demand of the movement was to maintain the right to free public higher education.

workers, farmers, indigenous people, city people, housewives, students, teachers, artists and intellectuals, honest religious workers, retired people, men, women, children and old people in other parts of Mexico. And it also reaches beyond the borders of our country of Mexico. . .

"On the radio and television and in the press that are at the service of lies and money, they say that these soldiers are here to build a highway that will bring benefits to the indigenous people. . . We know full well that the highways that have been built by the government have not brought one single benefit to the indigenous population. These highways have not brought doctors, they have not built hospitals, or brought teachers, or schools, or materials to improve housing, or to better the price of the products that the farmers sell or lower the cost of the merchandise the indigenous families buy. . . the highways have brought war tanks, cannons, soldiers, prostitution, venereal diseases, alcoholism, the rape of indigenous women and children, death and misery. . ." (Letter from the EZLN, August 1999)

The example of resistance and dignity shown by the Zapatista base communities in the fight to halt the construction of the highway through the Lacandón Jungle is worthy of studying. For whole months the Zapatistas stood guard twenty-four hours a day in front of the military headquarters. It was in Amador Hernández that the Zapatista Air Force made its debut. In response to the deafening sound emitted by the federal soldiers to drown out the protests of the indigenous inhabitants, the Zapatistas "bombed" the military headquarters with hundreds of paper airplanes. In Amador Hernández, hundreds of men and women from Mexico and different parts of the world endured cold, heat, hunger and fatigue to support the indigenous people's demands for the withdrawal of the army and the return of their lands.

At the same time as the people's resistance camp in Amador Hernández, solidarity with the student strike at the UNAM and meetings with diverse sectors of society were all going on, Subcomandante Marcos

sent out various articles on neoliberalism and globalization, the war, the national and international situation, and the role of intellectuals and the left. These texts were emitted in the name of the CCRI of the EZLN during the second half of 1999 and first months of 2000. They included a series of letters to many different people or groups, among them intellectuals, workers at *La Jornada* newspaper, mothers of the political disappeared, as well as a long missive directed to the UN Special Rapporteur for Extrajudicial, Summary or Arbitrary Executions, Asma Jahangir.

The situation by the end of the year was marked, on the one hand, by the increase in hostilities and the dirty war against the rebel villages and also against everyone, national or international, who participated actively with the Zapatistas; and on the other, by the large number of meetings—both face to face and in writing—between the EZLN and different sectors of the national and international community.

After seven years of war, the militarization and paramilitarization had grown to alarming proportions in the state of Chiapas (and in many other states, such as Oaxaca, Hidalgo and Guerrero). According to official figures, in 1999 there were 30,000 elements of the Mexican Army based in Chiapas. However, unofficial calculations set the figure at closer to 70,000.

The militarization of Chiapas, denounced by human rights organizations, peace camps and especially by the nongovernmental organization Enlace Civil, was and is alarming. On January 1, 1994, the federal government ordered close to 10,000 soldiers, 200 vehicles (armed jeeps and armored cars, among others) and forty helicopters into the conflict zone. Over the course of the ten days of war the number of soldiers increased substantially to 17,000. That year (1994), the federal government restricted the armed conflict to four townships: San Cristóbal de las Casas, Las Margaritas, Ocosingo and Altamirano. Later it was extended. By 1999 the Mexican army had broadened its range of action to sixty-six of the 111 townships in Chiapas.

To fight the ongoing war in Southeast Mexico (according to data contained in the EZLN essay about the Geostrategic War in Chiapas, dated November 20, 1999), the federal army is organized as the 7th Military region, made up of five military zones: the 30th based in Villahermosa, 31st in Rancho Nuevo, 36th in Tapachula, 38th in Tenosique, and the 39th in Ocosingo. It also has the following military air bases: Tuxtla Gutiérrez, Ciudad Pemex and Copalar.

The federal army's main force, the so-called Rainbow Task Force, officially had 11 units in Chiapas: San Quintín, Nuevo Momón, Altamirano, Las Tacitas, El Limar, Guadalupe Tepeyac, Monte Líbano, Ocosingo, Chanal, Bochil and Amatitlán. However, a tour of the zone revealed many other stations not officially included, such as those in San Caralampio, Calvario, Laguna Suspiro, Taniperla, Cintalapa, Monte Líbano, Laguna Ocotalito, Santo Tomás, La Trinidad, Jordán, Península, Ibarra, Sultana, Patiwitz, Garrucha, Zaquilá, San Pedro Betania, Yulomax, Florida, Ucuxil,

Temó, Toniná, Chilón, Cuxuljá, Altamirano, Rancho Mosil, Rancho Nuevo, Chanal, Oxchuc, Rancho El Banco, Teopisca, Comitán, Las Margaritas, Río Corozal, Santo Tomás, Vicente Guerrero, Francisco Villa, El Edén, Maravilla Tenejapa, San Vicente, Rizo de Oro, La Sanbra, Flor de Café, Amador Hernández, Soledad, San Quintín, Río Euseba (in the Selva region); Chenalhó, La Limas, Yacteclum, La Libertad, Yaxmel, Puebla, Tanquinucum, Xoyeb, Majomut, Majum, Pepentik, Los Chorros, Acteal, Pextil, Zacalucum, Xumich, Canonal, Tzanen Bolom, Chimix, Quextik, Bajoventik, Pantelhó, Zitalá, Tenejapa, San Andrés, Santiago El Pinar, Jolnachoj, El Bosque, Bochil, San Cayetano, Los Plátanos, Caté, Simojovel, Nicolás Ruiz, Amatenango del Valle, Venustiano Carranza (in Los Altos); Huitiupán, Sabanilla, Paraíso, Los Moyos, Quintana Roo, Los Naranjos, Jesús Carranza, Tila, Emiliano Zapata, Limar, Tumbalá, Hidalgo Joexil, Yajalón, Salto de Agua, Palenque, Chancalá, Roberto Barrios, Playas de Catazajá, Boca Lacantún (in the Norte region).

According to several indigenous and social organizations in Chiapas that are not part of the EZLN, in 1999 the Mexican army had 266 military positions in the state—up considerably from the seventy-six posts it had in 1995. In a letter to Ernesto Zedillo and Secretary of National Defense Enrique Cervantes Aguirre, grassroots and indigenous groups in the Selva zone of Chiapas stated that just in the townships of Ocosingo, Altamirano, Las Margaritas, La Independencia and La Trinitaria there were 37,000 soldiers. In these five townships, they noted, the population is less than 300,000, which means one soldier for every nine inhabitants.

Apart from the "regular" army and air force units stationed in the Chiapas military zones, of the government's fifty-one Mobile Air units of the Special Forces at least five operated in Chiapas. A corps of the Rural Defense Infantry, six infantry battalions, two motorized regiments, three groups of heavy artillery, and three non-stationed companies also operated there, in addition to twelve roaming companies of infantry in Salto de Agua, Altamirano, Tenejapa and Boca Lacantún.

The growth of paramilitary presence in the zone six years after the Zapatista armed uprising showed equally alarming figures. Seven paramilitary groups were known to be operating: Máscara Roja, Paz y Justicia, MIRA, Chinchulines, Degolladores, Puñales and Albores de Chiapas.

The year ended and the Zapatistas had more than enough reason to dance: they were alive, the communities had firmly resisted the aggressions, they had broadened their influence to more villages and regions, and they had linked up with a growing circle both within Mexico and abroad. Zapata lived and the struggle continued.

2000

The Zapatista silence during the electoral storm.
Solidarity with student prisoners.
Position on the presidential elections.
Farewell to Ernesto Zedillo and the
announcement of the March of 23 commanders
and one subcommander to Mexico City.

Mexico greeted the new century in the midst of a pre-electoral storm seldom seen before. Immersed in the battle for the presidency, the major political parties began to define their strategies with respect to the war in Chiapas—an inescapable issue although only addressed in campaign speeches.

After a bare-knuckled fight for the candidacy, Francisco Labastida Ochoa, who helped promote and implement the dirty war in Chiapas, was elected (designated) candidate of the Institutional Revolutionary Party (PRI). In the National Action Party (PAN), the former manager of Coca-Cola and ex-governor of the state of Guanajuato, Vicente Fox, won the contest over more doctrinaire PAN leaders with the support of a group called "Friends of Fox." Cuauhtémoc Cárdenas of the Party of the Democratic Revolution (PRD) prepared to compete for the third time in presidential elections.

During the campaign months, Vicente Fox adopted a marketing-based strategy that advised not confronting the Zapatista movement and maintained a stance in favor of dialogue in Chiapas and respect for the rebels. Labastida repeatedly badmouthed the conflict. As in the past, Cárdenas tried to keep a "safe distance" with respect to the insurgent group.

The EZLN refused to enter into the electoral game and once more opted for silence as a weapon and a strategy. During the first months of the year, Subcomandante Marcos continued to send letters to noted intellectuals and cultural figures: a posthumous letter to the writer, historian and journalist Fernando Benítez; a greeting and homage to Pablo González Casanova; an essay on the intellectual right and liberal fascism titled "Oxymoron!"; a greeting to the musician and social activist René Villanueva; and a message to the insurgent women on International Women's Day.

In February 2000, the Federal Preventive Police (PFP) violated the autonomy of the National Autonomous University of Mexico by entering its grounds to break the student strike. Several students from the General Strike Council were taken prisoner. Days later, the EZLN manifested its unconditional solidarity with the university movement, its rejection of the use of violence to break the strike, and a call to free the jailed students.

All Zapatista correspondence stopped in April, and the group main-

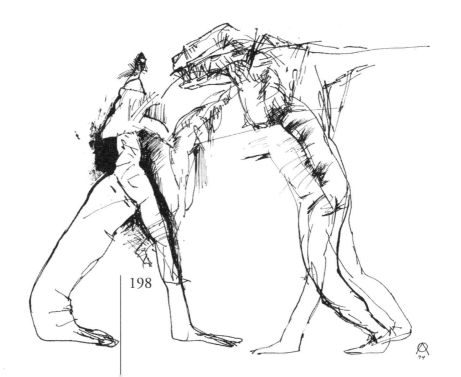

198

tained absolute silence over the next two months. Finally on June 19, 2000, the EZLN released its position on the presidential elections. It warned that in the first place, the elections would take place in the middle of a war—in Chiapas, but also in Guerrero, Oaxaca, Hidalgo, Puebla, Veracruz, San Luis Potosí, and other areas with indigenous populations. In these places, tens of thousands of federal government soldiers and various police forces wage a war of extermination against the indigenous peoples of Mexico. Due to extreme poverty, persecution and the lack of recognition of indigenous rights, the EZLN stated, "the Zapatista resistance continues, the guerrillas of ERPI and EPR remain active, and other armed groups with demands for justice and democracy are emerging." (EZLN essay, June 19, 2000)

They also denounced the indiscriminate use of voter surveys that replace the citizen's vote as elector and make it far more important to win in the headlines of the written press, radio and television than to run for election in the voting booths.

Foretelling the possible triumph of an opposition party, they warned that even if the opposition won the presidency it would not lead to a transition to democracy as long as power remained concentrated in a single person and the powers of the legislature and the justice system continued to be merely decorative.

The Zapatistas emphasized that an autonomous legislative power, independent of the executive branch, is an indispensable part of a democracy and declared themselves against a vote of unity in favor of the right-wing project led by Vicente Fox and in favor of holding clean, fair, honest and pluralistic elections.

Finally, they reiterated the political position they had asserted for the past six years. "The electoral period is not the time of the Zapatistas. Not only because of our masked faces and armed resistance. But above all,

because of our effort to find a new way to do politics that has little or nothing to do with the current forms. . . according to the Zapatista way of thinking, democracy is something that is built from below and with everyone involved, including those who think differently than we do. Democracy is the exercise of the power of the people all the time and everywhere."

On July 2, 2000, the day of presidential and legislative elections, the Zapatistas allowed the installation of voting booths in rebel zones and abstained from carrying out any acts of sabotage or any actions against electoral installations, officials or voters. They did not endorse any of the candidates or their parties, and urged the people of Mexico to view the elections as a possibility for struggle, to fight for change in this way and with these means, and to defend the vote.

The night of July 2, 2000, put an end to over seventy years of continuous administrations under the Institutional Revolutionary Party.

PAN member and former Coca-Cola executive Vicente Fox won the presidency. Pablo Salazar, the candidate of an alliance of all major parties against the PRI, took the governor's election in the state of Chiapas.

After a silence of nearly six months, the EZLN came back on the scene. In late November 2000 the Zapatistas said goodbye to the outgoing president Ernesto Zedillo in a letter similar to the one they sent to welcome him at the beginning of his presidency. In the document Subcomandante Marcos summed up the nightmare that Zedillo's term had been for millions of Mexicans: "political assassinations, economic crisis, massive impoverishment, illicit and brutal enrichment of the few, the sale of national sovereignty, public insecurity, tightened ties between the government and organized crime, corruption, irresponsibility, war. . . and bad jokes poorly told." (Letter from the EZLN, November 28, 2000)

With respect to the armed conflict, the EZLN noted that Zedillo's strategy over the six years of his term had been a dual strategy of pretending to be willing to enter into dialogue while continuing to propagate violence. During his term the chief executive "tried to repeat the history of the betrayal of Chinameca with the government offensive against the Zapatistas on February 9, 1995; spent millions of pesos trying to buy the consciences of the rebels; militarized indigenous communities (not only in Chiapas); expelled international observers; trained, equipped, armed and financed paramilitaries; persecuted, imprisoned and summarily executed Zapatistas and non-Zapatistas; destroyed the social fabric of the Chiapas countryside; and followed the slogan of its alleged offspring, the paramilitary group 'Red Mask' (Máscara Roja): 'We will kill the Zapatista seed' by massacring children and pregnant women in Acteal on December 22, 1997."

The letter ended with an eloquent "You are now going into exile. We are still here." Two days later, on December 1, 2000, the EZLN presented its interpretation of the electoral process. In an essay titled "Mexico 2000: Open Windows, Doors to Be Opened," dedicated to the insurgent leader Lucha, who died on September 9 of the previous year, the rebels evalu-

ated the elections. "The common point of reference in these campaigns was a profound disrespect for the citizen. More like product marketing, the presidential campaigns conceived of the citizen as a consumer, who pays in cash, doesn't ask questions, does not demand a guarantee and has no memory. In its stubborn march away from the citizenry, the Mexican political class made it clear that there is a huge disparity between its offers and the people's expectations."

The victory of the opposition after seventy-one years of PRI government was seen by the Zapatistas as the result of widespread citizen sentiment that said NO to more of the same in the system: "an anonymous multitude of Mexicans rejected a political system that for over seven decades sowed catastrophes and cadavers in national history. The dead along the way are many: justice, democracy, liberty, national sovereignty, peace, life with dignity, truth, legitimacy, shame and above all, hope. These dead come back to life every so often: 1965, 1968, 1985, 1988, 1994 and 1997." (EZLN essay, December 1, 2000)

Furthermore, the EZLN argued against confusing power changing hands ("because that's all Fox's victory is") with a real transition, and noted that those responsible for the fact that the majority of citizens linked democratization of the country with the defeat of the PRI were the PRI members themselves, due to their economic and social policies, their discretionary handling of the budget and their ties to drug trafficking.

On the PRD presidential campaign led by Cuauhtémoc Cárdenas, the insurgent group stated that it was a campaign that began obsessed with the center (and in politics, they said, the center is nothing more than the right moving in) and later shifted left, but leaving certain casualties along the way: its credibility, confidence, coherence and hope.

Finally, Subcomandante Marcos said that with Fox's rise to power—first within the PAN, then in the campaign, and now with his winning presidential bid: "the ultra-right found the umbrella, the reflector and the pulpit it had been seeking. A struggle took place between ultras and moderates of the right within the National Action Party. In the course of the power struggle the party itself began to disappear, losing its profile, and now it seems it can only offer the triumphant Fox two things: the color blue and the entity that will have to take responsibility for the mistakes of the new federal executive.

"On July 2 the PRI not only lost the presidency, it also suffered a historic defeat. This defeat is the product of many struggles. Not facing up to that fact and acting in consequence is petty stubbornness."

The indigenous rebels called an unusual press conference for December 2, the day after the new president took office. This raised widespread interest, and dozens of journalists from nearly all the accredited media in the country and many members of the foreign press who had come to Mexico to cover the presidential inauguration traveled to the village of La Realidad, curious to hear the word of the indigenous rebels.

As rarely had happened in the past, the Zapatistas arrived right on time. Subcomandante Marcos appeared along with Major Moisés and Comandante Tacho and began the press conference by reading four communiqués. The first welcomed President Fox, in the Zapatista manner: "With the Zapatistas you begin at zero as far as credibility and confidence

(. . .) There should be no doubt about it—we are your opposites. What is at stake here is whether that opposition will express itself in civil and peaceful channels or if we must continue in arms and with masked faces to get what we seek, which is, Mr. Fox, democracy, freedom and justice for all Mexicans. . ." (Letter to Vicente Fox, December 2, 2000)

In the same letter, Subcomandante Marcos described the 2,525 days of the war: "For nearly six years of war the Zapatistas have resisted and we have confronted two federal executives (self-named 'presidents'), two secretaries of national defense, six secretaries of the interior, five peace commissioners, five 'governors' of Chiapas and a host of mid-range officials. . . During these nearly six years the Zapatistas have insisted, time and time again, on dialogue. We have done this because we have a commitment to civil society, which demanded that we put down our arms and try for a peaceful solution."

Somewhere in Mexico City the new president listened to the voice of the rebels telling him, "If you choose the path of sincere, serious and respectful dialogue, simply show it in acts. Be assured that you will find a positive response from the Zapatistas. This way we can reinitiate the dialogue and soon begin to build true peace."

In the second communiqué, the EZLN stipulated three signals that they considered minimal conditions for resuming dialogue: approval of the Cocopa law on indigenous rights and culture, liberation of all Zapatista prisoners in Chiapas and other places, troop withdrawal and closure of seven of the 259 positions maintained by the army in the state—Amador Hernández, Guadalupe Tepeyac and Río Eusteba (near the Aguascalientes of La Realidad); Jolnachoj (near the Aguascalientes of Oventik); Roberto Barrios, (near the Aguascalientes of the same name in the Norte zone); La Garrucha (near the Aguascalientes of the same name in the Selva), and Cuxuljá (near the community of Moisés Gandhi).

In the third communiqué, the Zapatista Army of National Liberation announced that a delegation of rebels would march to Mexico City to demand that Congress approve the Indigenous Rights and Culture law drafted in November 1996 by the Cocopa. The Zapatista delegation would be made up of twenty-four members of the CCRI, representing Tzotzil, Tzeltal, Tojolabal, Chol, Zoque, Mam and mestizo communities. Their names were Comandantes Esther, Fidelia, Susana, Yolanda, Abel, Abraham, Alejandro, Bulmaro, Daniel, David, Eduardo, Filemón, Gustavo, Isaías, Ismael, Javier, Maxo, Mister, Moisés, Omar, Sergio, Tacho and Zebedeo, and Subcomandante Marcos.

Finally, in the fourth and last message of the afternoon, the Zapatista Army recognized the designation of Luis H. Alvarez as the new peace commissioner. It stated that once the government complied with the signals, the EZLN would accept Alvarez as a "valid interlocutor."

The organization of the march began the next day. Bulletins to the press, to the National Indigenous Congress and to national and international civil society followed.

On December 8, 2000 Pablo Salazar took office as governor of

Chiapas. As with Vicente Fox, the Zapatistas gave him the benefit of the doubt. "Mr. Salazar now has the possibility of contributing first to reinitiating dialogue and later to seriously and responsibly going forward to reach the end of the war and the beginning of the construction of peace with justice and dignity." (EZLN communiqué, December 8, 2000)

On December 22, 2000—three years after the massacre at Acteal where paramilitary groups murdered forty-five indigenous women, men and children—the EZLN demanded punishment of the real culprits, dismantling of paramilitary groups, and compliance with the signals required for a possible resumption of dialogue.

That same day the government ordered the withdrawal of the army from its position in the community Amador Hernández where it had been since August of 1999. It also announced the derogation of the expropriation decree dictated by the Zedillo government that had stripped the indigenous inhabitants of their land in this Tzeltal community.

For sixteen months, day after day, minute by minute, thousands of indigenous rebels in Amador Hernández had staged one of the most important demonstrations of organizational genius, creativity and peaceful resistance to protest the military base. They did not want the construction of a highway that would facilitate the arrival of military vehicles, prostitution and the looting of natural resources from the jungle. Through their resistance they were finally able to achieve their objective.

The EZLN was glad to see the military withdrawal but as always remained cautious. It called on national and international civil society to continue to mobilize for compliance with the rest of the demands.

The end of the year arrived and with it the festivities of the seventh anniversary of the armed uprising. Once more, thousands of indigenous people gathered in the five Aguascalientes to celebrate with song and dance seven years of being alive, of fighting back and, above all, of perseverance.

2001

The Color of the Earth March,
hope and mobilization.
Mexico and the world welcome the Zapatistas.
Betrayal by the political parties and the counter-
reform on indigenous rights and culture.
More harassment and persecution, now under the
government of "change."

The year and the century began, perhaps as never before, with hope and optimism. Year seven was beginning, the seventh year of the war against oblivion, the year of the "Color of the Earth March." The Zapatistas greeted the dawn of the first day of the year, as is customary, dancing to the tunes of the marimba and electronic keyboards. Peace looked like a real possibility and the rebels, although somewhat distrustful, were betting on attaining it.

In the speech on the seventh anniversary of the uprising, the Zapatistas recounted, year by year, reflections of the decision to rise up in arms.

"In the first reflection we were wind rising up from below, an unexpected awakening. . . From far back in time, memory became the breath of fire. . .

"With the second reflection, we were lips for the word and ears to listen to the hearts of others. The fire died down and the chest swelled as the collective 'we' grew. . .

"With the glint of the third reflection we made an agreement with the one who rules so that we who are the color and blood of the earth could have a dignified place among all people. The one who rules did not keep his word, but we became a bridge to other worlds. . .

"It was on the fourth reflection that those who govern us and sustain us took the first step. One thousand one hundred and eleven times we saw our solitude at last defeated. However, the stupidity that ruled with blood sought to blind our vision. 'Acteal' is the name of the place where the eyes will never close again.

"The fifth reflection was of growing resistance, of making resistance our school and our lesson. On the side of he who said he ruled there was war, destruction, lies, intolerance. Here, quiet dignity, rebellious silence, a government of our own.

"The sixth reflection was a long walk. Five times a thousand went out to all the lands of those who call themselves brothers and sisters. We asked them questions, we listened to them. We stored their words so they could mature and find their time.

"The seventh reflection came at last and with it that which was already wavering finally fell. 'The other' arrived with many faces but without a face, with a name but unnamed, and completely anonymous came what was not the end but a stop along the way. They spoke to us and told us that the seventh was the moment to go to the land above." (EZLN speech, January 1, 2001)

Although the words at the beginning of the year showed optimism, the EZLN also stated its mistrust. "Today he who rules says he wants peace. That's the same thing the one before him said, and all he did was try to destroy those whose very lives challenged him. So today we want to remind everyone and the government that there are many injustices still pending. . ." (EZLN speech, January 1, 2001)

The days that followed were intense. The organization of the march began in earnest and the Zapatistas announced the creation of the Center for Zapatista Information (CZI), an office designed to serve as a bridge between the EZLN and national and international civil society. Once again, they announced, they themselves would handle organization.

The flow of messages sent directly from the Lacandón Jungle increased. The National Indigenous Congress, Mexican civil society, the international community, the Commission on Concordance and Pacification, the Congress of the Union, and the press were among the recipients.

On January 10, 2001, the army withdrew from Cuxuljá, the second position on the list of withdrawals demanded. "We are pleased but not pleased," said the base communities, always mistrustful.

On January 12, 2001, the seventh anniversary of the ceasefire, the indigenous rebels again took the city of San Cristóbal de las Casas. Thousands of Tzotzils, Tzeltals, Tojolobals, Chols, Zoques, Mams and mestizos with masked faces invaded the streets of the city to deliver their word:

"For the past seven years we have demanded that the rulers recognize the rights and culture of those who have given history and honor to this country that is Mexico. For the past seven years, we have urged dialogue for all who truly want peace. . . Now that the new century and a new millennium are beginning, we are insisting on the path of dialogue to end the war." (EZLN speech, January 12, 2001)

By this time, the EZLN's announcement that it would send a delegation to Mexico City had stirred a nationwide debate. On January 23, 2001, the president of the Chamber of Deputies, Ricardo García Cervantes, declared that the mobilization was illegal and the rebels should be detained.

But preparations for the march continued and on January 24, 2001, the EZLN revealed the route they would take to the capital.

Three weeks before the march set off, Vicente Fox—eloquent as always—stated: "The country is more than Chiapas (. . .) If there is a march, there's a march. If they don't want to march, then don't march. Whatever."

Several days later, however, the presidential discourse changed. The results of surveys and international attention forced the switch. "My priority these days is that the EZLN march go well. I'll stake my presidency and all my political capital on it. We must give Marcos an opportunity," said President Fox on February 23, 2001.

The Chiapas peace commissioner Luis H. Alvarez considered it a positive sign that the EZLN sought to open up a dialogue with Congress. But mere days before the start of the march, the International Committee of the Red Cross, which had agreed to accompany the Zapatista delegation along its journey to Mexico City, retracted its commitment. It explained that the federal government had asked it not to participate.

The Zapatistas denounced the government's contradictory statements. On the one hand, it publicly applauded the Zapatista initiative and on the other, blocked security efforts. "We will be there with you. Nothing will stop us," the EZLN reassured civil society.

And so it was. On February 24, 2001 at noon, twenty-three members of the EZLN *comandancia* left for Mexico City from five different points in rebel territory, with a first stop in San Cristóbal de las Casas, Chiapas. With their faces covered and only their words and the legitimacy of their cause as weapons, the twenty-four members of the Clandestine Revolutionary Indigenous Committee (CCRI) were received by a crowd made up mostly of members of Zapatista communities to bid then farewell.

In a traditional ceremony, the delegation received the ruling staffs of each one of the indigenous villages present. And from the stage where the journey would depart, the EZLN announced that it needed the support of "a grassroots activist, someone who has dedicated all his life to transforming the living conditions of poor Mexicans, someone who has suffered persecution and prison for the Zapatista cause, someone who has the virtues of personal sacrifice and honesty." These characteristics were embodied in the architect Fernando Yáñez Muñoz, whom the EZLN asked to accompany

them on the delegation's march and to serve as a liaison between the EZLN and the deputies, senators and leaders of the political parties.

"We welcome him and tell him that it is an honor for us that people of his stature are on our side," said the Zapatistas. (Speech by Subcomandante Marcos, EZLN, February 24, 2001)

In his address to the crowd, Subcomandante Marcos stated, "With us go the steps of Indian peoples from all over and the steps of all men, women, children and old people in the world who know that the world holds all the colors of the earth."

At six in the morning the next day, the caravan of indigenous dignity began its long trip to Mexico City. More than forty buses and more cars—not even counting the vehicles of the national and international press—started their motors to accompany the Zapatista delegation. It was just the beginning and the caravan already had more than 3,000 persons from various organizations and nationalities.

The next stop was the capital of the state, Tuxtla Gutiérrez, headquarters of the state powers that had done so much to fight the rebels. This stop provided one of the first surprises on the march. No one expected the large crowd that came out to greet the Zapatistas, or that the residents would fill the streets with yells and slogans of support, not just for the Zapatista delegation but also for the whole caravan that swelled as the hours passed.

After a brief event, thousands of indigenous people—accompanied by national and international civil society—continued on their way to Juchitán, Oaxaca. Along the road, thousands of Oaxacans showed their support, greeting the caravan with fruit, water, sandwiches, tortillas—whatever they had.

The caravan stopped for a brief event with regional indigenous groups in a place called La Ventosa. Huaves, Mixes, Zapotecos and Chinantecos asked them to carry their word with the caravan and integrate the demands of people in the Isthmus with their own.

Finally, the day of February 25, 2001, ended in Juchitán, Oaxaca, where Comandanta Esther spoke of the difficult situation of indigenous women: "As a rule we the women are triply exploited. First for being indigenous women, and because we are indigenous we don't know how to talk and we are looked down on; for being women they say we don't know how to talk, they say we are stupid, that we don't know how to think. We don't have the same opportunities as the men. And three, for being poor women. We are all poor because we don't have good food, decent housing, education; we don't have good health. Many women watch their children die in their arms from curable diseases." (Speech by Comandanta Esther, February 25, 2001)

On February 26, 2001, in the morning the Zapatistas called a press conference. The purpose: they had received death threats from a mercenary group in the area and wanted to respond. "No threat will stop us from our objective of arriving at the seat of federal legislative power to promote the constitutional recognition of indigenous rights and culture."

Following the announcement, the march continued on its way, and by nightfall it had reached the state capital, where the delegation was received by a packed plaza of indigenous peoples and mestizos from all over the state of Oaxaca. "We are amazed by your capacity for organizing, your combativeness, your sincere pride in the roots that give us color and name in these lands. . . The indigenous Oaxacans make all indigenous peoples in all parts of Mexico proud to be indigenous. . . We hope what all indigenous people of Mexico seek will now be possible, and that the indigenous peoples of these lands have an important place there," said the Zapatistas during the central event in the city of Oaxaca. (Speech by Subcomandante Marcos, February 26, 2001)

The fourth day of the march began on the road to Tehuacán, Puebla, where thousands of Nahuas, Mazatecos, Popolucas and Mixtecos received the caravan. That same day the growing parade of vehicles was on its way to Orizaba, Veracruz, where probably the most surprising and emotional event of the caravan took place.

Before a plaza full of indigenous people, workers, urban residents, children, members of grassroots organizations and a wide range of individuals from civil society, Comandante Ismael explained, once again, the concept of autonomy that the Indian communities were defending. "What we want with autonomy is not to divide our country Mexico; what we want is to build a different Mexico, where all the poor are included. To build a Mexico with a future where not just a few get rich while millions live with misery, hunger and death." (Speech by Comandante Ismael, February 27, 2001)

The day ended with a gathering in the central plaza of the city of Puebla, where once more people filled the streets. Young people carrying black and red flags, as well as teachers, workers, city dwellers, debtors from the organization El Barzón, women and children, all came out to greet the Zapatista leadership and members of the National Indigenous Congress.

"In the four days of our March of Indigenous Dignity, in passing through the different villages and cities, along with thousands of brothers and sisters from national and international civil society, we have been joined by the hearts and steps of thousands of Mexican brothers and sisters and people from other countries who have joined our journey

215

to accompany us on our long road, and along with you our struggle will be even bigger and stronger," said Comandante David, visibly affected by the outpouring of support. (Speech by Comandante David, February 27, 2001)

The Zapatistas spent the night in the Convent of the Carmelitas, and at dawn the next day left for the state of Tlaxcala. There Comandante Mister spoke: "We have been resisting for over 500 years and we have been divided by the imposition of their ideologies, but now that we are united we won't go through another 500 years of misery and abandonment; now they will have to recognize and respect us as Indian peoples who form part of this nation." (Speech by Comandante Mister, February 28, 2001)

After an early morning meeting in the kiosk of the central square of Tlaxcala, the march left for Pachuca, going through the townships of Tepatepec, Emiliano Zapata and Ciudad Sahagún, where they held short but very well-attended demonstrations.

In Pachuca, Comandante Zebedeo, famous for his colorful prose, took the stand: "Let's all use our awareness to commit ourselves to seeking a peaceful solution to the conflict; it should be the people of Mexico who chart the course toward a dignified social and cultural harmony." (Speech by Comandante Zebedeo, February 28, 2001)

The day's events did not end there. After that were forums and speeches in Actopan and Ixmiquilpan, where a torrential downpour caught the crowd who simply remained where they were to listen to the words of the Zapatistas. The end of the day found the caravan in the township of Tephé, where the delegation slept in an area known for its hot springs owned by an Otomí indigenous collective from the community.

On March 1, 2001, the Color of the Earth March suffered its first accident. En route from Tephé to Querétaro, a bus ran into one of the vehicles of the Zapatista Information Center. In the accident a member of the Federal Highway Police was run over and four members of the Zapatista support team were injured. The ELZN sent a message of con-

dolence for the death of the police officer and an investigation was opened to determine if it was an accident or an attempt on their lives.

The caravan continued along its route. In the capital of Querétaro the EZLN delivered one of the harshest speeches against a state governor, Governor Loyola, who had openly threatened the members of the caravan. In that same place, the EZLN greeted two Zapatistas unjustly imprisoned by the governor. "Since we have not yet been executed we take this opportunity to send a message to our Zapatista brothers imprisoned in the Querétaro jail, Sergio Jerónimo Sánchez and Anselmo Pérez Robles, not to be sad, that they will soon be freed, and that their place in the prison will be filled by those who now govern without knowing the history of their state." (Speech by Subcomandante Marcos, March 1, 2001)

The next day, the caravan met up with thousands of people who filled the streets and the plaza of Acámbaro, Guanajuato. They went on to Zinapécuaro and Pátzcuaro in the state of Michoacán. At these stops they had to improvise events to meet the demands of the people. One stop more in the township of Uruapan and they arrived at the final destination—the Purépecha community of Nurío where the Third National Indigenous Congress was being held.

On March 3, 2001, the Congress formally began with representation from forty indigenous peoples from all over the country. Amuzgo, Cora, Cuicateco, Chiapa, Chinanteco, Cholcholteco, Chol, Chontal,

Guarijío, Huasteco, Huave, Kikapú, Kukapa, Mam, Matlazinka, Mayo, Maya, Mazahua, Mazateco, Mixe, Mixteco, Náhuatl, Ñahñú, O'odham, Pape, Popoluca, Rarámuri, Purépecha, Tenek, Tlahuica, Tlapaneco, Tojolabal, Totonaco, Trique, Tzeltal, Tzotzil, Wixaritari-Huichol, Yaqui, Zapoteco and Zoque filled two days of intense work with their languages, their colors, their thought and their resistance.

Among the resolutions made by the National Indigenous Congress were:

"First, constitutional recognition of our rights as Indian peoples, in the terms of the initiative for constitutional reform drafted by the Commission on Concordance and Pacification (Cocopa);

"Second, constitutional recognition of our existence as Indian peoples;

"Third, constitutional recognition of our inalienable right to self-determination as expressed in autonomy within the framework of the Mexican state;

"Fourth, constitutional recognition of our ancestral territories and lands;

"Fifth, recognition of our indigenous systems of norms in the construction of a pluralist legal system;

"Sixth, demilitarization of all indigenous regions in the country;

"Seventh, freedom for all indigenous prisoners in the country that are deprived of their liberty for having fought in defense of autonomy and for respect for our individual and collective rights."

On March 5, 2001, the caravan left for Morelia, capital of the state of Michoacán, where a crowd gathered in the central plaza for a morning demonstration. Comandante Abel spoke of attacks and invasions of their territory: "Autonomous townships and offices have been dismantled by the system that causes so much suffering to all the poor people in Mexico. In spite of all this, our villages have grown stronger, they continue to resist and fight back, converting fiestas and songs into blows against the enemy." (Speech by EZLN Comandante Abel, March 5, 2001)

The next stop was the township of Temoaya in Mexico State, and by the end of the day, the long caravan had arrived in Toluca, the capital of Mexico State.

By this time the march's warm reception from millions of Mexicans and, above all, the protest and rebellion against the government that the march registered all along its route, was worrying not only Vicente Fox and his cabinet but also parts of the business community. Some business leaders saw their interests threatened by a crowd that called not only for recognition of indigenous rights but also justice and equality for all Mexicans.

In Toluca the Zapatista Central Command sent a message to the masters of money: "You are scared because they say that as we go by the poor will rise up and call for retribution for all the wrongs committed against them. You are scared because you recognize that the living conditions of the majority of Mexicans—not only indigenous—are very bad and that could lead to rebellion. . ." (Speech by Subcomandante Marcos, March 5, 2001)

On March 6, 2001, the caravan arrived in Cuernavaca, Morelos, where the Zapatistas from Chiapas spoke and left a floral offering at the foot of the statue of General Emiliano Zapata. The next stop was Tepoztlán, and there Comandante Isaías reiterated the mistrust they had in the government: "We don't want any more deceit because Mr. Fox tries to deceive the people of Mexico. Once again he is saying there is already democracy and already change. And no, compañeros, we the Zapatistas say the same thing we've been saying since January 1, 1994: Enough is enough! . . ." (Speech by EZLN Comandante Isaías, March 6, 2001)

The next day, the city of Iguala, Guerrero, opened its doors and hearts to the unstoppable march of colors. Thousands of Amuzgos, Tlapanecos, Náhuatl and Mixtecos left their communities to unite their voices and demands with those of the Zapatistas and the rest of the Indian peoples of the nation. The CCRI extended a respectful greeting to the armed organizations ERPI, EPR and FARP. March 7 ended in Cuautla, Morelos, where they talked about the old and the new Zapatista movements: "We will walk the same road of history, but we will not repeat it. We are from before, yes, but we are new." (Speech by Subcomandante Marcos, March 7, 2001)

On International Women's Day, March 8, 2001, the caravan passed through Anenecuilco, the town of birth of General Emiliano Zapata, where the delegation was received by the children of the revolutionary leader. The route continued through Chinameca, where Zapata was assassinated by betrayal, and Tlaltizapán, where they visited the general headquarters of the first Zapatistas. The arduous revolutionary journey culminated in Milpa Alta, in the Federal District, where they talked about indigenous and peasant women.

On March 9, the people of San Pablo Oxtotepec received the long line of vehicles with tens of thousands of people on board. The march had reached the outskirts of Mexico City, where people were already preparing to receive the indigenous people, peasants, workers, members of the

urban popular movement, artists, teachers, retired persons, students and youth from all over Mexico and many other countries.

A day before entering the heart of Mexico City, the Zapatista delegation and its thousands of followers stopped in Xochimilco, where again Subcomandante Marcos referred to the declarations made by the business community: "Fear has distorted the already poor vision of the business people. That and their minimal intellectual quotient prevents them from realizing that the century called "twentieth" has ended and the second millennium is behind us. . . But you should know, men of money, that the times of yesterday will not return today or tomorrow. We will no longer listen to your insults quietly. . ." (Speech by Subcomandante Marcos, March 10, 2001)

After fifteen days on the road and twelve states, the march that had left from San Cristóbal de las Casas was not the same. Millions of people accompanied its journey, hundreds of declarations had been made in favor and against, the first from the voices of the dispossessed, the second from the government and the business class, powers that felt threatened.

People flooded into Mexico City. The streets filled with indigenous people, workers, peasants, teachers, city dwellers, chauffeurs, fisherfolk, taxi drivers, office workers, employees, street vendors, religious workers, athletes, activists and a long etcetera made up of tens of thousands of men, women, children, youth and old people.

221

A huge white trailer with the command of the Zapatista Army of National Liberation on board wheeled through the streets of the city from Xochimilco to the Zócalo—the heart of the nation's capital. There, in front of the gigantic flag that waved in the center of the Plaza of the Constitution, the Zapatista rebels spoke: "Mexico—we didn't come here to tell you what to do, or to lead you anywhere. We came to humbly, respectfully, ask you to help us, not to allow another day to dawn without this flag having a dignified place for us, we who are the color of the earth." (Speech by Subcomandante Marcos, March 11, 2001)

The General Command of the EZLN had made it to the Federal District, specifically to the National School of Anthropology and History (ENAH). There the community offered the Zapatistas lodging during their stay in Mexico City. The days that followed were intense. Problems arose in the preparations for Congress to hear the arguments on the recognition of indigenous rights and culture. The deputies and senators invited the Zapatista delegates to speak in a joint meeting of the commissions on Constitutional Points, Indigenous Affairs and Legislative Affairs. This proposal was deemed totally unacceptable by the CCRI and the indigenous movement. "We do not accept a shameful dialogue with the legislature, off in a corner with a small group of legislators, that only serves to avoid allowing the National Indigenous Congress and the Zapatistas to speak to the full legislature." (EZLN communiqué, March 13, 2001)

The legislators tried to ignore the historic dimension of the national and international mobilization. Without mind to race, economic position, color, sex, ideology, religion, age or size, the people of Mexico had demonstrated in favor of the recognition of indigenous rights in the constitution and compliance with the three signals demanded by the EZLN

222

as a prerequisite to initiate dialogue with the government. But none of this seemed to matter to the deputies and senators.

While the politicians attempted to assimilate what was happening, the rebel delegation continued to meet with national and international civil society. During the first week in Mexico City, the CCRI met with the National Indigenous Congress, intellectuals, workers, rock fans, theater groups, teachers and students, and with its hosts (the ENAH community and the residents of the Isidro Fabela neighborhood). They also went to the National Polytechnic Institute and visited villages and neighborhoods throughout the Federal District.

A week after the EZLN announced its demand to be heard on the floor of the Congress of the Union, the legislators had still not responded. Every indication was that the conservative wing of the PAN and PRI would prevail, so on March 19, 2001, the Zapatistas announced that they were returning to the mountains of Southeast Mexico and a farewell ceremony was held in front of the Legislative Palace on March 22.

"Forced to choose between the politicians and the people, the EZLN does not hesitate: it is with the people, from them we have received an attentive ear and respectful words. We will never bow our heads to the politicians or accept humiliation or deceit. We will not wait in line to receive seals of 'received' on our historic demands. . . the political class's refusal to listen is obvious. The people, the Indian people, national and international civil society are convinced of the fairness of our demands and have supported us unconditionally. The EZLN will continue to seek and build inclusive spaces for the participation of all who want a truly new Mexico. . ." (EZLN communiqué, March 19, 2001)

That night, President Vicente Fox announced the army's withdrawal from Guadalupe Tepeyac and said he would send a message to the Zapatista command. The letter did not arrive, and the rebels continued the tour planned for before leaving the city. They visited the three campuses of the Autonomous Metropolitan University (UAM) and participated in one

223

of the most emotional gatherings of the tour—the one held at the National Autonomous University of Mexico (UNAM).

As promised, on March 22, 2001, the Zapatistas stood outside Congress to denounce the blindness and racism of part of the political class that refused to hear them. While they explained the situation and said goodbye to thousands of people gathered in the street next to the Legislative Palace, inside the building the deputies and senators discussed whether or not to let the Zapatistas speak before them.

The agreement arrived, and against the entire parliamentary group of the president's National Action Party, legislators from the rest of the political groups made it possible to have a meeting with the Zapatistas on the full floor of Congress.

On March 28, 2001, when everyone thought that Subcomandante Marcos would take the tribune, the Zapatistas again surprised not only the politicians but much of national and international civil society. An indigenous woman, Comandanta Esther, took the floor and gave the central message in the name of the Clandestine Revolutionary Indigenous Committee–Central Command of the EZLN.

Comandanta Esther spoke of the terrible situation of indigenous women, their poverty, exploitation, repression and exclusion. She spoke of their triple marginalization: to be poor, women and indigenous. She referred to the benefits that the approval of the Cocopa's legislative proposal would bring, she defended the right to difference and finally, she opened up the possibility of a real dialogue with the executive branch. The architect Fernando Yáñez, she announced, would communicate with the peace commissioner Luis H. Alvarez to certify compliance with the three signals demanded. (Speech by Comandanta Esther, March 28, 2001)

With this important and historical act the delegation of twenty-three Zapatista leaders said goodbye to the millions of people from Mexico and the other countries that had accompanied them. The road to peace, perhaps as never before in those seven years, looked like a real possibility.

The Color of the Earth March went for a total of thirty-seven days and 6,000 kilometers. The Zapatista delegation and the tens of thousands of indigenous and nonindigenous fellow marchers went through thirteen states: Chiapas, Oaxaca, Puebla, Veracruz, Tlaxcala Hidalgo, Querétaro, Guanajuato, Michoacán, Mexico State, Morelos, Guerrero and the Federal District and held a total of seventy-seven public events to over-flowing audiences. Who in their right mind could be capable of ignoring this level of mobilization? Who could be so blind and deaf? Would economic and political interests prevail over citizens' calls? Would the politicians turn their backs on the indigenous people of the country and millions of people who in Mexico and throughout the world demanded the recognition of indigenous rights and culture?

On April 25, 2001, the answer came. The Senate of the republic "unanimously" approved a constitutional reform on indigenous rights and culture that denied the principal points of the legislative proposal drawn up by the Cocopa. With 109 votes in favor from the PRI, PAN, PRD and Green Party, they refused to respect the main points of the San Andrés Accords.

Even before the Zapatistas responded to this move, indigenous representatives from all over the country, from social organizations and human rights groups, academics, national and international intellectuals, artists and legal experts warned against ratifying the reform on the floor of Congress, considering it a measure designed by the most backward forces in the nation. The reforms to the Cocopa proposal finally were ratified and President Vicente Fox, knowing perfectly well the consequences, rushed to welcome them.

On April 29, 2001, the EZLN released its position. It noted that first, the recently approved reform did not respond at all to the demands of the Indian peoples of Mexico, the National Indigenous Congress, the EZLN, or to the demands of national and international civil society that mobilized in the march.

Second, the Zapatistas noted that the reform betrayed the San Andrés Accords in general and in particular it betrayed the Cocopa legal initiative in its primary points: autonomy and free determination, Indian peoples as entitled to public rights, land and territory, natural resource use, election of municipal authorities, and right to associate on a regional basis, among others.

"Mr. Fox accepted the current reform knowing full well that it is not remotely similar to what he presented as his own. In this way, it is obvious that Fox only pretended to promote the Cocopa initiative while negotiating with hardcore sectors of Congress to pass a reform that does not recognize indigenous rights." (EZLN communiqué, April 29, 2001)

This was another decisive moment in the rebel path of the Zapatistas. From there on in, nothing would be the same. As they noted in the communiqué, with this reform the federal legislators and the Fox government closed the door on peace and dialogue. Since they failed to resolve one of the root causes of the Zapatista uprising and invalidated the process of dialogue and negotiation, they basically justified the existence of the different armed groups in Mexico. They evaded their historic commitment to pay the debt Mexico had for nearly two hundred years of sovereign and independent existence, and they tried to split the national indigenous movement by passing on to the state congresses the obligations of the federal legislature.

The EZLN therefore refused to recognize the constitutional reform on indigenous rights and culture. With this law, they said, all hope for a negotiated solution to the war in Chiapas was betrayed. The organization announced its total divorce from the political class when it came to promoting popular demands.

As a consequence, the rebels declared that Fernando Yáñez Muñoz would completely suspend his work as a liaison between the EZLN and the administration. There would be no more contact between Fox's government and the EZLN, until indigenous rights and culture as defined in the Cocopa initiative were constitutionally recognized. The Zapatistas would continue in their resistance and rebellion.

Ernesto Zedillo was only two months into his term when he revealed his real strategy in Chiapas; Vicente Fox took a little while longer. But in the end, not only did he not resolve the conflict "in fifteen minutes" as promised in his campaign, but four months into his presidential term he lost any possibility of dialogue with the indigenous Zapatista movement.

There is no legislative initiative in memory that has stirred so much debate in nearly all parts of society. Academics, legislators, indigenous peoples, analysts, social organizations, anthropologists, legal experts, experts in indigenous affairs from other countries, political scientists, journalists and columnists, among other sectors of civil society, debated and reflected for four long years on the pros and cons of an initiative that, although it did not include all the San Andrés Accords, was legitimated by the EZLN, the Indian peoples of the country, and by millions of people in national and international civil society.

The next step for the federal government consisted of mounting a smear campaign against the Zapatista, accusing them of being intransigent and not wanting dialogue. In this context, the peace commissioner

in Chiapas, Luis H. Alvarez, persisted in his calls to resume the negotiations, after noting that "silence does not help to correct the harm that indigenous communities undoubtedly have suffered for too long."

On May 24, 2001, the Commission for Concordance and Pacification (Cocopa) requested a meeting with Vicente Fox "to analyze the possible scenarios that would enable them to break the impasse in the conflict." The move by a group that had become an accomplice to the reforms made to its own initiative and consequently no longer had a role to play, showed a lack of political sensitivity.

The reform was then voted on in the state congresses. It was ratified during the months of May, June and July, 2001, in the midst of protest demonstrations against local deputies who were called "traitors" and "Judas." In some states, members of angry crowds threw eggs. Some representatives had to leave through the back door of the legislative building following the ratification vote. They could not even show their faces, but still they consummated the act of betrayal against indigenous peoples.

Parallel to the federal campaign to discredit the Zapatistas, attacks by paramilitary groups increased in the zone and military patrols and harassment intensified against rebel communities.

Starting in May 2001, military actions were registered throughout the zone of conflict, including the establishment of new checkpoints, patrols, and increased harassment and interrogation. According to testimonies gathered by human rights organizations, the army went around inquiring what kind of people lived in the communities, about the Zapatistas and about "strange persons" who weren't from the region.

The permanent checkpoints that were "officially" removed under Fox's administration were replaced by intermittent checkpoints at the crossroads in Palestina, Cintalapa, Paraíso and Chocoljá, just to mention a few. Furthermore, the patrols that before were carried out with military vehicles now were executed with more than six artillery cars three times a day.

Examples of the increase in military action in the state included new patrols from Caté to San Cayetano in the township of San Andrés Sacamch'en de los Pobres; a checkpoint and military operation from Caté to Simojovel; military patrols from Laguna Santa Clara to Cintalapa, Francisco León and Palestina in the autonomous township of Ricardo Flores Magón on May 27, 2001; and reinforcement of military camps in Cintalapa and the Palestina Crossroads. Between June 2 and 4 the military carried out an operation in Tzaclum, a mostly Zapatista community, under the pretext of searching for drugs.

During the first week of July 2001, low-flying planes buzzed San Miguel (Ocosingo township), while in the Zapatista community of Prado Payacal a civilian plane flew over and dropped an object that exploded. During the same month, the community of Roberto Barrios denounced military harassment and several communities of Yajalón were victims of a disarmament operation that failed to uncover any arms and violated the human rights of the population.

The federal and state governments affirmed in the media that all was calm in Chiapas and that the federal army was withdrawing, when in fact on July 11, 2001, they increased the number of troops in the fourth headquarters of Cintalapa. The Network of Community-based Human Rights Defenders denounced new military incursions and harassment against the inhabitants of the Autonomous Township of Vicente Guerrero.

The new reform on indigenous rights and the increase in military harassment formed and form part of a general plan whose main objective is to move toward the privatization of the natural resources in the zone. For example, the autonomous authorities of the township of Roberto Barrios denounced the opening of a highway for a golf course and tourist center.

During this period, several human rights organizations denounced the critical conditions of political prisoners in the different state jails, as well as the repression they suffered for defending their rights and demanding full compliance with the three signals demanded by the Zapatistas for resuming dialogue with the government.

During the following months, demonstrations against the Congress of the Union and the Fox administration continued, as the government repeated its line that a state of calm prevailed in Chiapas. The double discourse of the Chiapas strategy became even more evident when the commissioner for indigenous affairs, Xóchitl Gálvez, declared that it was understandable that "not everyone is satisfied with the constitutional changes."

Finally, on August 14, 2001, Vicente Fox formalized the reforms to the constitution by publishing them in the Official Diary of the Federation. This decree marked the betrayal of the original peoples of Mexico.

Protests continued and became action when indigenous people and civil society began to pressure townships and state governments to present a series of constitutional challenges before the Supreme Court of Justice of the Nation to keep the constitutional reform on indigenous matters from going into effect.

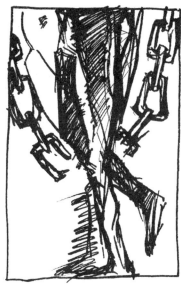

Between July and October of 2001 a total of 330 challenges were presented before the Supreme Court by townships from the states of Oaxaca, Chiapas, Guerrero, Morelos, Veracruz, Michoacán, Jalisco, Puebla, Tabasco, Hidalgo and Tlaxcala against the reforms to Articles 1, 2, 4, 18 and 115 of the Mexican Constitution and against the procedures used for approval. The first township to protest was Molcaxac, in Puebla, which claimed that the reform violated Convention 169 of the International Labor Organization, signed by Mexico.

While the Supreme Court decided on the challenges, in Chiapas the situation of thousands of indigenous refugees, mostly members of base communities or sympathizers with the EZLN, continued and continues to be unresolved. Nevertheless, in August of 2001 the International Committee of the Red Cross prepared to withdraw from Chiapas under duress from the federal government, with the supposed claim that its assistance was no longer necessary.

In the context of the civilian resistance against the constitutional reforms on indigenous rights and culture, on September 6, 2001, the independent union of *La Jornada* newspaper (SITRAJOR) and of the National Autonomous University of Mexico (STUNAM) presented a grievance against Mexico before the International Labor Organization in Geneva for noncompliance with Convention 169 on Indigenous and Tribal Peoples in Independent Countries.

That same day, PRD senators who had ignored the demands of indigenous people and supported the reforms promoted by more conservative and backward legislators in the country demanded that the discussion on the constitutional reform on indigenous matters be reopened. The people of Mexico had called them to task for the betrayal of indigenous people and the PRD senators were responding.

Nearly a year into the Fox administration, the disappointment could be felt among the majority of the population of the country. Everyone felt that nothing had changed, and now a new event confirmed that this was true. On October 19, 2001, the lawyer and human rights defender Digna Ochoa was assassinated in her office.

The General Command of the Zapatistas broke its six-month silence and issued a statement: "We just learned of the assassination of Digna Ochoa y Plácido, so long warned of and so irresponsibly ignored. The crime that ended this life reaches beyond causing indignation in any honest person. When social activists are eliminated, Power celebrates, it wears its finest clothes and showers a few coins around so its handouts can buy indifference. Up above the only change is in who dictates the fashion of the day, and below injustice and misery are repeated in every face and step. Below there is once again pain and rage, but there will no longer be impotence." (Letter from the EZLN, October 2001)

In early November, with a cynicism born of its futility, the Cocopa proposed a permanent recess until it actually had something to work on.

That same month, six indigenous people who had been accused of having participated in the massacre of forty-five Tzotzil Indians in Acteal on December 22, 1997, were released. The inhabitants of Chenalhó protested the freeing of the paramilitary members, while Zapatista prisoners were still held as hostages of the state.

2002

The Supreme Court decides against
the Indian peoples of Mexico.
Debate over the EZLN, the struggles
in Basque Country and ETA.
The Zapatistas continue to organize autonomy.
The Casa-Museum of Doctor Margil is
inaugurated and the magazine *Rebeldía* is born.

Dawn's first light caught the Zapatista communities still dancing as they celebrated the eighth anniversary of the uprising and the beginning of the ninth, as they would say.

During the first months of the year it seemed that the General Command would not break its silence, but the autonomous townships continued to speak out against military incursions in Zapatista communities.

The 330 challenges to the constitutional reforms on indigenous matters were still pending. The executive and legislative branches had denied the recognition of indigenous rights and cultures. The judicial branch, represented by the Supreme Court of Justice of the Nation, had the next word.

In the meantime the rebels continued to organize for autonomy, a process that began in December of 1994 and that, eight years later, continued to be a major challenge.

As part of this process, and to give an example of the difficulty of simultaneously building autonomy while resisting attacks, the Zapatista base communities of the autonomous township Olga Isabel refused to allow the construction of a road designed to serve the army and facilitate illegal logging activities. In July 2002 they organized a roadblock at the entrance to the community of Nichteel. There, near the village of Bachajón which forms part of the official township of Chilón, some 200 Zapatista men, women and children announced that the roadblock would last until the machinery was withdrawn.

Human rights violations continued in Chiapas. Representatives of Amnesty International decided to carry out a tour to gather testimonies from human rights activists and victims of aggressions from the federal and state authorities or paramilitaries.

The Special Rapporteur of the United Nations on the human rights of indigenous peoples, Rodolfo Stavenhagen, declared that in Mexico the rights of campesinos were abused through violations, abuses, selective violence and errors in the administration of justice, but above all, by the old problem of land tenure. Stavenhagen noted the obvious: "It will be very difficult to achieve peace in Chiapas because the indigenous believe that this government, like the one before it, is not complying with its duties."

In July 2002, in the city of Monterrey, Nuevo León, the architect and grassroots activist, Fernando Yáñez Muñóz inaugurated the Casa-Museum of Doctor Margil. The new museum houses the history that ultimately led to the creation of the Zapatista Army of National Liberation.

Subcomandante Marcos sent a message to the inauguration ceremony. "As we know, you work, along with other honest men and women to tend the memory of the struggle of our people. An important part of that memory is kept in the Casa-Museum of Doctor Margil, in the City of Monterry, Nuevo León, Mexico. In this house and museum are kept the testimonies of a fundamental part of our history as Zapatistas, a history of which we are proud and which, to the best of our abilities, we try to honor." (Letter from the EZLN, July 2002)

236

While the Supreme Court of Justice delayed the decision on the constituitional challenges to the indigenous reform, violence in Chiapas increased. On August 7, 2002, José López Santiz, a small farmer from the Tzeltal Zapatista base communities, was executed outside the community "6 de Agosto," in the autonomous township of "17 de Noviembre." His twelve-year-old son witnessed the crime and stated that Baltazar Alfonso, a transportation businessman from Altamirano, assassinated his father with a rifle.

Attacks by paramilitary groups and the military, as well as police harassment, did not stop autonomous organization from proceeding. Far from it. Hundreds of thousands of Zapatista base communities continued to build new forms of government. Autonomous projects on health, education and marketing, among other topics, continued to function. More and more autonomous municipalities created sister relationships with towns, city councils or governments of other countries, mostly in Europe.

In this context, local officials from the autonomous township "Tierra y Libertad" (Land and Freedom) decided to take back a plot of land called La Paz in the governmental township of Motozintla, near the border with Guatemala. The land, they noted, was "the property of our compañero Guillermo Pompilio Gálvez Pinto, of the ejido Belisario Domínguez, who has placed it at the disposition of the autonomous residents of the ejido."

By mid-August 2002, a threatening atmosphere had once again taken hold in Chiapas. The Zapatista indigenous communities were warned that they could be displaced from the Biosphere Reserve of Montes Azules. The rebel response to this threat would come later.

The violence continued to increase and the government "of change" was an accomplice to the impunity with which the paramilitary bands acted. On August 18, 2002, perhaps the worst paramilitary attack since Acteal took place in the autonomous township of San Manuel. The attack carried out by the paramilitary organization OP-DIC at the crossroads of Quexil resulted in one resident arrested and tortured, four residents shot and wounded, and several badly beaten. In spite of the aggression, the Zapatista base communities made it clear that the checkpoint they had installed there to stop illegal trafficking of timber, stolen cars and alcohol would continue to operate. And it did.

The paramilitary groups, initially upset by the electoral defeat of the PRI in the state and nation, regrouped and launched offensive actions against the autonomous townships.

On August 25, 2002, two farmers, supporters of the EZLN, were shot and killed in the settlement of Amaytik by PRI paramilitaries from that community and the neighboring village of Peña Limonar. This happened just a few kilometers from Cintalapa, where the Army operated. In the attack, which the autonomous council called an ambush, seven more indigenous Zapatistas were wounded, one of them seriously.

Faced with this situation, national and international solidarity networks went into action. After the attacks on the autonomous townships that had resulted in four dead, more than twenty wounded, displaced families and high tension in the indigenous communities, civilian groups of human rights and environmental activists, solidarity committees, cultural figures and academics began to demonstrate in different ways against the government "of change" headed by President Fox and initiated a series of protests in front of Mexican embassies abroad.

On September 6, 2002, the Supreme Court rejected 322 of the 330 constitutional challenges to the indigenous reform presented by the same number of Indian townships in Chiapas, Guerrero, Hidalgo, Jalisco, Michoacán, Morelos, Oaxaca, Puebla, Tabasco and Veracruz. These challenged the procedure followed to approve the constitutional reforms on indigenous rights and culture.

By a majority of eight to three, the highest court in the nation decided to declare that it was beyond its jurisdiction to address the legitimate demands of the indigenous population of Mexico. In this way, the judicial branch, the last legal hope of indigenous people for recognition of their rights, culminated its betrayal. The three branches of government—the executive, the legislative and the judicial—failed to respond to the just demands of indigenous peoples and of society in general.

The Supreme Court argued that it did not have the faculties to review reforms and additions to the Constitution or the procedures followed. Eight justices voted to not even consider the arguments and the content of the 330 challenges submitted, while the other three indicated that they should be analyzed.

The process of the Supreme Court in this case was unprecedented and so the case opened up an opportunity to move forward in a real separation of powers. However, the majority of the justices preferred to subordinate themselves to executive power as had been the custom in the past. The message to the indigenous population was clear: the legal paths to exercising your rights are blocked.

Once again Chiapas was the focus of national debate. The consequences of the Court's decision were unpredictable and the future did not look hopeful. The General Command of the EZLN maintained an anti-climactic silence, while diverse sectors of national and international civil society protested the decision.

A joint pronouncement signed by 100 organizations of indigenous people, human rights activists, intellectuals and academics warned, "legal measures have been exhausted and peace is even farther off now that the last door to the State has been slammed in the face of indigenous peoples."

"God help us! They have dealt the final blow," exclaimed the Bishop of Tehuantepec, Arturo Lona. The singer Manu Chao published the following text: "And now? Where to? What's next? What solutions? The Supreme Court seems to have decided that there is none! Shame continues to dictate its laws. And from Barcelona, I deplore it with all my soul. . ."

For their part, forever loyal to their political strategy, the legislators of PAN and PRI applauded the Court's decision while the writers José Saramago and Ernesto Sábato expressed their disappointment and disagreement with the resolution and reproached the Mexican government and President Vicente Fox for their menacing posture against the indigenous peoples of the nation.

Mexican intellectual Pablo González Casanova warned that the decision of the Supreme Court would have predictable consequences including "a redistribution of national territory as dictated by the Plan Puebla-Panama and the Free Trade Area of the Americas." Philosopher Adolfo Sánchez Vázquez commented that the resolution "leaves open the path to violence by blocking legal paths." The rejection of the Court "reflects the racism and contempt of the Mexican state for Indians," declared Ricardo Robles, a Jesuit priest committed to the indigenous cause for the past thirty-nine years.

Dressed in mourning, members of the National Indigenous Congress, the National Association of Democratic Lawyers, the Union of Jurists of Mexico, the Civic Alliance and villages of Morelos that had submitted challenges, all made statements in front of the Supreme Court. Solidarity groups from several European cities condemned the decision; in Madrid, Spain, the Platform of Solidarity with Chiapas organized a twenty-four-hour protest in front of the Ministry of Foreign Affairs; and several groups in Germany sent messages protesting the violence in Chiapas and the judicial decision of Mexico's highest court.

Church representatives from Veracruz and Michoacán also protested the decision and members of indigenous and civic organizations from Chiapas marched in the streets of San Cristóbal de las Casas demanding a solution to the conflict.

While all this was happening, the legal adviser to the Presidency of the Republic, Juan de Dios Castro Lozano, affirmed: "The country should be pleased that now the institutions are functioning as they should."

Martha Sahagún de Fox, the president's wife, declared that the federal government "is betting on peace and development, never on division and egotism, because we should learn from the indigenous peoples their values and their traditions."

The protests did not cease. Indigenous municipal presidents from Oaxaca, Veracruz and Chiapas, leaders of grassroots organizations, and local officials charged with management of communal goods expressed their pain, indignation and the offense caused by the Supreme Court resolution. "What they did to us is a joke. Our hope for justice was responded to with absolute denial and authoritarianism," they stated.

The National Meeting of Indian Peoples, which gathered 200 delegates of organizations in thirteen Mexican states in Chilpancingo, Guerrero, announced coordinated mobilizations for October 12, 2002. These would include marches to the capital, demonstrations in Guerrero, Oaxaca, Morelos and Michoacán, and roadblocks in Veracruz, Yucatán and Campeche to continue the struggle for constitutional recognition of the San Andrés Accords.

At the inauguration of the Third National Forum for Defense of Traditional Medicine, some 500 participants from twenty-nine Indian peoples in twenty states rejected the "indigenist" constitutional reform of April 28, 2001. The Forum declared that given the breakdown of the state of law they recognized "the San Andrés Accords as the only Constitution on indigenous matters."

As protests continued, on the morning of Mexican Independence Day, September 16, 2002, the main statues of the heroes of the independence in Mexico City woke up with black face masks, red bandannas, and flags of the Zapatista Army for National Liberation.

The Fox administration continued its discourse calling for dialogue, but in deeds a new military camp was installed in the Norte region of the state at the entry to the autonomous township of La Paz. This military mobilization occured just a short while after at least 1,000 more troops were dispatched to the northern part of the Lacandón Jungle and around Montes Azules, in late August.

In Oaxaca, representatives of the indigenous Triquis protested ratification of an indigenous law that did not represent their interests, and warned that "violence not only comes from bullets, it also exists when there is no water or education." This prompted President Vicente Fox to call on Indian peoples of the country to avoid "violence and intransigence."

At the same time, in an unusual move in Rome, 275 Italian members of Parliament from political currents that ran from the government to the opposition, and even from the party of the prime minister Silvio Berlusconi, published a letter to Mexican legislators that stated that, with "due respect for the autonomy and sovereignty" of the Mexican Congress, we urge the approval of the indigenous proposal of the Commission on Concordance and Pacification (Cocopa) that translates the San Andrés Accords."

In this turbulent context, on November 17, 2002, the nineteenth anniversary of the birth of the EZLN, a new publication of the left came out: the magazine *Rebeldía*. The new editorial endeavor was hailed by the indigenous rebels through Subcomandante Marcos.

The new magazine made no bones about its position: "We are Zapatistas. We do not pretend to have a hypocritical, false neutrality. We are committed to the end. We want to help build a tool for all those who don't struggle for power and who declare themselves willing, against reason, to defy the law of gravity."

Subcomandante Marcos sent seven stories of Durito—the famous Zapatista philosopher-beetle—for the first seven issues of the new publication, in which he referred to the Zapatista movement and its relation to Power, among other themes. Some fragments of these texts:

"Durito says that the Zapatistas sowed the apple tree so that one day when they were no longer there, someone could pick a ripe apple and be free to decide to eat it in a fruit salad, in applesauce, in juice, in cake or in one of those horrible (according to Durito) apple sodas." (*Rebeldía* No. 1, November 2002)

"When a rebel arrives at the Seat of Power (like that, with capital letters) he or she stares at it, analyzes it, but instead of sitting in it, goes for a file, like a nail file, and patiently starts filing down the legs until they seem so fragile that they'll break every time someone sits there, which immediately happens. Just like that." (*Rebeldía* No. 2, December 2002)

"Durito says that the Zapatistas are really strange pedestrians. Because instead of looking on with indifference at the arrogant passage of the train, a Zapatista goes up smiling to the track and sticks out a foot. He or she probably thinks, naively, that the powerful machine will be tripped up and immediately run off the track." (*Rebeldía* No. 3, February 2003)

"Durito says that while the politicians get together and fight over the key to the door of power, the Zapatistas walk right by, stop in front of one of the walls of the labyrinth that doesn't even have anything to do with the room where power lies, and with a black pen, mark an x. . ." (*Rebeldía* No. 4, February 2003)

"Durito says that all the multiple choices that Power offers hide a trap: Where there are many roads and we are given the possibility of choosing, something fundamental is forgotten—all these roads lead to the same place. So freedom doesn't mean choosing our destination, the route, the speed, the rhythm and the company—just the road. And what's more, the freedom that Power offers is just freedom to choose who will walk representing us, says Durito." (*Rebeldía* No. 5, March 2003)

"Durito says that rebellion in the world is like a crack in a wall: its first aim is to peek over to the other side. But later, this little glance weakens the wall and ends up breaking it down completely." (*Rebeldía* No. 6, April 2003)

"Like a bird, the Zapatista movement is born, it grows, it reproduces over and over, it dies and, as is the law of birds, it shits on statues." (*Rebeldía* No. 7, May 2003)

At the inauguration of the "Aguascalientes" in Madrid, Spain, in November 2002, the EZLN again broke its silence with a letter greeting the new space of rebellion, which, like the five Aguascalientes in Chiapas, would be a political and cultural meeting place.

When their message was read to the organizers and participants at the event, another episode began of their more than a decade of struggle and rebellion. The Zapatistas criticized the Spanish royalty, President José Aznar, Felipe González and Judge Baltasar Garzón, whom they accused of "carrying out terrorism of the State that no honest man or woman could view without becoming indignant."

The "clown Garzón," stated Subcomandante Marcos, "has declared the political struggle of the Basque Country illegal. . . and shown his true fascist vocation by denying the Basque people the right to struggle politically for a legitimate cause. . ."

Judge Garzón's response came quickly. In the Mexican newspaper *El Universal* he replied: "I challenge you when and wherever you like,

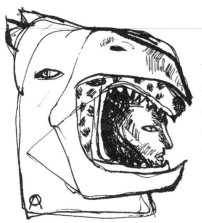

without masks or disguises, to talk about terrorism, rebellion, dignity, struggle, insurgency, politics, justice, all those values that serve to build a country and a democracy and defend the rights of those who have the least."

On December 7, 2002, it was the EZLN's turn. Subcomandante Marcos accepted the challenge and set conditions for the meeting: the debate would be on the island of Lanzarote, and there, but not at the same time, a meeting would be held among all the political, social, and cultural actors on the Basque issue who wanted to attend.

If Subcomandante Marcos lost the debate, specified the Zapatista military chief and spokesperson, Garzón could unmask him then and there. But if the Spanish judge lost he would have to commit himself to providing legal advice to the EZLN on the demands for recognition of indigenous rights and culture pending before international courts.

"An Opportunity for the Word"—to talk about the complicated situation in Basque Country—was what Subcomandante Marcos asked of the Spanish government, the ETA, Spanish and Basque societies, and especially the left (*abertzale*).

Subcomandante Marcos made his position on terrorist acts clear to the Basque political-military organization Euskadi Ta Askatasuna (ETA): "We consider the struggle of the Basque people for sovereignty just and legitimate, but neither this noble cause, nor any other, can justify the sacrifice of civilian lives. Not only does it not lead to any political gain, even if it did, the human cost is unpayable. We condemn military actions that hurt civilians. And we condemn them equally, whether they come from ETA or from the Spanish state, or Al Qaeda or George W. Bush, from Israelis or Palestinians, or anyone who under different names or initials, claiming state, ideological or religious reasons, makes victims of children, women, old people and men who have nothing to do with the matter."

246

On December 15, 2002, the Basque pro-independence political party Batasuna thanked the EZLN for "its interest, solidarity and support for the Basque cause" and communicated its willingness to "participate in any initiative that could seriously and democratically have the objective of creating the necessary political conditions" to guarantee the right to decide freely and democratically the future of the Basque Country.

This produced one of the most widespread and least understood polemics of the conflict. Most of the media took advantage of the confusion to publicize that the EZLN supported the terrorist group ETA, a version that intellectuals and academics utilized to disassociate themselves from the Zapatista movement.

While the debate covered the front pages of the newspapers and broadcast news, the indigenous community of Arroyo San Pablo in Montes Azules was forcibly relocated by the federal government. This community was not Zapatista but was among the indigenous communities that had been threatened with displacement from the region.

The Fox administration had finally carried out its threats made in August to remove indigenous communities located in the Lacandón Jungle, specifically in the area of Montes Azules, in order to impose its neoliberal project. The alleged reason for the displacement was to preserve the ecological reserve. However, the real interests behind it were all business. The real problem in Montes Azules is that the indigenous communities there impede the Fox government from promoting tourist development in the zone that includes plans for hotels and spas, among other attractions designed to attract foreign tourists.

The problem was presented as an ecological conflict and later it became an issue of agrarian law. The Montes Azules Reserve forms part of the over 600,000 hectares that were ceded by presidential decree to a few families of Lacandón Indians in the 1970s. These families now reclaim their property. It should be noted though that according to a study by the organization Wood for the People, the Lacandóns received the land from then-President Luis Echeverría and for decades allowed and propitiated its exploitation and the looting of precious woods.

The communities threatened with displacement belong to several indigenous organizations; some are Zapatista-affiliated, others work with the independent Rural Association of Collective Interest (ARIC) and others with the PRI.

On December 29, 2002, two days before the festivities of the ninth anniversary of the insurgent uprising, the EZLN fixed its position on the relocation, without revealing which of the threatened communities formed part of its organization so as to avoid "leaving those who aren't Zapatistas in a vulnerable situation," the EZLN warned. "It's good for everyone to know right away—in the case of the Zapatista villages, there will be no peaceful relocation."

Furthermore, the rebel indigenous army explained that the Zapatistas living within the Montes Azules region "are not there because they lack land or have the morbid pleasure of destroying the jungle, but because they have been forced to leave everything behind, so as not to swell the silence with which the Powers that be and its intellectuals bury the misery and the death of indigenous Mexicans." (Letter from the EZLN, December 29, 2002)

The notice signed by the spokesperson and military chief of the EZLN went on: "We have talked with the representatives of these Zapatista communities and with the authorities of the autonomous townships they belong to. They have communicated their decision to remain there, even at the cost of their lives, as long as Zapatista demands are not satisfied. We have replied that we will back them up completely."

Although the threat persists, for now the relocations have been interrupted.

On December 30 and 31, 2002, tens of thousands of men and women came out of the jungle, the north, and the highlands of Chiapas, their destination, as nine years before, the city of San Cristóbal de las Casas.

2003

Definitions of the Zapatista movement with respect to the political class.
The Caracoles and Good Government Boards are born.
The EZLN consolidates autonomy and launches initiatives to build national and international networks of resistance.

The dawn of the ninth year of the indigenous uprising saw tens of thousands of Tzotzil, Tzeltal, Tojolabal, Chol, Zoque and Mam Indians leaving their homes. San Cristóbal de las Casas, the colonial city where up until recently indigenous people were prohibited from walking on the sidewalks, received them, as it had nine years before, with their faces covered—but this time unarmed except for the conquered word.

In one of the largest demonstrations of the nine years, more than 20,000 indigenous members of base communities of the Zapatista Army of National Liberation took over the city of San Cristóbal. Organized in columns and with machetes and torches in hand, men, women, children and old people of the rebel villages filled the streets along with thousands of people from other parts of Mexico and the world.

This major show of strength and organization concluded with a demonstration presided over by members of the EZLN General Command, who had remained hidden since their return from the Color of the Earth March in April of 2001. Comandantes Esther, Fidelia, David, Tacho, Omar, Mister and Brus Li gave seven speeches in which they redefined their position on the Mexican political class and the Fox administration. They talked about indigenous issues, women, resistance in other parts of the world and intellectuals, and they made special mention of the vital role of everyone in the Zapatista Army.

The Zapatista speeches on the ninth anniversary culminated a process that had begun on February 16, 1996, when the EZLN and the Mexican government signed the first agreements toward ending the war in Chiapas. Following tense negotiations, the Zapatistas achieved an agreement for the Commission on Concordance and Pacification (Cocopa) to draw up a legislative proposal. In November of that year, the Cocopa presented its proposal and although it did not include everything in the Agreements on Indigenous Rights and Culture, it was endorsed by both parties. In January of 1997, the administration withdrew its support for the proposal and it was frozen for the four years that followed. During this period the rebels devoted their efforts to bringing the proposal to a vote and implementing its terms.

Throughout the four years they organized an endless number of mobilizations to support the legislative proposal. A debate began that had no precedent in Mexico or in any other part of the world. As part of the efforts to obtain constitutional recognition of the rights of Indian peoples, 1,111 members of base communities marched to Mexico City in 1997. In 1999, the EZLN held a national and international consultation, and in 2001 the General Command marched to Mexico City on a journey in which millions of Mexicans joined in with their support and demands.

In December of 2000, without encouraging approval, the president sent the Cocopa proposal to Congress. In April of 2001, following the Color of the Earth March, the senators of the three main political parties (PAN, PRI and PRD) changed the initiative and voted for a law that rejected the San Andrés Accords. The full Congress ratified the counter-reform and President Fox immediately welcomed the betrayal. A few months later, he decreed its promulgation in the Official Diary of the Federation.

The next step was taken by more than 300 indigenous townships throughout the country, which, indignant over the legislative reform that stripped them of the achievements made in the San Andrés Accords, submitted constitutional challenges to the Supreme Court of Justice of the Nation. In September of 2002 the judicial branch threw out the challenges and consummated the betrayal.

During January 2003, the EZLN defined its position on this series of events. Comandante Tacho said: "The three main political parties of Mexico, the PAN, the PRI and the PRD, made a mockery of the demands of all indigenous peoples of Mexico, all the people who supported the recognition of our rights, and people of the world who also supported them. . . The executive, legislative, and judicial branches rejected a peaceful, political solution to the demands of the Indian people of Mexico.

"All this history of deceit and betrayal does not end with us being defeated. We as Zapatistas will continue to seek ways for the people to become sovereign and to comply with the mandate 'to rule by obeying,' so we will continue to know ourselves, and above all we will continue to know that the Zapatistas are not forgotten, do not give up and will not sell out. . ." (Speech by Comandante Tacho, January 1, 2003)

The party for the ninth anniversary of the uprising was long and in it the indigenous Zapatista comandantes endorsed the work of Subcomandante Marcos, military chief and spokesperson for the insurgence. "We want to tell you that when Subcomandante Marcos says he supports the political struggle of the peoples, all the Zapatista men, women and children are saying it too," said Comandante Mister, clearly alluding to the debate caused by the Zapatista initiative "An Opportunity for the Word," which sought a dialogue and meeting on different political options in Basque Country.

"We the indigenous peoples do think internationally, and we the indigenous peoples have the right to state our opinions and decide what we want to do. . . That's why we say to the powerful of the world that if they unite to globalize with the globalization of death, then we also are going to globalize freedom." (Speech by Comandante Mister, January 1, 2003)

Defining their position on "Mr. Vicente Fox" fell to Comandanta Esther who, wrapped in the same Tzeltal shawl she wore when she addressed the Mexican Congress, said: "I only want to say to you that the people are disappointed with the cheating that you do. . . You said you were going to resolve the problems, mainly of the struggle of the EZLN. That in 15 minutes you'd change the situation of the poor. . ." (Speech by Comandanta Esther, January 1, 2003)

Referring to the polemical silence of the Zapatistas, Comandante David took the mike: "Our silence has been used to say that the Zapatistas are finished, that we are divided that our leaders gave up or sold out, that the commanders are alone, and that the Zapatista villages are with the government. . . Then if that's true, who are we all here? Aren't these thousands of men, women, children and old people protesting here today Zapatistas, and the dozens of thousands that stayed behind in the villages because they don't have money or transportation to come to the demonstration?" (Speech by Comandante David, January 1, 2003)

In front of the Cathedral of San Cristóbal de las Casas where the first dialogue with the federal government had taken place nine years earlier, Comandanta Fidelia spoke on women: "I want to invite women to organize so that together we can defend our rights and also we can have equality. Sisters, we must no longer allow the government and the president to cheat us because there are many things happening to us as women." (Speech by Comandanta Fidelia, January 1, 2003)

Comandante Omar spoke to the millions of young people in Mexico and the world who have joined the Zapatista struggle. "For the youth of these Mexican lands and the world we will never stop fighting

to challenge the governments of the world because this is our hope, that together we can change these neoliberal governments." (Speech by Comandante Omar, January 1, 2003)

Comandante Brus Li spoke to the indigenous peoples of the country: "It's time for us all to organize and form our autonomous townships. Don't wait until the bad government gives permission. We should organize as real rebels and not wait until someone gives us permission to be autonomous, with or without the law."

The demonstration was more militant than most. It ended near midnight in a sea of lit torches and amid the roaring sound of the clash of thousands of machetes, axes and other tools. "Let's make the light strong so that the villages see that we are still in rebellion," said Comandante David at the end of the crowded event.

After this major indigenous demonstration, the debate continued on

the initiative "An Opportunity for the Word" on the issue of Basque Country and the supposed sympathy (built up by the media and some intellectuals) of the Zapatistas for the political-military organization, ETA.

In a second letter to ETA in response to a message sent by that organization, Subcomandante Marcos was clear: "Our arms are not for imposing ideas or lifestyles, but to defend a way of thinking, and a way of seeing the world, and relating to those who are open-minded enough to learn from others' thought and lives but also have a lot to teach. It's not from us that you need to demand respect. You must earn the respect of the people. And respect is one thing and another very different thing is fear. . . We don't see why we should ask you what to do or how to do it. What would you teach us? To kill journalists because they criticize the struggle? To justify the death of children for the 'cause'? We don't need or want your support or solidarity. We have the solidarity and support of many people in Mexico and the world."

The rebel spokesperson made clear the huge differences that separate the methods of struggle of the Zapatista and those of the ETA. "Our struggle uses an honor code, inherited from our warrior ancestors, that states, among other things: to respect the life of civilians (although they hold posts in the governments that oppress us); to not fall back on crime to get resources (we don't even rob the corner store); and not to respond to words with fire (even though they hurt us or lie to us). You might think that by renouncing these traditional revolutionary methods we renounce the chance to advance in our struggle. But, by the dim light of our history it seems that we have advanced more than those who recur to these arguments. . ." (Letter from the EZLN, January 7, 2003)

The debate continued, and meanwhile the EZLN command released a "calendar of resistance." There were twelve documents, one for each

256

month of the year, in which the insurgent military chief and spokesperson presented an x-ray of the struggles and acts of resistance in an equal number of states of the republic.

The path of the struggles that hundreds of organizations were carrying out in different parts of the country began in Oaxaca and went through Puebla, Veracruz, Tlaxcala, Hidalgo, Querétaro, Guanajuato, the North Pacific Region, Mexico State, Guerrero, Morelos and Mexico City—the same route of the Color of the Earth March, which draws a snail's spiral on the map.

In each one of the documents, called *estelas* (referring to pre-Hispanic carved stones, sculpted in bas-relief, that contain representations of personages, dates, names, ceremonies and prophecies), the EZLN General Command gathered together the many examples of resistance against the privatization of historic monuments, in defense of the earth and respect for human rights, in demand of justice for undocumented workers (braceros) and a long etcetera. It was an x-ray of innumerable struggles that came together in a rejection of the neoliberal policies handed down by a government that ignored or forgot the have-nots, that is to say, the vast majority.

In the Calendar of Resistance, the EZLN explained that "those who come from below and from far back in time have, it's true, many bonds and wounds. But these were inflicted on them by those who made wealth their god and their alibi. And also, those who walk with a slow and measured pace can see very far ahead and at that faraway point that their hearts can only guess at is another world—a new world, a better world, a necessary world, a world in which many worlds fit. . ."

In the twelfth document of the Calendar of Resistance, the EZLN abandoned the initiative "An Opportunity for the Word." With that it ceased plans to unite the social and political forces of Basque Country to study and discuss the issues, and to send a Zapatista delegation to Europe to participate in a meeting there and debate with Judge Baltasar Garzón, and to appeal to international organizations to try to obtain recognition of indigenous rights and culture that national entities had denied Mexico's indigenous peoples.

"The EZLN never proposed to mediate the Basque conflict, much less tell the Basque people what to do or not to do. We only asked to give the word a chance. Our proposal might have been clumsy or ingenuous or both, but it was never dishonest or disrespectful. That isn't our way. . . If we should now abstain from participating in the meeting "An Opportunity for the Word," it isn't because the criticism, reproaches or cheap accusations are keeping us awake at night. It is because in terms of our ethics we can't participate in a meeting that doesn't have the support of the all the nationalist forces in Basque Country," explained Subcomandante Marcos. He also closed the debate with Judge Baltasar Garzón: "Judge Garzón, in spite of being the challenger, preferred to remain silent. In this way he showed that he's good at interrogating tortured prisoners, taking pictures with families of victims of terrorism and doing self-promoting campaigns for the Nobel Peace Prize, but he does not dare debate with somebody halfway intelligent."

Zapatista statements regarding the Mexican political class and in particular the ELZN's questioning of the Party of the Democratic Revolution (PRD), a party supposedly of the left, motivated a new national polemic that included, among others, PRD leader Cuauhtémoc Cárdenas.

While the debate continued, the Zapatista base community of Flor de Café in the La Paz autonomous township of the Chol region in northern Chiapas, denounced threats of expulsion and violence from members of the organization Kichañ Kichañob, aligned with the PRD and the state government.

In the international terrain, the government of the United States headed by George W. Bush started a devastating war against the people of Iraq. Millions of people throughout the world protested, and Chiapas was no exception.

In Italy, more than a million people protested in Rome against the barbaric act, and Zapatistas raised their voice and their protest there: "This is a war of fear. Its objective is not to defeat Hussein in Iraq. Its goal is not to finish off Al Qaeda. Nor is it to liberate the Iraqi people. It is not justice or democracy or freedom that motivate this terror. It is fear. The fear that all of humanity will refuse to accept a policy that tells them what they should do, how they should do it, and when they should do it." (Message from the EZLN, February 7, 2003)

In April, the voice of the Zapatista rebels against the war was heard again, this time through a tape sent to the anti-war march in Mexico City: "It is a war against rebellion, against humanity. It is a world war in its effects and above all, in the NO that it has provoked. . . Iraq is in Europe, in the United States, in Australia, in Latin America, in the mountains of Southeast Mexico, and in this global and rebellious NO that paints a new map under the flag of dignity." (Message from the EZLN, April 2003)

Global rebellion has many manifestations. One group of cultural rebels met another on April 10, 2003. The theater company Tamèrantong (Tumadrenchanclas) made up of twenty-four child actors from the Paris barrio of Belleville, visited indigenous rebel children in the Aguascalientes of Oventik. In the context of the war in Chiapas and the war of the United States against Iraq, a group of poor rebel children from France met with thousands of Zapatista girls and boys.

In the month of April, against the backdrop of the war in Iraq, the EZLN supported the campaign against the war "Let's Work for Peace and Justice" and called on Mexican civil society and the world to mobilize and not let up on the protests. The signing of a declaration, among other things, allowed many voices to be heard.

Threats of forced relocation in the Montes Azules region continued but on May 7, 2003, the state government and Lacandón leaders signed a truce to not carry out relocation of communities in the Biosphere Reserve. "We don't believe the truce that the government and Lacandóns

have offered us," declared the representatives of the communities Nuevo San Isidro and Nuevo San Rafael, who refused all contact with government officials. "We don't want dialogue with the government until it complies with the law on indigenous rights," they said.

So in the terrain mined by counterinsurgency policies that attempted to "contain" and weaken the demands of indigenous rebels, the private-sector conservationist tourism projects pushed forward, especially in the south and east of Montes Azules.

The civic organization Maderas del Pueblo del Sureste (Wood for the People of the Southeast) wrote a report that noted: "Obeying the interests of multinational corporations that want to obtain water or oil and develop the biotechnology and ecotourism of the Lacandón Jungle, the government hides beind an 'environmentalist' discourse and threatens to violently relocate the populations of Montes Azules, 'for the good of humanity.'"

The study explains that "the so-called Lacandón Community was formed on March 1972 by presidential decree from Luis Echeverría Alvarez, based on a huge agrarian fraud, through which an illegitimate communal plantation was formed to favor three villages (two of which were not even there) and only fifty-five families of Caribe Mayas (falsely called 'Lacandóns'), violating the previous agrarian right granted to forty-seven indigenous villages and 4,000 Tzeltal, Chol, Tzotzil and Tojolabal families every bit as Mayan as the Caribes, and already settled in the territory since the 1950s and 1960s, of which seventeen already had presidential resolutions."

These villages, warned Maderas del Pueblo del Sureste, have been periodically threatened with relocation, accused first of "invading Lacandón territories" and later with "depredating" a natural protected area.

July 6, 2002, elections were held for representatives of the House of Deputies throughout Mexico. In Chiapas, the Zapatista autonomous townships did not allow election booths to be installed in their communities, and in some cases, burned electoral material.

Without issuing any formal declaration, authorities and spokespeople of several rebel townships in the Altos and Lacandón Jungle agreed that, as on previous occasions, on July 6, 2003, base communities of the Zapatista Army of National Liberation (EZLN) would oppose the electoral process sponsored by a political class that had betrayed the indigenous peoples.

Chiapas is calm, President Fox affirmed in different forums. However, days before and after the federal elections, new checkpoints were installed on the highways and roads of the region. Some were under the control of the Federal Agency of Investigation (AFI), with military personnel and Federal Preventive and Sectoral Police. Meanwhile, in the "calm" state, two new control points were established in the communities of San Antonio el Brillante and Tacitas, in the autonomous townships of San Juan de la Libertad (El Bosque) and San Miguel (Ocosingo), respectively.

In Ocosingo and the Norte zone, the movements of the army and state police intensified (in particular in Chenalhó, the northern jungle, the border region and near the Norte zone). Journalists confirmed that forty new checkpoints had been installed throughout the state that officially, of course, did not exist.

Following the elections in which abstention was the big winner, the EZLN released a series of important and defining communiqués that ratified, on the international level, their position on the Fox government, the three main political parties and the executive, legislative and judicial branches of government, and at the same time explained the new Zapatista initiatives and their internal reorganization.

On July 19, 2003, Subcomandante Marcos stated, "In our country, the Mexican political class (including all the registered political parties and the three branches of government) betrayed the hope of millions of Mexicans and of thousands of people of other countries of seeing the rights and culture of Indian peoples of Mexico recognized in the constitution. . . In this context, the EZLN decided to totally suspend any contact with the Mexican federal government and political parties; and the Zapatista villages confirmed their commitment to resistance as the main form of struggle." (EZLN communiqué, July 19, 2003)

During these months, they explained, the indigenous Zapatista villages prepared a series of changes in their internal functioning and their relationship with national and international civil society. To explain these changes, they said, thirty Zapatista autonomous townships asked Subcomandante Marcos to be the spokesperson for the autonomous townships, although only temporarily.

Faced with the increase in paramilitary activities in the region of Los Altos, Chiapas, particularly in the townships of Chenalhó, Panelhó and Cancuc, the General Command of the EZLN warned the leadership of these organizations that their crimes "would not go unpunished this time." The Zapatistas sent the following message to the paramilitary groups: "According to the law of Talon it is eye for an eye and tooth for a tooth, but we have a special offer of two eyes for each eye and a whole set of teeth for each tooth, so you decide if you take it." In the same commu-

niqué they warned that the Plan Puebla-Panama would not be allowed in rebel territories.

As spokesperson for the EZLN and the autonomous townships, Subcomandante Marcos announced that during the week they would release seven documents that made up the "Thirteenth Estela" (the continuation of the twelve-part Calendar of Resistance). In the first, he explained the essence of being Zapatista. These indigenous people, he said, "even make people who sympathize with their cause mad. They just don't obey. When you expect them to talk, they keep quiet. When you expect silence, they talk. When you expect them to lead, they step back. When you expect them to follow behind, they take off in another direction. When you expect them to talk just about themselves, they start talking about other things. When you expect them to conform to their geography, they walk throughout the world and its struggles." (EZLN Thirteenth Estela, July 2003)

In the second part of the Thirteenth Estela, the indigenous rebels explained the long learning process they went through when they began to have contact with national and international civil society, over almost ten years of struggle and resistance.

As to the "support" that diverse sectors of society had sent the rebel indigenous communities, they indicated somewhat indignantly that "in the Aguascalientes there are piles of computers that don't work, expired medicines, extravagant clothing (for us) that we can't even use for theater plays, and even shoes without their mates. And things like that keep arriving as if the people said, 'oh poor things, they really are needy, anything will be useful for them and these things are in my way.'"

They went on in Part Two to describe "a more sophisticated handout—the practice of some NGOs and international organizations. It consists basically in that they decide what the communities need and without even consulting them impose not only certain projects but also the times

and ways of implementing them. Imagine the exasperation of a community that needs drinking water and what they get is a library, one that needs a school for children and gets a course on herbal medicine."

They spoke firmly of the meaning of their resistance and of being armed. "Many Zapatistas have received offers to buy their consciences, but they remain in resistance, making their poverty (for those who learn to see) a lesson in dignity and generosity. Because we Zapatistas say 'everything for everybody, nothing for us,' and we say that is how we live. . . The kind of support we need from civil society is for the construction of a small part of this world of many worlds. It is then political support, not handouts."

In this context, the EZLN announced the death of the "Aguascalientes" for August 9, 2003, and with it the death of the "Cinderella syndrome" of some "civil societies" and the paternalism on the part of some national and international NGOs; this would "at least die for the Zapatista communities, which from now on will not receive leftovers nor allow the imposition of projects."

In the third part of the Thirteenth Estela, the Zapatistas announced their internal reorganization, through the creation of the Good Government Boards and the birth of five "Caracoles" (snails, literally), located in each one of the places where the Aguascalientes had been.

The Caracoles, they explained, would be political and cultural centers (like the Aguascalientes before them) and "will be like doors to enter into the communities and for the communities to leave through; like windows to look out of and into; like speakers to spread our word and to hear the word from afar. But above all, to remind us that we must be vigilant and aware of the full range of worlds that fill our world."

The names of the Caracoles, decided in assemblies in each region, were: "Madre de los Caracoles del Mar de Nuestros Sueños" (Mother of the Snails of the Sea of our Dreams) in La Realidad, a region of Tojolabal, Tzeltal and Mam Zapatistas; "Torbellino de Nuestras Palabras" (Tornado of our Words) in Morelia, made up of Tzeltal, Tzotzil and Tojolabal Zapatistas; "Resistencia Hacia un Nuevo Amanecer (Resistance Toward a New Dawn) in La Garrucha of Tzeltal Zapatistas; "Que Habla para Todos" (Speak for Everyone) in Roberto Barrios of Chol, Zoque and Tzeltal Zapatistas; and lastly, named on August 8, "Resistencia and Rebeldía por la Humanidad" (Resistance and Rebellion for Humanity) in Oventik of Tzotzils and Tzeltals.

The fourth message of the Estela series referred to Plan Puebla-Panama as "already extinct." To counter this global project to fragment Mexican national territory, the Zapatistas launched the Plan La Realidad–Tijuana, which "consists of linking all acts of resistance in our country, and with them, rebuilding the Mexican nation from below. In all the states of the federation there are men, women, children and old people who don't give up and, although they are nameless, struggle for democracy, freedom and justice. Our plan consists of talking to them and listening to them."

In the international terrain they announced for North America the Plan Morelia–North Pole; for Central America, the Caribbean and South

America, the Plan La Garrucha–Tierra del Fuego; for Europe and Africa, the Plan Oventik-Moscow and for Asia and Australia, the Plan Roberto Barrios–New Delhi. The objective for all, they stated, is the same: "to struggle against neoliberalism and for humanity."

The history and functioning, up to now, of the rebel Zapatista autonomous townships was explained amply in the fifth part of the Estela. "Although they were declared when we finally broke through the military circle in December of 1994, the Zapatista Autonomous Townships in Rebellion (MAREZ, by their Spanish initials) took a while to implement." Today, they said, "the exercise of indigenous autonomy is a reality in Zapatista lands, and we are proud to say that it has been led by the communities themselves. In this process, the EZLN has been only a companion and intervened only when there are conflicts or detours."

This extensive document details that "when the autonomous townships began, self-government not only went from being local to regional, it also moved out of the 'shadow' of the military organization. The EZLN does not intervene at all in the designation or destitution of autonomous authorities, and has pointed out that since the EZLN principles state that it does not struggle to take power, none of the military brass or members of the Clandestine Revolutionary Indigenous Committee can hold positions of authority in the autonomous townships. Whoever decides to participate in an autonomous government must resign definitively from their organizational post in the EZLN."

After explaining the workings of the MAREZ, they recognized that they are far from perfect. To rule through obeying, they said, "in the Zapatista territories is a tendency, and is not exempt from ups and downs, contradictions and errors, but it is a growing tendency."

Following the explanation of the new stage of internal organization, the EZLN announced the creation of the Good Government Boards in the sixth message. The Boards were created to correct imbalances in the development of the autonomous townships and the communities; to

mediate in conflicts that arise among autonomous townships and between autonomous townships and municipal governments; to attend to complaints against the Autonomous Councils for human rights violations, protests and grievances; to monitor projects and community tasks in the MAREZ and to promote support for community projects; to monitor compliance with the laws; to attend to and guide national and international civil society to visit the communities, carry out productive projects and install peace camps; and based on agreement with the CCRI-CG of the EZLN, to promote and approve the participation of compañeros and compañeras in activities or events outside the rebel communities. In sum, they explained, "to take care that in Zapatista rebel territory he or she who rules, rules by obeying."

Each Good Government Board has a name chosen by the Autonomous Councils: in the Selva Frontera region it is "Hacia la Esperanza" (Toward Hope) and includes the autonomous townships of "General Emiliano Zapata," "San Pedro de Michoacán," "Libertad de los Pueblos Maya" and "Tierra y Libertad"; in Tzots Choj the Board is called "Corazón de Arco Iris de la Esperanza" (Heart of the Rainbow of Hope) and includes the autonomous townships of "17 de Noviembre," "Primero de Enero," "Ernesto Ché Guevara," "Olga Isabel," "Lucio Cabañas," "Miguel Hidalgo" and "Vicente Guerrero"; in the Selva region the Tzeltal Good Government Board is named "El Camino del Futuro" (The Path of the Future) and is made up of the autonomous townships of "Francisco Gómez," "San Manuel," "Francisco Villa" and "Ricardo Flores Magón"; in the Norte region it is called "Nueva Semilla que Va a Producir" (New Seed That Will Produce) and is made up of the autonomous townships of "Vicente Guerrero," "Del Trabajo," "La Montaña," "San José en Rebeldía," "La Paz," "Benito Juárez" and "Francisco Villa." Lastly, the

Good Government Board of Los Altos was named "Corazón Céntrico de los Zapatistas delante del Mundo" (Central Heart of the Zapatistas to the World) and is composed of the autonomous townships of "San Andrés Sacamch'en de los Pobres," "San Juan de la Libertad," "San Pedro Polhó," "Santa Catarina," "Magdalena de la Paz," "16 de Febrero" and "San Juan Apóstol Cancuc."

In the seventh and last part of the series of communiqués, the Zapatista Army of National Liberation invited national and international civil society to "the celebration of the death of the Aguascalientes, the party to name the Caracoles and inaurgurate the Good Government Boards. The date: August 8, 9 and 10, 2003, in the Oventik autonomous township of San Andrés Sacamch'en de los Pobres." (Thirteenth Estela, Part 7, July 2003)

From August 7, 2003, thousands of members of base communities and persons from Mexican civil society and other countries began to gather in the community of Oventik, whose political and cultural center was remodeled for the new operations.

Hundreds of national and international organizations greeted the birth of the new stage of indigenous autonomy, built without asking permission from any government power, with the legitimacy granted it by thousands of indigenous people organized in thirty autonomous townships and innumerable rebel communities.

The call to accompany this new organizational effort of the Zapatista villages came to national civil society at a time of acute crisis in the political parties. It was also a time of profound social disillusionment reflected in high abstention in the last elections. The rebel organization meant, for many, the possibility of still believing that a better world was possible.

On August 8, 2003, Oventik was dressed for a party. Thousands of indigenous and nonindigenous people arrived at the Caracol to celebrate, accompany and be part of the new Zapatista challenge. The increase in military movements did not keep members of the EZLN General Command from fooling the surrounding forces and showing up at one of

the five new Caracoles. Highways and dirt roads were invaded by thousands of men, women and children from base communities who were headed to the party, to the celebration of autonomy.

On August 9, 2003 more than 10,000 people gathered at the festivities to pronounce the Aguascalientes "dead" and celebrate the birth of the Caracoles, as well as to inaugurate the five Good Government Boards.

In the main act that day, Comandanta Esther called on the Indian people to defend their rights as Mexicans. "Now they can never finish us off or betray us," she said, referring to the three major political parties "that reached an agreement among themselves to deny us our rights."

The same commander who two years before demanded recognition of indigenous rights and culture before Congress now called on the first peoples of the nation "to apply the law of the San Andrés Accords. Now is the time to apply it throughout the country. We don't need to ask anyone's permission. Even though the government has not recognized it, for us it is our law and we will defend ourselves with it."

Another comandanta by the name of Rosalía spoke at the demonstration about strength and organization. "Today we are demonstrating once again that we are strong for fighting. We know that we have resisted ten years in this struggle and we are ready to go on," she said, as if anyone doubted it. "The rebel townships are good and fucking cool because we know how to resist. Don't get scared away by threats of persecution from the bad governments. Our struggle has grown a lot. There are compañeros and compañeras in the entire world."

In the deeply meaningful and emotional event, Comandante David played host to the thousands of participants, spoke to his own people and knit together the many speeches. Comandante Tacho mentioned concretely the struggles of the small farmers of Mexico, while Comandante Omar spoke to youth and Comandanta Fidelia to women. Comandante Brus Li announced the Plan La Realidad–Tijuana, with seven agreements and seven national demands, and finally, Comandante Zebedeo talked to the crowd about rebels all over the planet.

In a taped speech produced by the EZLN's recently launched Radio Insurgente, Subcomandante Insurgente Marcos gave back "the ear, the voice, the sight" to the autonomous villages and townships in rebellion that had entrusted him with explaining the internal reorganization to Mexico and the world during this period. "The Zapatista Army of National Liberation cannot be the voice of those who rule, although they rule well and by obeying. The EZLN is the voice of those from below," said the military chief and spokesperson, now only of the EZLN.

To explain the challenges of the Plan La Realidad–Tijuana, Commander Brus Li presented seven agreements to be subscribed to and broadened by independent organizations throughout the country. Among them were respect for the independence and autonomy of grassroots organizations; promotion of forms of self-government and self-development throughout national territory; formation of a basic trade network among communities, and encouragement of civil peaceful rebellion against the designs of the bad government and the political parties.

270

The Plan La Realidad–Tijuana is composed of seven demands: defense of the ejido and communal land tenure, and protection and defense of natural resources; work with dignity and justice for all; and housing, public health, food and clothing, free lay education, and respect for the dignity of women, children and old people.

In the international realm, the Zapatistas saluted the struggles and acts of resistance taking place throughout the world, especially that of the Basque people and perhaps for the first time in public, they referred to Cuba: "We extend our admiration and respect to these people. As small as we are, there isn't much we can do. But we know well that the attack plans on the island are not lies nor is the decision of the Cuban people to resist and defend themselves from foreign invasion." (Speech by EZLN Comandante Zebedeo, August 9, 2003)

The inauguration of the Caracoles and Good Government Boards closed (or did it open?) a cycle that had begun seven months before, on January 1, 2003, when the EZLN General Command announced in San Cristóbal de las Casas its firm position *vis à vis* national political power, its decision to implement the San Andrés Accords that were betrayed by the three branches of government, and its plan to continue weaving networks with the struggles and resistance led by others in Mexico and other parts of the world.

The announcement came seven months before, but the cycle really began nine months earlier in November 2002 when the Zapatista Army of National Liberation began the twentieth year of its existence.

The government's response to the Zapatista challenge came quickly. In rhetoric, but only in rhetoric, the federal government noted that the Good Government Boards fell within the constitutional framework and greeted the Zapatista proposal as a political and not a military measure. However from then on, according to reports from several nongovernmental organizations, the government has been encouraging the reactivation of paramilitary groups to work directly against the Good Government Boards.

271

The denunciations made by the Good Government Boards since they began operating make it clear that there is a military offensive against the centers of civil resistance. However, nothing seems to faze the thousands of organized villages of the EZLN. Nothing, they assert, will stop the process of consolidating autonomy.

In rebel territory, every day and at any time, hundreds of men, women and children are working to build an alternative: building, brick by brick, a better world, one world in which many worlds fit.

Ten years have passed since the uprising. A decade in which there has been plenty of pain and disappointment in Southeast Mexico, but a decade marked by the encounter of indigenous peoples with a world that never fails to surprise them by its willingness to join them in their struggle and also to undertake their own struggles and build together.

The Zapatistas completed twenty years since their founding and ten since the uprising. "We can see the horizon now," says the Zapatista hymn, and "the road will be marked for those who follow."

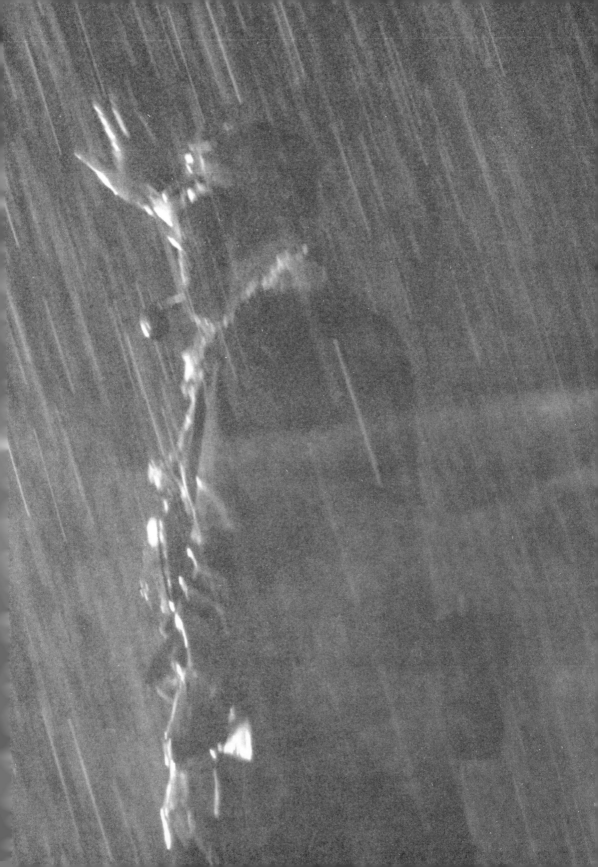

A Time to Ask,
a Time to Demand,
and a Time to Act

On November 17, 2003, the Zapatista Army of National Liberation celebrated twenty years since its founding somewhere in the Lacandón Jungle. On January 1, 2004, it completed ten years of public life—of resistance, creativity, and the paradoxes of a movement that's here to stay. The two celebrations were a time of festivities and remembrances, of looking back, of evaluating, of talking about achievements and mistakes, strategies and surprises; a time of reflecting on the ground covered so far.

It has been twenty years now that hundreds of rebel villages and hundreds of thousands of indigenous people have been fighting back. The first ten years were spent underground, weaving a political web, person by person, family by family, community by community. How were these years possible without anyone knowing about it? How did they manage to keep a secret that included thousands of indigenous rebels? Twenty years later, the story of the heroism and determination of these first villages has still not been fully told. It's a story that can only be imagined if you realize that everything that followed, and what will come, is possible due to the existence and resistance of that founding nucleus that celebrates its twentieth and tenth anniversaries of the fire and the word.

In the first interview following the Color of the Earth March, in September 2003, the EZLN's military chief and spokesperson evaluated the first decade of Zapatista struggle and resistance in response to questions sent to him from the magazine *Rebeldía* and the newspaper *La Jornada*.

Marcos accepted the suggestion that instead of answering in writing he audio record his responses. Alone in front of the microphone, he talks without pauses. These are, we imagine, questions he answers without his face mask with no other witnesses but the rain and the firecrackers that can be heard in the distance.

El Sup recalled the beginning of the war, he spoke of the first twelve days, of the initial battles, and later, he refers for the first time in an interview to Subcomandante Insurgente Pedro and his death in combat during the early hours of January 1, 1994.

Transcript of an audio recording made by Subcomandante Insurgente Marcos, September 2003:

The Beginning of the War: Motives, Memories and Confrontations

Today, nine years and nine months into our struggle—and it's important to mark the date because circumstances change—we continue to view the war that began January 1, 1994, and still goes on, as a war that was begun out of desperation, but that we then saw as necessary. Nine years and nine months later, we still see it as necessary.

We think that if we hadn't launched the war, if we hadn't started the armed uprising of the Zapatista Army of National Liberation, many things that have benefited indigenous peoples and the people of Mexico, even the world, wouldn't have happened the way they happened.

On the one hand, the memory of those first days of combats and conflict is a painful memory. We remember our companions who were killed during those first days, in Ocosingo, Las Margaritas, Altamirano. Compañeros who shared many years with us prior to that First of January

preparing and thinking about how it would be when the war began and what would happen later. Compañeros with whom we shared many things. Among them, I recall Subcomandante Insurgente Pedro, who was then head of security and second in command of the EZLN. He died in Las Margaritas in the first hours of January 1, 1994. I also remember Comandante Hugo, or Mr. Ik, as we called him, who died in Ocosingo in the battle with the federal army in the central plaza. We remember Alvaro and Fredy, insurgent compañeros in the War Materials division who also died in Ocosingo. . . we also remember militia members who fell in many places.

There is also the memory of the Mexican Army's brutal response— lacking all military honor—that did not just concentrate on fighting our troops, which is what we were there for, but which began to kill civilians and count them as if they were our dead, shooting here and there, all over, especially in the massacre of Ocosingo in the first days. I remember the lack of military honor shown by the federal army then, and that would later be repeated throughout the ten years of off-and-on war that we have waged with them. We've encountered (and this is the memory we have of the feds) this lack of military honor in battle and in the dirty tricks that they resort to in attempt to raise their fallen prestige.

On our side, we remember our combatants, not just those who were killed, but those who remain fighting, notably the women insurgents who in many cases turned out to be better fighters than the men. There is also the attitude and conviction of our commanders, the members of the Clandestine Revolutionary Indigenous Committee, the vast majority of whom marched to the front in combat along with the rest of us and demonstrated what few demonstrate today in organizations—that the leadership should join with its people, not stand aside from them or behind them. This is what we remember now.

280

After nine years and nine months from the start of the war, our reading is, to sum up, that it was a desperate but necessary war for the Indian people of Chiapas and Mexico who had been forgotten. And it was the only way to change things, not only how the federal government viewed them but also how Mexican society and international society saw them.

The beginning of the war represents for us pain, but also hope. As we see it now, the war is what made possible everything that happened afterward. The successes over the past nine years wouldn't have been possible without those first hours of armed uprising.

Our evaluation of the beginning of the war, apart from an internal evaluation, is also something that will mark the public history of the EZLN up to now. Aside from the confrontations between the EZLN and the Federal Army, we see another confrontation that isn't in itself aggressive, namely between the EZLN and what we call civil society. This encounter begins in the first minutes of the uprising and, in some ways, pushes the federal army completely to the sidelines.

If you look at the pictures from January 1, 1994, you see the almost promiscuous relationship between the Zapatista troops and civil society. What I have in my mind's eye now is the surprise of the civilians surrounding the insurgents, their surprise at seeing them and also the surprise and amazement that we showed, in our looks and in our faces, at meeting these people. There wasn't exactly camaraderie, but there wasn't aggressiveness either. As if both sides were convinced that the other was not the enemy.

From the outset, this characterizes what will be the relationship throughout all these years of meetings, clashes and reconciliations between the EZLN and civil society. It's important to point out that this encounter happens right away; so from the very beginning the government and the army start to be pushed to the sidelines. They are there, as an aggressive force you have to fight against. But they have little or nothing to do with what will be built—not what will be destroyed—over these nearly ten years. It's a surprising relationship, like, "oh, there you are!" on both sides, Zapatistas and civilians, from January 1, 1994, on.

This is going to be important, I repeat, because during the days of combat the attitude of civil society toward the insurgents was to try to find out who they were, what they're like, what they thought, what they wanted. Meanwhile, the attitude of the federal government and the army was to wipe them out, bury them, destroy them, eliminate them. And after the first battles where we took the municipal seats, we were just busy fighting, planning retreats, and surviving.

In most cases, civilians were there—in the town squares where we fought, in the plazas where we mobilized, in the places where we fought battles. Most of the civilian population didn't flee in the presence of our troops.

That's been going on for ten years now, from the first hour of this war, there has been this encounter, and the federal government and its troops were displaced from being the most powerful counterpart. I think this has been decisive for many things that have since happened.

There's another thing—the Zapatista way of making decisions, of building things from the ground up, not making decisions from the top down. This is what gave us the strength and confidence that we were doing the right thing when we started the war. It's one of the doubts a combatant usually has, among many others—is it the right thing to do or not. We had a lot of doubts—if we'd be able to do it, if we would have the capacity, what people's response would be, how the enemy army

282

would respond, the media's reaction. We had many doubts, but we never doubted the legitimacy of what we were doing. I don't mean the personal decision of each combatant—that's a huge burden, having to decide to fight to the death to get something. No, I'm referring to what it meant to us to carry out an action with collective support, in this case, the support of tens of thousands of indigenous people and thousands of combatants.

Ten Years: The Fire and the Word, Consolidating Autonomy

Instead of dividing this period into big stages, we distinguish three main strategies over the last ten years. The strategy we call fire, which refers to military actions, preparations, battles, military movements. And the one called the word, which refers to meetings, dialogues, communiqués, wherever there's the word or silence, which is the absence of the word. The third strategy would be the backbone of everything else—the organizational process that the Zapatista communities evolve over time. These strategies—the fire and the word, articulated by popular organization, are what mark the ten years of public life of the EZLN.

The fire and the word appear with greater or lesser intensity and last longer or shorter depending on the specific period, and they have more or less impact on the life of the EZLN, its surroundings, or in the national or international arenas. But the two strategies are always determined by the structures developed by the villages. As we've said many times: the communities are not only the sustenance of the EZLN but the road that the EZLN walks along. The rhythm of its step, the interval between one step and the other, the speed—both for the fire and the word—has to do with the organizational processes of the villages.

Sometimes fire, that is, the military part—combat training, mobilizations, maneuvers, battles, advances or retreats—is the most important or what appears most visible. In other cases, it's mostly the word or the silences built around the word, or speaking silently, as we say. Throughout these ten years, one or the other has prevailed but always they are predicated on the way the villages are organizing.

The EZLN bases of support don't organize the same way for war as for dialogue with the government or with civil society, or to resist, or to build autonomy, or to build other forms of government, or to relate to other movements, or to other organizations, or to people not from movements or organizations.

The Zapatista base communities have adopted styles along the way that aren't in any book or manual, or, of course, in anything we've told them. They're forms of organization that have a lot to do with their experience, and I don't just mean the ancestral and historic experience that comes from centuries of resistance, but also the experience they've gained already organized as Zapatistas.

In this sense, 1994 was characterized mostly by the strategy of fire; not only for the beginning of the war and combats but also because 1994 was full of military movements, both the government's and ours. The word was still incipient, still just murmured.

The major military mobilizations happened in January 1994 and December of the same year, when we broke through the military enclosure surrounding us. Both imply large mobilizations of thousands of combatants.

Throughout the year, whenever there were public appearances of the EZLN they always emphasized or noted the military aspect. There were marches and military movements to underline the fact that we are an army.

The word, meanwhile, was used in important meetings, but in retrospect, these were incipient efforts compared to what would come later.

For example, there was the Cathedral dialogue, which was more than a dialogue with the government, it was a dialogue with civil society. It was the continuation of the surprising encounter between the EZLN and civilians that I talked about, that started on January 1, 1994. But during the Cathedral dialogue things happened in a more refined way, because more than a dialogue with the government, the EZLN decided

to talk to the people, in this case, through the media. Members of the EZLN gave many interviews, there were meetings, etc. where the EZLN tried to say: this is me. But we still hadn't formulated the question "and who are you?" to civil society.

In the National Democratic Convention we kept up the part of "this is me." The EZLN had realized that the administration was not interested in ending the conflict but in maintaining it within limits that would allow it to finish out its term, although in the end it couldn't finish well due to the internal ruptures caused by the assassinations of Colosio and then Ruiz Massieu. . . But as part of the word that's the other thing that happened, the National Democratic Convention (NDC).

At any rate, even with the dialogue, the NDC and meetings with politicians, I see 1994 as a year marked by the line of fire.

The year 1995 continued with the line of fire, marked by the Zedillo administration's betrayal of the dialogue that was just beginning. The government launched the military offensive against EZLN positions in the Lacandón Jungle, there were battles, our people died, enemy soldiers died, and there was this huge military mobilization, the militarization that not only continues today but has increased over the years.

All of 1995 was defined in this way. So even though the dialogue with Zedillo started, it was still shadowed by the military threat—in this case from the federal government, because in August the EZLN held a consultation before formally entering into the San Andrés dialogue.

The EZLN held the consultation because we figured that if we went into the dialogue, it would be because we meant it. In the consultation, a good part of the people—1,200,000—said yes, it was necessary to become a political force. So the EZLN had to enter into the dialogue with that perspective, but there was the problem that the word was still in a nascent stage. During 1995, the line of fire still predominated, although the consultation pushed us closer to the word than the National Democratic Convention had in 1994. In 1995, the EZLN received some serious blows.

286

Then we get to 1996. The EZLN began to build the word more systematically, as a weapon but also as a meeting place. The National Indigenous Forum was held in 1996, which later became the National Indigenous Congress. There was also the Forum on Reform of the State, and the Continental and Intercontinental Gatherings. Thanks to the Zapatista communities, and these meetings, the EZLN began to ask "who are you?" and get a response from part of civil society. The word began to grow stronger.

In 1997 the EZLN responded to this new form of organizing in the communities that was progressing rapidly, and launched another initiative for dialogue. This time it did not name commissions but sent a large contingent. This was the march of the 1,111 that passed through most of the country and arrived in Mexico City with the aim of demanding compliance with the San Andrés Accords.

From then on, compliance with the San Andrés Accords, which is the goal of the Zapatista war, became a very important axis of EZLN mobilizations. However, faced with its own internal defeats, to stop the progress the government reactivated paramilitary groups, which became more and more belligerent, and finally, in December of 1997 with Acteal, the year took a definite turn toward the line of fire. And this wound, this scar, has lasted until today.

Nineteen ninety-eight was above all, the line of fire. The EZLN and especially the communities suffered a brutal offensive on the part of the government, attacks on autonomous townships, clashes, confrontations with dead on both sides in various regions of the Zapatista movement, confrontations of thousands of base community members against the federal army to block new military bases. All this defined 1998 as the line of fire.

In 1999, the EZLN tried, as always, to turn things around. It once again insisted on the word, because it was finding answers to the question of "who

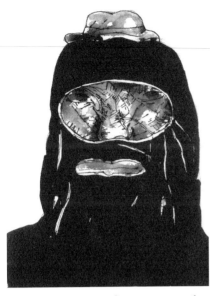

are you?" from the side of civil society, and also from the political class. The kind of political class that will be definitive in 2001 and 2002 begins to become clear.

In 1999 the National Consultation for Indigenous Rights and Culture was launched and the Zapatista villages provide a show of strength to those in power by sending out 2,500 men and 2,500 women to travel the breadth and width of the country. The National Consultation represented an organizing effort not only of the EZLN, which had been organizing for years, but of many people who were not organized and who organized for the consultation and to receive the delegates, transport them, and prepare information and consultation activities. In addition to providing fundamental support for the law on Indigenous Rights and Culture, all this mobilization gave the EZLN an accurate thermometer to gauge the relationship it had been building with civil society.

For us, 1999 was an answer to the federal government and the aggressive policy it had carried out in 1998; it's a response to the politically powerful on the importance of the indigenous law, but above all, it's a response to the EZLN from a big part of society that had been waiting to build a political relationship with us.

In the year 2000, before the electoral period, the EZLN withdrew and again used the word, but now in silence. The elections came, the defeat of the PRI, the triumph of Fox, and the EZLN played its card. After evaluating the National Consultation and the meetings with many groups in 2000, we launched the Color of the Earth March.

In the Color of the Earth March, the EZLN began to try to get even closer to that society it perceived in the national consultation in 1999, the society that's interested in building something new, which is also what the Zapatistas want. And also the EZLN was asking a basic question about the Mexican political class—if it's worth it or not to build a relationship like that. The march takes place that year, with all the events that I won't go into here.

After the vote in the Senate and in the Congress of the Union, the EZLN got a definite answer on the nature of the Mexican political class.

In 2002 it dedicated itself to preparing encounters with civil society and to building, de facto, what it had been asking for for years.

In 2003, when the construction of the Good Government Boards was announced, it represented progress toward indigenous autonomy and the EZLN became an alternative not just in words but in practice. I'm not talking about an example to follow or a guide to action, but of a point of reference. The EZLN has a practical political profile to offer when it engages in dialogue with others. A political-practical reference point, civil and peaceful, because the reference point we had before was as an armed organization that had to organize and rise up in arms.

The creation of the Good Government Boards and the autonomous townships meant there was another alternative, another option or reference point for society.

Throughout those years, from 1994 to 2003, but especially in 1996 and 1997, the EZLN began to build a relationship with the world, with people and movements on the international level, a relationship that has its ups and downs but is important for the process of building a civic and peaceful alternative. A kind of dress rehearsal for another possible world, which is what we're trying to build in the indigenous communities.

That's more or less, in general, what I can say about those three axes. The axis of fire and the axis of the word both hinged on the central axis—the organization of the people. And based on this a relationship with its own characteristics was built with civil society. And then there was the process with the politicians, which ended with their refusal to recognize indigenous rights and culture in 2001.

Surprises in Ten Years, Accomplishments, Encounters

So, in chronological order, the first surprise is that the world we had imagined in the mountains had nothing to do with the world we later discovered. From there, the most important thing that we realized was that, contrary to what you might think—that the people are basically apathetic, that they don't care or whatever—the people were in fact really interested; in this sense, we were really lucky to meet this Mexico, with its people ready to listen and to find out what was happening with the Zapatistas. That was one of the big surprises.

Another surprise was the young people. We thought they would be completely skeptical, reluctant, cynical, not very receptive to any movement, more egotistical, more wrapped up in themselves. And it hasn't been like that at all. They have been generous, open, eager to learn and eager to devote themselves to a just cause.

Another surprise is the high participation of women in all of the initiatives and at all levels. The determination and commitment of these

women, of these sisters as we say, was a big surprise at both the national and international level.

Another political surprise has been the international impact of the Zapatista word, and I don't mean just the intellectual aspect, but also the impact it had on movements and organizations all over the world.

Another surprise, and we have to recognize it, is that the Mexican political establishment has deteriorated to such a degree that we'd go so far as to say it has no remedy. We used to think there were groups we could work with, but we found out that on the whole, there are not.

If I had to sum up everything I'd say: the big political surprise was that we discovered a common ground,

290

or a channel of communication, between the villages' organizing process and what was happening from below nationally and internationally. And the last big surprise was the openess that was there in the beginning in the media (although the majority closed up as the years went by) to tell what was really happening in the indigenous communities, not only in Chiapas but in all Mexico.

I think our biggest accomplishment is the willingness and capacity to learn, first to learn to fight, then to learn to recognize the enemy, to learn to recognize who isn't the enemy, to learn to talk, to learn to listen, to learn to walk together alongside others, and to learn to respect and recognize difference. And above all, to learn to see ourselves as we are and as others see us. That, I think, is the biggest accomplishment of the Zapatistas; we've learned to learn, although it sounds like a pedagogical slogan.

Self-criticism, What We Wouldn't Do Again

If we could turn back the clock, what we would not do again is allow and. . . encourage. . . the figure of Marcos to get so blown out of proportion.

What other things wouldn't we do again? I think, honestly, that all we did—the good and the bad—we did thoughtfully, and after evaluating it, we realize that at the time it was the best decision. If in that moment we could have taken into account other factors that we didn't see then, maybe we would have made another decision, but in that moment we couldn't have done anything else. We did what we thought we could do. Sometimes we were wrong and other times we were right.

On Learning

Among other things that we learned is the wealth of diversity.

The great advantage of having come in contact with civil society is having come into contact with many different ways of thinking. And that

291

has helped us reach the conclusion that, confronted with homogeneity and hegemony, it's preferable to respect and tolerate those who are different. Another thing we've learned is to value, respect and take into account, always, the nobility of the majority of the people—people who have come through for us at crucial times in the life of the EZLN and the indigenous communities without asking anything in exchange, and not only that, they also did a lot on their own, in some cases risking everything to support a cause they consider just.

The process of meeting up with civil society—which I talked about in the Thirteenth Estela of Chiapas—has been an encounter marked by our learning and civil society's learning to meet mutually and recognize ourselves. To begin building a language, a bridge of communication, a way of understanding each other.

The Word as a Weapon and Silence as a Strategy

We didn't realize the value of the word, really, until the Cathedral dialogue or a little afterward. There we start to put out a lot of words, especailly through the media, and later we saw that it had good results. We discovered silence later, when we discovered that the government was more interested in having us say anything—it didn't even matter if we were insulting them—because they thought that then they would know what we were up to. When we are silent they don't know what we were doing. When an army that has used the word as a major weapon goes quiet, it makes the government worry. I don't know when exactly silence began to be important. . . it was definitely important during Zedillo, around 1996–1997, when it became a strategy. It was most effective in 1998, right before the second meeting with civil society in San Cristóbal de las Casas.

The Path of the Word

The war, the Cathedral dialogue, the National Democratic Convention, the First National Consultation for Peace, the San Andrés Sacamch'en de los Pobres Dialogue, the Special Forums on Indigenous Rights and Culture and Reform of the State, the Continental and Intercontinental Gatherings for Humanity and against Neoliberalism, the construction of the Zapatista National Liberation Front, the participation in the founding of the National Indigenous Congress, Comandanta Ramona's trip to Mexico City, the march of 1,111 Zapatistas, the national and international consultation for the recognition of Indian peoples when 5,000 Zapatistas went all over the country, the Color of the Earth March and finally, the installation of the Good Government Boards and the birth of the Caracoles, among many other events, calls, greetings and invitations.

These are all public initiatives—although some are missing that fell flat or had little impact—that are built up from the grassroots as part of the organizing process of the Zapatista villages, in the development of their own ways of organizing. We're talking about an organization that is so fused to the people, to its base of support, that it can hardly take any initiative apart from it, or that doesn't involve or have a relationship with that grassroots base. In both the line of the word and the line of fire, the process of building, advancing, organizing forms in Zapatista communities has a lot to do with recognition of the other, in this case, civil society. A good part of the initiatives mentioned are attempts, complete or not, successful or not, on the part of the EZLN communities to build a two-way dialogue.

In the construction of this conversation, in finding out what the other is like and showing ourselves as we are, at the same time, the EZLN—along with the communities—builds the legitimacy of its movement, explaining the causes, the conditions that originated it, its forms of orga-

nizing, and inviting everyone not to follow us but to follow their own paths, both the ones that exist and those in the making.

Sometimes the conversation with society happens by sector, and given the indigenous roots of the EZLN, especially with Indian peoples. Also due to the impact that the EZLN has had and the international repercussions and support it has received, special attention is placed on the conversation with persons and movements on the international level. More generally, with civil society—without defining a class or social group in particular. Always giving preference to interlocution with indigenous peoples, women and youth. The strategy up to now is to build the legitimacy of the movement, to get to know each other, to get to know our context, to get to know the situation on the national and international level.

Evaluation of the Dialogue in San Cristóbal de las Casas and Carlos Salinas de Gortari

Carlos Salinas de Gortari is a cynical thief, that's what defines him then and now. The first dialogue with his government in San Cristóbal helped us to see the other side. That's when the EZLN strategy to turn the tables really began, that is, to end the "customer service window" style of dialogue and to use the opportunity to engage in dialogue with others, with the people, with civil society.

In the case of the Cathedral dialogue in San Cristóbal de las Casas, since we didn't know the right way and we couldn't even imagine how we were going to dialogue with civil society, the dialogue with civil society was mainly with the media. What we wanted to say was, "this is me, this is what I want, and this is what I was." This is what the Cathedral dialogue was good for.

It was a dialogue that helped a lot; it was very exhausting and very intense. It was a lot of work crammed into a few days and in retrospect we think that what came out of it was good, because as a result of that dialogue many people had a better idea of us. These were our intentions and our goals and it was the point of departure for the EZLN to build the legitimacy we now have.

The San Andrés Dialogue and Ernesto Zedillo Ponce de León

Zedillo is a criminal who is also an economist—or pretends to be. The evaluation of the San Andrés Dialogue with his administration is very positive for us, because it allowed us to polish what we tried in San Cristóbal. We managed to seat at the negotiating table everyone we could invite and, without taking into account the accords themselves, it represented an experience that still hasn't been fully appreciated in Mexico or in the world.

The main contribution of San Andrés was the way in which the dialogue between the government and the EZLN transpired. But furthermore, on the EZLN side, it opened the door to others, including to organizations and ideas that were very critical or rivals of the EZLN.

In regards to the accords reached on indigenous rights and culture, they expressed the main point that the January 1994 uprising put on the national agenda—the situation of Mexico's Indian peoples. They signified the possibility of incorporating not only the experiences of the Zapatistas but of peoples in all parts of Mexico, and synthesized them in the demand for constitutional rights. Due to the way the dialogue was structured and the way results were reached, compliance with the San Andrés Accords meant no less than the full incorporation of the EZLN into public life. That's why, as will be seen later, the political class joined forces to block the recognition of indigenous peoples, of their rights, and to impede the action of the EZLN in the civic and political arenas.

Vicente Fox, the Failure of the Politicians

As for Vicente Fox, to put it succinctly, I'd just say that the process of negotiation was a failure of the whole political class—not just Vicente Fox, but of all the branches of government, all the political parties, the entire political class. If we had triumphed it would have been an example not only for Mexico, but for the world. It would have been a break with the past, a precedent to orient dialogues and negotiations all over the world. But instead, they preferred to shut themselves up in their room and count their money, instead of resolving the problem and establishing a precedent for international conflicts.

The EZLN and the Indigenous Struggle

Some groups have said that the EZLN took up the indigenous struggle after the uprising, when the movement was already strong. According to this version, the National Indigenous Plural Assembly for Autonomy (ANIPA), for example, says that when the EZLN realized that the indigenous issue was popular, it began to reorient its discourse toward that issue. The accusation is ridiculous, like everything that ANIPA does. If you take into account the founding act of January 1, 1994, the speech of the First Declaration of the Lacandón Jungle explains who we are. "We are the product of 500 years of struggles, etc.," and there is no other social group that can say that in Mexico except indigenous people—not workers, not peasants, not intellectuals—none can say they've been around 500 years. . .

The other reason you have to bear in mind is that the EZLN is comprised of two or three mestizos and thousands of indigenous people. I don't think it's even necessary to say that the indigenous issue is important. When the EZLN later opens its borders, so to speak, to grant the press access to the indigenous communities, reporters start talking to the people—all this at the same time that we're fighting battles. That's much more eloquent than any declaration of ANIPA's leaders or advisers.

The EZLN has never presented itself as the representative, leader or guide of all the Indian peoples of Mexico. Only those who fight over the bone of representing the indigenous out of pure economic interest or to gain a quota of power, those who are called professional indigenous people, those who live off appearing or pretending to be indigenous, can accuse the EZLN of that. The EZLN has always said that it only speaks for the Indian peoples that are organized in the EZLN, specifically, in Southeastern Mexico.

Well, anyway, this critical comment or calumny that circulates in some sectors is always made behind our backs, never to our face, because they know they can't back it up.

Following history—our history—when the revolutionary laws were being discussed in 1993 in the Clandestine Revolutionary Indigenous Committee (among the leaders of the different Indian peoples: Tzeltal, Tzotzil, Tojolabal, Chol, Zoque and Mam), it was debated whether we would emphasize certain indigenous demands of the EZLN in the moment of the uprising, and the side that argued better and won said that we had to give it a national character so that the movement wouldn't be seen as having just regional or "ethnic" objectives. The danger was that they would see our war as a one of Indians against mestizos, and that was a danger to be avoided. I think the decision was correct, that the First Declaration of the Lacandón Jungle is convincing and clear, that the clearer definition of the indigenous issue as the movement advanced after becoming public, after the start of the war, was also correct and very modest. We never tried to take the lead or speak in the name of all the Indian people of Mexico.

Now, the EZLN does not publicly present itself or conceive of itself as a watershed in the indigenous struggle. We present ourselves, as it says in the First Declaration, as part of a struggle that goes way back and that can be found in many places. In the case of Mexico, the indigenous struggle didn't start in 1994 or in Chiapas. Before January 1994 there were many acts of resistance, many valuable experiences, among other Indian peoples in many parts of Mexico. And the EZLN has always said that.

The talks in San Andrés on Indigenous Rights and Culture did not represent the EZLN. If we thought we were the leaders of the national indigenous movement, we would have gone alone. But we invited organizations, groups, intellectuals—all those who've worked with and know the demands of Indian peoples. The group included diverse viewpoints that can loosely be called pro-autonomy. This was important to say from the outset, because at the start of the movement, in the first months, the political class and much of the media affirmed that the main problem or the fundamental indigenous issue in Mexico was a problem of charity. That is, that the indigenous people are poor and should be given handouts—in this case, more handouts and more pity.

[Marcos continues talking into the tape recorder. Suddenly from far away you can hear the sound of fireworks from celebrations.] What you hear exploding in the background is because they are celebrating the cry of independence in the Good Government Boards. It's the dawn of September 16 and we're celebrating Mexican independence. Well, not me because I'm off in a corner, but there in the Good Government Board.

Well, at first the indigenous problem was described as a problem of material poverty and not how the EZLN and before it other indigenous peoples and organizations in the rest of the country had defined it—as something more complex that implied cultural issues, self-government, autonomy and not just the need for more handouts. At first much of national and international public opinion saw the problem as "poor Indians, we have to help them a little, so they have a good house and a good education"—thinking that education is the way for the indigenous to stop being indigenous, learn Spanish, forget their language, become mestizos (mixed blood) or Ladinos as they used to say, and the moment they stopped being indigenous everything would be better.

299

So that's the first stage of the indigenous struggle. It is recognized that in Mexico and in the world the living conditions of indigenous peoples are disastrous, prehistoric. And one compares this situation with Salinas de Gortari's plan, a project to become part of the First World, of a country capable of competing under globalization. But evidently, the indigenous problem wasn't the only thing in this comparison.

In the second stage, around the dialogues of San Andrés, all these experiences and demands coalesced when EZLN explicitly renounced the role of vanguard of this rich and varied indigenous movement. The people then realized that the indigenous problem is not only economic but also cultural, political and social. And they began to look at experiences in other places, began to get to know each other and articulate their views in the San Andrés Accords, which eventually came to include the demand for autonomy and self-government, and cultural issues. This is what will later be incorporated in the Zapatista autonomous townships and in the Good Government Boards, not only as a product of the Zapatista experience but also gathering all that we learned from our contact with the national indigenous movement and in some cases with the international movement.

In this second stage, the indigenous movement builds a kind of bridge or common cause, that unites us all with what will be the San Andrés Accords in Mexico. This happens alongside the EZLN, but not directed by it, and is the constitutional recognition of Indian peoples to govern and be governed on their own terms. When things are thought of only in terms of charity, the PRI, the PAN and the PRD say, "if it's about giving more money, fine, we keep a part of it and give them the other, we can buy votes like that, etc." As demonstrated in the Congress and now in their campaigns, when Indian demands are couched in terms of political organization and forms of government, the political parties no longer agree.

In the second stage we began to build a consensus on indigenous demands to publicize within the national indigenous movement and outside, through civil society, the media, and other social organizations. This

stage ends when the Mexican Congress legislated against the rights with the support of the executive branch, and later this decision was validated by the Supreme Court. At that moment, the second stage ended and the current stage began. In sum, in the first stage, certain rights were claimed as necessary; in the second, we demanded these rights; and in the last stage we exercise these rights. That's where we are now.

The Political Class

The EZLN came into the public spotlight and, somewhat dazzled, began to stutter and explore who's who in this new terrain. With respect to the political class, the EZLN began a long learning experience.

An organization that puts so much stake in the word assumes that the other side does too, and we took a while to understand that no, for the politicians the word has absolutely no value. But for us to learn that, several moons went by, as a compañero puts it.

So we went stuttering along, talking to different sectors, and the first thing we learned was that the word has no value for the politicians. The second thing we learned is that there are no principles, not to mention morals, that they uphold. One day they say one thing and the next they say another. They even look down on people who do the opposite. I'm referring generally to all politicians without distinguishing which political party they belong to. The difference between one and the other could be that there are some honest ones, that is, those who don't steal. I'm not referring to their integrity, because there are very few of those. What makes them politicians, this disdain for keeping their word, this lack of principles and of political goals, is true, in general, for all of them. I wouldn't make any distinction. They're all the same in that there are no principles or morals. They can be right-wing one day if that's where the ratings are, left-wing if the rating changes, or in the center. That's why there's this search for the center, because that way it's easier to run in one direction or the other, and there are parties that do this with great agility.

We learned all this little by little. Still, with the bitterness of knowing what we were up against, in the Color of the Earth March we tried to in some way oblige them to come to their senses by confronting them with not only the EZLN but with all the Indian peoples and with a national and international mobilization. Even with all that, they still kept behaving like politicians.

The main lesson during this decade has been that you can't do anything with the Mexican political class, not even laugh at it.

Changes in Mexico from 1994 to Now

There is a fundamental difference between Mexico today, in 2003, and in 1994. Things started to happen after January of 1994, things that hadn't happened in a long time in the history of modern Mexico: the assassination of the presidential candidate of the ruling party, the assassination of the party secretary, infighting disguised as legal battles and indictments, the defeat of the PRI after so many years. All this within the political class.

At the same time, the public too was going through a change. Today the public is more critical, more willing to participate and mobilize, than years ago. But thanks to the work of the political class the people are more skeptical now, but this skepticism isn't like before, when they said "the PRI always wins." Now there is some resentfulness and anger in the majority of the people against the politicians.

And what's happening is that the media (most of them) are embracing the political class without realizing that they're falling instead of rising. Without realizing that the discredit, lack of credibility, lack of interest, and rancor that the political class is accumulating is also being accumulated by the communications media, which are so wrapped up in their new job of Public Ministry that they forget that their escort is illegitimate. Legality has no base if it lacks legitimacy.

The most fundamental change we've seen has been in the people. In terms of the political system, alternating the presidency is a change, but that doesn't mean democracy at all. The economic model that the PRI had in 1994 not only continues, but has been extended. There is an abandonment of the basics of national sovereignty. In social terms, the process of decomposition is accelerating due to economic policies that destroy the social fabric. That's the cynicism of the politicians, who offer no real alternative for the majority of the people.

In short, in both politics and society, Mexico is a deeper crisis now than it was in 1994.

The World Between 1994 and 2003

We had thought about and imagined the world we found in January 1994. The break-up of the socialist camp had happened and armed struggle wasn't very popular in Latin America, let alone in other parts of the world. That's what we expected. But the advance of neoliberalism and globalization throughout the world turned out to be a surprise, because we saw that not only had the process of destruction and reconstruction that we mentioned in some of our texts advanced, but the birth and maintenance of forms of resistance and struggle throughout the whole world had done the same. The socialist or communist internationals, or the international mutual networks to oppose capitalism had disappeared, but foci of resistance had emerged in various places and were multiplying.

This is why the uprising has been so well received in much of the international community, among organized people and people who want to be organized. And I'm referring to something beyond the feeling of pity or compassion for what the EZLN uprising meant and the revelation of the outrageous conditions that indigenous people lived in before

January 1, 1994, which was totally legitimate. That's what it was for many people. But for others it also meant a serious political project.

The world we discovered in 1994, even if we had imagined it, we didn't quite understand it, and so we didn't understand the way we were received by many groups, especially by groups of young people of all political tendencies and convictions. We didn't completely understand why the Zapatista movement caused this sympathy and why they created solidarity committees on all five continents.

The world of today, ten years later, is more polarized. This is what we predicted: that globalization is not producing a global village but a world archipelago that is sharpening differences, not only in the economic, political and social interests of this huge society, of power in general, to divvy up, conquer and destroy the world. But also in the growth of resistance, rebellion that grows autonomously, independently, not in a consequential line, not like a resistance that can be spread to all parts of the world, but one that acquires its particular form in each place.

The Anti-globalization Movement—We Weren't the First

The anti-globalization movement is now calling itself alternative globalization because it's not about opposing the world as it is but about creating another world. We don't think it's a linear movement, with precedents and consequences, or that it has to do with geographic situations or calendars, dates like first Chiapas, then Seattle, then Genoa, and now Cancún. It isn't that one precedes the other and inherits it.

We conceived of our movement, and this is what we declared in 1994, as a symptom of something that was happening and was about to happen. We used the image of the iceberg: we are, we said, the tip of the iceberg that is sticking up and soon other tips will emerge in other places, and something larger below will surge up to the surface.

In this sense, Chiapas doesn't precede Seattle as much as it announces Seattle. Seattle is the continuation. Seattle is another manifestation of this world rebellion that is gestating outside of political parties, outside of traditional channels of politics. And it's that way with every one of the demonstrations, and I don't mean only those that have followed the WTO around and have become its worst nightmare, but other kinds of more lasting demonstrations or mobilizations or movements against the globalization of death and destruction.

We are more modest as to our place. We are a symptom and we think that our duty is to maintain ourselves as much as possible as a handle, a point of reference. But not as a model to follow. That's why we never argued, nor will we say, that Chiapas and the Continental and Intercontinental Meetings were the beginning. The rebellion in Chiapas is called Zapatista; but in Seattle it's called something else; in the European Union something else; in Asia something else; in Australia something else. Even in Mexico, in other places the rebellion has other names.

We like this alternative globalization movement in the sense that it doesn't repeat the vertical model of top-down decision-making, and that helps it not to have a central command, directives or something like that. And because the movement has known how to respect the differences within it—the thoughts, the currents, the styles, the interests and the form of decision-making.

Based on the little I know of Cancún up to now, from what's in the press, especially in the newspaper *La Jornada*, it looks like that dynamic is still going on and it's still a diverse movement, not really massive but that's understandable because it moves all over the globe. It's not the same to mobilize here, in Chiapas, for someone who's really close, as to mobilize for someone who's in South Korea, just to give an example, the most famous one now. [Author's note: Lee Kyung Hae, a South Korean farmer, took his own life at the Cancún Fifth Ministerial meeting of the World Trade Organization just a month before this interview.] But there's still a diversity of interests, of forms of struggle, and of ways of expressing it.

In this sense, we view the anti-globalization or alternative globalization movement as rich in experiences, with much to contribute, and we think that it will give a lot, as long as it doesn't fall into the temptation of structures or showcasing. The risk that always exists is that a movement is converted into a personality parade when these personalities don't even have the support of mobilizations on their own home turf.

We think that this movement is translating not only into a critique of the model that the WTO and others represent, but also that it's building alternative forms of grassroots organization in many places where there are seeds of this other possible world.

It's often said that movements in Mexico and other parts of the world have found in the Zapatista movement an example of struggle and even that some have taken up its principles to build their own resistance.

We say to them: to those who follow our example, don't follow it. We think everyone has to build his and her own experience and not repeat models. In this sense, the Zapatista model offers a mirror, but a mirror that isn't you, it just helps you see how you are, to comb your hair in a certain way, to fix yourself up a little. We say, look at our mistakes and achievements—if there are any—the things that can serve to build your own processes. But don't try to export Zapatismo or import it. We think that the people have enough courage and wisdom to build their own process and their own movements, because they have their own histories. This should be not only welcomed, but encouraged.

Challenges, Mistakes, Risks: What's Next?

So then, you want to hear the plan of action? Mmmm. . . First it has to be clear that not all the Zapatista campaigns or initiatives met with a massive response from civil society, nationally or internationally. We think that when that has happened it wasn't the people's fault but our errors, in this case mine, because it's my job. Because here in the EZLN the mistakes are conjugated in first person singular and the achievements in third person plural. To mention two of these Zapatista calls to action that didn't have a mass response: one was "An Opportunity for the Word," referring to the situation in Basque Country that was also going to be the EZLN entry into Europe; and the other was when the media reported the war of the United States against Iraq. In this context we launched an initiative to sign a declaration by a group of intellectuals. We called on the people to organize roundtables, discussions, but there was no echo. These two campaigns failed to get a big response—at least these two, but there might be more too. This is to say that I haven't hit the mark with everything I've done, because the mistakes are in first person singular.

But really, this part is asking about what's next, and the objective of the EZLN now is to consolidate the exercise of community rights,

307

because, as I explained at the beginning, the main axis or the backbone of these two lines of action—the fire and the word—is the axis of political organization and development of political, social and cultural organization in the communities. And now it is all about the Good Government Boards and the autonomous townships. That's a tall order.

Anyway the wager was clearly defined in the speeches made by the Command on August 9, 2003, the day the Aguascalientes died and the Caracoles were born. These are international efforts. There is a clear national effort aimed at spreading forms of self-government or self-management—that are possible here, in a way—to other places.

As far as the government or the political class are concerned, it's not worth it to spend much time on them since they don't spend time on us. So better not to lose sleep over it.

The Zapatista Villages, the Resistance

In general, the backbone of the Zapatista movement is the organizing process of the villages.

You have to go back to the time when the villages organized into a political-military organization and all that implies, always in the collective. In this case, it implied going from the family nucleus to that of the community, then from the community to the region, then from the zone to all the EZLN in all the different Indian villages that form parts of it.

After the uprising, due to the contact with national and especially international civil society, the villages broadened their cultural experience, their horizons as we say, and can confront the process of self-government more comfortably, far from the temptation of ethnic fundamentalism that is so expensive and so admired by ANIPA.

So the most advanced forms of self-management and self-government that already functioned on the community level even before the EZLN got to Chiapas began to build, then afterward advanced to a

308

higher level—the level of autonomous townships, around 1995–1996. But the progress has been uneven. Some townships are more experienced in the process of self-government; they build it and it's a product of their own struggle and their own development, and they push the EZLN to learn from them and adjust.

In other places it's not like that. There are places where supposedly there are autonomous townships, but they don't really operate. In other places, they do develop as a government and with the characteristics of ruling by obeying, with rotation in local authorities, removal from office, sanctions for corruption, etc. In the Zapatista communities, it isn't just work or a promise or a utopia, but a reality, and it's not our contribution—it's the contribution of the communities from before we arrived. This continues developing more and more, but unevenly.

From two years ago to now, after the Congress of the Union and the federal administration betrayed the national and international mobilization in favor of indigenous rights and culture, we started to try to even up the development in the autonomous townships, consolidate the ones that exist and develop those that are a little behind. Since the decision of the Supreme Court of Justice that pre-empted recognition, we've been moving toward this new stage of Good Government Boards, which govern inter-municipal relations between autonomous townships and solve problems that have been identified throughout their existence.

As I said in the Estelas—especially in the Thirteenth Estela—all this happened in the context of war, persecution, harassment, paramilitary attacks, media campaigns against us, sicknesses, natural disasters and all you can imagine in terms of obstacles.

The Zapatista villages confronted all of this and still built this alternative of good government, the Boards, although we still have to see if they come through, as we say.

The villages have organized collectively. This is easy to say but hard to understand and even harder to put in practice. Here what helps a lot is the communities' ancestral experience, from centuries ago, first in developing their cultures and later in surviving the many attempts at annihilation and ethnocide they've suffered though history, from the "discovery" of America to our days.

This collective way that has allowed them to develop culturally, socially and economically, then to survive the conquest, colonization, independence and modern periods in Mexico, is what allows them to build resistance within the model of the communities. The fundamental aspect of this resistance is that it's possible because it's collective. Furthermore, it has the advantage that, with the relationship that the Zapatista movement built with national and international civil society, the resistance began to generate the possibility of building an alternative, and not only resisting until some day the Accords were complied with, but parallel to that resisting, building the means of compliance and of exercising the rights they were demanding.

What prevents the Zapatistas from giving up to the different governments, is the experience, the history and the consciousness of that history. Everything that happened before, the words, the promises and what happened after the promises, makes us believe firmly that the government is always trying to cheat us. That's why we are not asking them to give us something, but that they let us live without giving up being who we are— indigenous and Mexican.

The same collective, political work, control, development of forms of communication that we have within our communities—all this makes it possible for the community to protect each and every one of its members who by choice decide to resist.

We just did an investigation, and the PRI villages do not have better living conditions than the Zapatista villages, for instance. The rebel Zapatista communities, although not all, are the only ones that have free health services. There isn't one community outside the Zapatista villages, even if not all of them have it yet, that can say that.

In education, it's not about whether you pay or not, but whether you have schools or not. The Zapatista communities, on average, have more educational centers than the PRI communities. That's just health and education. Food is about the same for both. The aid that the government gives the PRI communities is spent on liquor and does not improve nutrition or clothing. In terms of access to the land, that's the same for everybody, although the fact is that the Zapatista way of encouraging, promoting and fostering collective production has, little by little, made conditions less harsh than in the PRI communities.

We are not in the best conditions, but we are better off since the uprising. And these improvements are not the product of handouts or having sold out, but the product of the internal organization of the communities, of the organization between communities and of the heroic support of national and international civil society.

It isn't what we want, we still have a long way to go to get what we want, but we are in better conditions than before the uprising and we have the conviction that our poverty and our shortages have a direction and an end, that is, we have hope.

Women in the EZLN

As for the struggle of the rebel indigenous women—their triple marginalization as women, indigenous and poor—the compañeras organize on two levels. Historically, the women in the communities are the most marginalized, but when young indigenous women go to the mountains and develop their capacities more, it has consequences in the communities.

Insurgent women became more advanced, or in better condition as women, than those in the villages, and this began to have an impact on their communities.

311

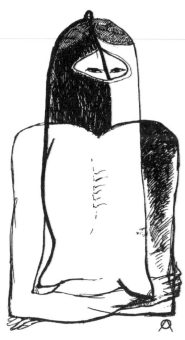

Within the communities the process of organization has advanced a lot, although it's far from what it should be.

From what we can see, generally, in zones where there weren't any women's committees or women commanders until about two or three years ago, such as in the Tzeltal zone, there are now compañeras in leadership positions, because the women in the villages organized to choose their own representatives, or "responsibles" as we say. This has been going on for a long time in the Tzotzil zone. But in other places it wasn't until two or three years ago that more women start to appear. You can see more where the Zapatista educational system is well-established, where women and girls who usually stayed home cooking and caring for younger brothers and sisters now go to school, although it's still not complete.

It's now almost nonexistent to find marriage by payment in Zapatista communities, that is, that a compañera is married off to someone she doesn't want. But domestic violence still exists against women, and sexual harassment, although that term doesn't exist in the legislation of the communities. The women tell us about the problems they face.

In the EZLN we think that the liberation movement—the emancipation of women—has a lot to do with their material conditions. A woman can't be independent and free if she depends economically on a man. In this sense, the progress made in the indigenous women's cooperatives allows them to have an income and gain economic independence; it allows them to do many things they couldn't do before. And we are trying to spread that. But we're still very far because it's so tied up with economic conditions in the Zapatista communities.

We see that there is more women's participation in the CCRI. From three years ago to now the percentage of women comandantas has grown to over 30 percent, and before it was between 10 and 15 percent in the whole committee. Now there are women comandantas in all the Indian villages. It didn't used to be like that. More are participating, they hold their own separate meetings. I perceive more respect from the men comandantes for the women comandantas. This didn't use to happen, but we still have a long way to go. We hope that some day we will have more good news to report on this issue.

Challenges for the Good Government Boards

The main challenge is the same one we've always faced: learning. The Good Government Boards are now in a learning process; they have to learn to delineate their functions with respect to the autonomous municipalities, because in the first few days there were cases of invasion of functions. The Good Government Boards are starting to make decisions that correspond to the autonomous townships, and in other cases functions that they should take on are being delegated to the autonomous townships.

Now they are in the process of settling in, of defining their horizons and range of action with the autonomous townships, with other townships that aren't Zapatista, and with other Good Government Boards. So they are organizing and learning. Each autonomous township has representatives, accompanied by a delegation from the CCRI of each zone who explains to them and helps them to explain to everybody else. The role of the CCRI is to make sure everything is transparent toward the communities, that they know what is being done every moment, what money is being received, where it's going, so that the oversight mechanisms that worked for centuries can continue to work: the collective watches over so that the individual won't be corrupted.

The problem that we're encountering now is that people who come to talk to the Good Government Boards think that they are the EZLN, and they ask them questions that correspond to the EZLN and not about forms of government. But you can't forget that there are more Zapatista communities than those that are organized in autonomous townships and Good Government Boards. There are indigenous communities that haven't reached that level of cohesion, or that haven't yet managed to weave together a territory to have the capacity to be an autonomous township and much less to have a Good Government Board. Proportionally these are the majority, the ones that don't have autonomous representation in a township or a Good Government Board.

So to think of the EZLN as the same as the Good Government Boards is still to not understand what the EZLN is proposing. Demanding the Good Government Boards to give out positions, opinions, functions that fall in the realm of the EZLN, is to not understand that these are organizations from groups of villages in resistance. This is something that civil society still has to learn.

We think that all this is going to be resolved with that capacity that we talked about at the beginning, the capacity Zapatistas are so proud of—the capacity to learn.

The Next Step:
The Sixth Declaration of
the Lacandón Jungle

By Hermann Bellinghausen and Gloria Muñoz Ramírez

In the sixth month of 2005 the EZLN released the Sixth Declaration of the Lacandón Jungle. It invited "indigenous peoples, workers, peasants, teachers, students, housekeepers, farmworkers, small landowners, small businesspeople, micro-entrepreneurs, retirees, the handicapped, clergymen and clergywomen, scientists, artists, intellectuals, youths, women, elders, gays, lesbians and children to individually or collectively participate directly with the Zapatistas in a national campaign to develop a different way of doing politics, a national program of struggle from the left, and a new Constitution." The Declaration reaffirmed the EZLN's conviction not to become a political party or to struggle to take power.

The Other Campaign is the Sixth Declaration in practice. In its first stages, it consists of tours by delegations of the Zapatista insurgents to visit places throughout the Mexican nation—to meet with leftist political organizations, landless peasants, the families of murdered women, repressed teachers, forsaken fishermen, exploited sex workers, jobless or underpaid workers, youths at risk, ostracized gays, lesbians and transgender persons, and a long list of people that covers the entire spectrum of Mexico from below. For the first time, a Zapatista initiative includes the other Mexico that resists north of the border.

The Other Campaign was born at a crucial political moment in Mexico—during the presidential campaigns of July 2006. Its name reflects this moment and represents a different way of organizing from below to change the system.

The Other Campaign's relationships with leftist political organizations are driven by an ethical stance:

"Never to make agreements from above and impose them below, but to agree to join forces to listen and to organize indignation; never to create movements that can then be negotiated behind the backs of those who built them, but to always take into account the opinions of their participants; never to seek giveaways, positions, personal advantage or public appointments from the structures of power or from those who aspire to them, but to look beyond electoral calendars; never to attempt to solve the nation's problems from above, but to build an alternative from below to neoliberal destruction, a left alternative for Mexico."

Subcomandante Marcos, now referred to as Delegate Zero, was designated for the first tour and left La Garrucha, Chiapas, on January 1, 2006. Surprisingly, he set off riding a motorcycle and wearing a helmet over his ski mask (and carrying an upright chicken known as the "Zapatista penguin" on the back of his bike.) He headed first toward San Cristóbal de las Casas, where thousands of Zapatistas from the base communities met to celebrate the first steps of the EZLN's new proposal.

Comandanta Kelly "handed" Delegate Zero to civil society in the name of the Zapatistas and the tour started, with a caravan that traveled first through the various regions of the state of Chiapas. Only six days had gone by when suddenly Comandanta Ramona, an emblem of Zapatista women's resistance, died of kidney failure in Los Altos. The tour was sus-

318

pended and the Zapatistas' entire high command attended the funeral. "Never again a Mexico without us" was the heritage left by this tiny Tzotzil woman who, together with other *comandantas*, wrote the Women's Revolutionary Law.

After paying homage to Ramona, the tour continued through the states of the Mayan Peninsula: Yucatán, Quintana Roo and Campeche. From there, it headed to Tabasco, Veracruz and all the way to the north— to Tijuana, Sonoyta and the industrial wastelands along the Río Bravo in Nuevo Laredo. Marcos arrived at the lands of the Cucapá, the Yaqui, the Tohono O'odham, the Rarámuri. At the border he met with migrants, Chicanos, and other U.S. adherents to the Sixth Declaration, challenging the U.S. authorities at various points along the border.

Since its early days, the Other Campaign discovered the existence of an Other geography, very different from that imposed by the borders drawn by those above. At several points on the border between Mexico and the United States, Chicanos and Mexicans from "both sides" met and

listened to each other. Perhaps for the first time in over a decade of Zapatista struggle, those from the "other side" (the United States) felt truly committed to a political initiative of the EZLN, not only as groups in solidarity with indigenous peoples, but as an important part of a common struggle that includes Mexicans and Chicanos without walls or documents between them.

In 2006, the Other Campaign toured Mexico as thoroughly as possible. It covered every state and went through capital cities, mountains, coasts, lakes, rivers, dams, forests, canyons, jungles and deserts, towns and villages, roadsides, borders, mines, wastelands, pockets of internal refugees, brothels, private homes, universities, and the poorest and most aggrieved neighborhoods.

With few exceptions, the Sixth Commission of the EZLN met with practically all indigenous peoples living in Mexico. The Nahuatl welcomed the Other Campaign in Guerrero, Jalisco, the Huasteca region, the Federal District, Puebla and Michoacán. It encountered the Zapotecs, Mixtecs and Triquis in Oaxaca and beyond—in Baja California, Sinaloa, the valley of Anáhuac and southern Veracruz. In "internal refugee regions" it met forgotten or negated peoples—Pames, Pimas, Teenek, Huachichiles, Caxcanes. The Wirrárika, Rarámuri, Maya, Mixe, Purépecha, Totonaca, Com'cac, Amuzgo, Chontal, Popoluca, Tzeltal, Tzotzil, Chol, Ñahñú, Mazahua, Tepehuano, Yaqui Yoreme and Mayo Yoreme welcomed the Other Campaign in their ancestral lands. The tour met the very last members of the Cucapá, Kumiai, Kiliwa and Kikapú, and along the way it was received by Mazatecos, Guarijíos, Mames, Chinantecs, Huaves, Tojolabales and Zoques.

The Other Campaign saw the same tendency toward gross inequality not only in rural areas, but also in cities, industrial zones and nonindigenous regions. In some cases, the transfer of resources from the poor to the rich is almost complete (in Cancún, Los Cabos, Huixquilucan). Many capital cities are already "American style," or at least their owners would like to think so. A few, like San Luis Potosí, Nuevo Laredo or Torreón, are already in the process of dying from lead, arsenic and other industrial poisons.

But the tour also revealed that forms of resistance multiply from below. And that indigenous peoples constitute the first ramparts against government policies to privatize land. They have a clearer vision and a sacred attachment to the soil they walk on. Migration cuts through them like a sword, yet they don't easily abandon their land. It is not merchandise. It does not belong to them; they belong to it. As an indigenous saying goes, "We do not inherit the land from our ancestors, we borrow it from our children." They affirm that the land must be owned and worked in common so that it may continue living for everyone.

In some places, the Mexican government responded to the Other Campaign with violent repression. Brutal and hateful government attacks took place against the Front of the Peoples in Defense of Land in the town of San Salvador Atenco, in the state of Mexico, and against the extraordinary people's movement of Oaxaca. These aggressions sparked a large number of mobilizations of solidarity in Mexico and abroad. They were hard times, during which the Other Campaign tested its ability to organize nationally, its international legitimacy, and its capacity to convene international solidarity (for Atenco alone there were 209 mobilizations in 77 cities of 30 countries). The Zapatista communities expressed their unconditional support for Atenco and Oaxaca not only with words, but, for the first time, tens of thousands of Zapatistas mobilized against the repression of another movement, in accordance with the Other Campaign's principle "if they hit one of us, they hit us all."

The Zezta Internazional

The Sixth Declaration contains an international component that is a result of an analysis of how the Zapatistas perceive the world:

"The form of capitalism related to neoliberal globalization is based on exploitation, pillage, contempt, and repression of those who oppose it. In other words, the same as before, but now on a global scale. . . But it's not that easy for neoliberal globalization, because those who are exploited in every country don't sit back and resign themselves—they rebel; and those who don't fit and get in the way of neoliberalism resist and refuse to be eliminated."

The Zapatistas are convinced that, "just as there is a neoliberal globalization, there is a globalization of rebellion."

The Sixth Declaration explains: "And so it happens that capitalism today isn't like it used to be, the rich happily exploiting the poor in their own countries; now it's at a stage called Neoliberal Globalization. This globalization means that workers aren't dominated only in a single country or in several of them, but that capitalists are trying to dominate the whole world, the Planet Earth, which is also called the "globe," and that's why it's called globalization, because it encompasses the whole world. . . Neoliberalism is like the theory, the plan, to make capitalist globalization work. And neoliberalism has its economic, political, military, and cultural plans. The objective of each of these plans is to rule over everyone, and those who don't obey are repressed and excluded, to keep them from contaminating others with their rebellious ideas."

The EZLN warns: "In neoliberal globalization, major capitalists living in powerful countries like the United States want to turn the whole world into a great enterprise where merchandise is produced and goes into a market where it's sold. A global market, a market to buy and sell everything and to hide all exploitation around the world. That's why we Zapatistas say that neoliberal globalization is a war to conquer the whole world, a world war, a war waged by capitalism to rule over the Earth. This conquest is sometimes done with armies that invade a country and conquer it by force. But sometimes it's done with the economy, when large capitalists put their money in another country or lend it money, but with the con-

322

dition that those countries obey what they say. And they also bring their ideas, their capitalist culture, which is the culture of merchandise, profit, and the market."

In the summer of 1997 the First Encounter for Humanity and Against Neoliberalism took place in the Zapatista community of La Realidad. Almost a decade later, the Zezta Internazional reiterated the international invitation to resist and struggle against globalization. The challenge is still to transform mobilization into organization. In Brazil the challenge is taken up every day by the Landless Peasant Movement (MST); in Bolivia and Ecuador by indigenous peoples; in Argentina by unemployed workers; in Paraguay by indigenous peoples; by the Mapuche in Chile; in the United States by migrants, Chicanos and other U.S. Americans. And of course in Cuba by the Cuban people, and in Mexico by the Other Campaign. In Europe there are organized struggles for job security, for migrant rights, for gender equality, for the defense of

323

agricultural lands, and to strengthen free and autonomous spaces, among other forms of resistance. Among other things, the purpose of the Zezta Internazional is to get to know each other, share experiences, create ties and organize these struggles without losing autonomy.

The Zezta calls for solidarity among peoples, not only from the world to the Zapatistas, but from communities in rebellion to the rest of the world: "We want to tell all of those who resist and struggle in their own ways and in their own countries that you're not alone, that we the Zapatistas, as small as we are, support you and will find the way to help you in your struggles, to talk to you and to learn from you, because in fact that's what we've learned best all these years: how to learn."

In that context, the Zapatista's first direct action of support was for the people of Cuba, a people that has been resisting imperialism for over forty years. In the spring of 2006, the Zapatistas sent a surprising ship-ment of corn and gasoline "from the indigenous Zapatista communities to the proud people of Cuba." While the Zezta clearly relates to other Latin American struggles, it also invites European movements and seeks to learn about and meet with struggles in Africa, Asia and Oceania.

"And we want to tell the people of Cuba, who have been resisting many years, that you're not alone and that we don't agree with the block-ade you suffer, and we're going to figure out a way to send you something, even if it's only corn, to help in your resistance. And we want to tell peo-ple in the U.S. that we don't lump everyone together, we know the differ-ence between the bad governments you have, which hurt the whole world, and the people who struggle in your country and in solidarity with struggles of other peoples. And we want to tell our Mapuche brothers and sisters in Chile that we watch your struggles and learn from them. And we want to tell Venezuelans that we see how you defend your sovereignty, that is, your nation's right to decide its own path. And to indigenous brothers and sisters in Ecuador and Bolivia, we tell you that you're giving all of Latin America a lesson in history by resisting neoliberal globalization. And to the *piqueteros* and the youths of Argentina, we only want to tell you that we love you. And to those in Uruguay who want a better country, that we admire you. And to landless peasants in Brazil, that we respect you. And to all youths in Latin America, that what you're doing is good and that you give us great hope."

The Zezta also posits the need for another "intergalactic" encounter, for which preparatory activities have taken place in many parts of the world. In only a year, from July 2005 to July 2006, nineteen meetings were held in sixteen cities of nine countries—Spain, Italy, Germany, Canada, United States, El Salvador, Uruguay, Argentina and Brazil—and in all of them local struggles were discussed as well as means for international networking.

In its first year—from December 2005 to December 30, 2006—the Zapatistas' international initiative received more than 3,386 adherents, individual and collective, from 74 countries from all the continents, according to a report by EZLN Insurgent Lieutenant-Colonel Moisés.

The report also notes that, up to that moment, the country with the largest number of adherents was Argentina, followed by the United States, where the new initiative was well received by the Chicano movement, by migrant workers and by other U.S. Americans who struggle against empire. At a time when the basic rights of mostly Mexican immigrant workers are decreasing alarmingly, while the border is militarized and migrant work is criminalized, the Sixth Declaration was perceived as an alternative for local struggle in the United States, as well as a reinforcement of a Mexican identity. This led many people on the "other side" of the border to identify with the national component of the initiative (the Other Campaign) rather than with the Zezta Internazional (in many cases organizations and collectives participate in both).

During the last days of December 2006 and the first days of 2007, when the EZLN celebrated the thirteenth anniversary of its armed uprising, the Zapatista communities organized the first Encounter between the Zapatistas and the Peoples of the World in the Caracol of Oventik. There,

325

the Good Government Boards and the autonomous municipal councils of the five Zapatista regions explained with great detail their experiences in self-governance, production and struggle. They offered simple and forthright presentations describing their thirteen years of building their autonomy. Before more than 2,000 people from forty-three countries, the Zapatistas described their efforts in autonomous organization, an accomplishment without precedents in Mexico and in most of the world. It is a very concrete praxis that, as they explained, follows no manual or theory, but is built with the everyday experience of resistance of tens of thousands of Tzotzil, Tzeltal, Tojolabal, Chol, Zoque and Mam men and women.

In an unprecedented event in their thirteen years of public struggle (and twenty-three years since the foundation of the EZLN), representatives from the communities in resistance expressed in simple terms what autonomy means for them: "For us it means that the people determine their forms of struggle and political, economic and social organization; it is the people who decide the way they live based on their language and their culture." The Zapatistas explained that one of their greatest challenges is the struggle for equal rights of women. "Machismo exists, we can't deny it, but we want to be respected as women, and because of that we are organizing ourselves and making agreements with our husbands and children. We want to make sure that all of us have the right to participate in our organization, for example, with collective work. Not only men should have that freedom."

A new generation of Zapatistas introduced themselves during the four days of the gathering. Very young men and women, born shortly before or after the 1994 uprising, described the immense challenges they face as they build, with practically no resources, an autonomous system of governance. The vaccination campaigns, the community health centers, the hospitals and microclinics, despite their precarious conditions, are today a reality in the communities in rebellion, as are the schools and the training centers for education promoters, where education is related to

327

the Zapatistas' thirteen demands in four areas of knowledge: language, math, life and environment, and history.

Concerns and challenges were expressed in relation to the defense of land. "We Zapatistas will not allow our land to be taken from us again. We will defend it so our children can have no bosses and live without suffering humiliation and contempt."

During the following months, the Zapatistas' international efforts increased with the beginning of the International Campaign for the Defense of Indigenous, Peasant and Autonomous Lands and Territories of Chiapas, Mexico and the World, announced on March 25, 2007. João Pedro Stédile, leader of the Landless Peasant Movement of Brazil, and Rafael Alegría, from the Campaign for Agrarian Reform of Vía Campesina, participated in the event that launched the initiative through video messages.

"We call for this international campaign of mutual support among rural peoples and others who support our rights and our struggles for the right to life and dignity, to join forces with others," said Subcomandante Marcos during a gathering in San Cristóbal de las Casas. This event also marked the beginning of the second phase of the Other Campaign.

One of the first concrete actions of the international campaign was the elaboration of a document signed by 202 organizations from twenty-two countries and 1,104 people from forty countries. The document demanded that the land held by autonomous communities of Chiapas, threatened by the imminent seizure of over 5,000 hectares, be guaranteed. The demand was supported by Vía Campesina and the Continental Network for the Demilitarization of the Americas, as well as worker, peasant, indigenous, human rights and environmental organizations, research centers and religious groups in Brazil, Spain, Italy, France, Palestine, Cuba, Paraguay, Argentina, Switzerland, United States, Bolivia, Canada, Germany, Costa Rica, Guatemala, Catalonia, the Basque Country, Portugal, Thailand, Sweden, India and Greece, among others.

As announced by the Sixth Declaration ("we will build more relationships of respect and mutual support with people and organizations that resist and struggle against neoliberalism and for humanity"), the EZLN expressed in mid-June its "admiration" for the Landless Peasant Movement (MST), in a letter sent to the closing ceremony of the Fifth Congress of the Brazilian organization. The MST "has our support, our love, and our respect, but also our admiration," stated the Zapatistas' spokesman and military chief. Subcomandante Marcos related the MST's struggle to that of General Emiliano Zapata and announced new initiatives to coincide with the hundredth anniversary of the Mexican Revolution: "Soon it will be a hundred years since his cry shook the countryside and the cities of Mexico. So it will be again."

At the same time, complying with the agreement made during the Other Campaign's tour in the northwest of the country, the Sixth Commission of the EZLN, representatives of the National Indigenous Council (CNI) from various states, and some indigenous tribes and nations of the United States met in Punta Peñasco, Sonora, in the terri-

tory of the Tohono O'odham (Papago) peoples. There they announced the Encounter of Indigenous Peoples of the Americas, to take place in the Yaqui territory of Vicam, in October 2007.

"The wars of independence and the revolutions that throughout history have taken place in our continent haven't modified our condition as colonized peoples, nor have they brought about the full recognition of our rights in the national states formed in the last two centuries," reads the continental invitation. The purpose of the encounter is to meet each other, since "the strength and unity of the struggles for liberation of indigenous peoples of the Americas will only be possible if our people meet and join forces."

Later, in July, two public debates were held prior to a second international encounter, with delegates from several organizations from Vía Campesina and the National Indigenous Council. The topic of the debates was "Facing capitalist plunder and the defense of land and territories."

330

"In order to affect capitalism, we need to take over the means of production. The land must be in the hands of those who work it, so they can decide how to work it and so the benefits are for the working people. This is one of the characteristics of our organization, the EZLN, and one of the most important aspects of the Sixth Declaration of the Lacandón Jungle, which guides our steps in the Other Campaign and in the Zezta Internazional: anti-capitalism," said insurgent Lieutenant-Colonel Moisés during one of the roundtables.

The second Encounter between the Zapatistas and the Peoples of the World took place in July 2007 in the Zapatista regions of Oventik, Morelia and La Realidad. Once again the Zapatistas shared with more than 2,000 people from around the world the everyday organization of their autonomous government, education, health, collective work, commerce and, notably, the participation of women in the construction of autonomy. This time, in addition to authorities from the Good Government Boards and the autonomous municipal councils, the presentations were made members of Zapatista base communities: education and health promoters, municipal agents and officers, members of cooperatives, and coordinators of collective work, as well as comandantas and comandantes from the Clandestine Revolutionary Indigenous Committee of the EZLN.

Born on December 19, 1994, the eighteen autonomous Zapatista municipalities in rebellion (MAREZ) started to grow at different rates depending on the region, the culture, their economic resources and their internal organization. Today there are more than forty autonomous municipalities divided into five large regions, each with its own autonomous government seat (caracol), which is both a cultural and political center. "We never thought we would get this far," says Manuel, a Tzeltal elder who recalls how, prior to 1994 when the EZLN still operated clandestinely, the Zapatistas started to "look after health in the villages."

The EZLN, still an armed guerrilla but one that promotes only peaceful, civilian political initiatives, narrated pieces of a history that is

331

continuously being written: "We tried to negotiate, we tried everything, but we all saw what happened with the San Andrés Accords (signed in February 1996 and never put in effect). Because of that we stopped asking permission and started to build. We believe that the organization of our people is much more important than money, because too much money corrupts, but our organization is never corrupt. The ideas we develop in our search for life cannot destroyed either in prison or in death," said Comandante Moisés.

The purpose of this encounter was for "people, groups, collectives and organizations that struggle against neoliberalism in Mexico and the world to learn, directly from the EZLN's base communities, the process of building autonomy in the Zapatista indigenous communities of Chiapas." People came to the encounter from Argentina, Australia, Austria, the Basque Country, Belgium, Bolivia, Brazil, Canada, Chile, Colombia, Costa Rica, Croatia, Czech Republic, Denmark, El Salvador, England, France, Germany, Greece, Guatemala, Holland, Ireland, Israel, Italy, Japan, Lebanon, Luxemburg, Mexico, New Zealand, Nicaragua, Norway, Panama, Peru, Poland, Portugal, Spain, Sweden, Switzerland, Turkey, United States, Uruguay and Venezuela.

Representatives from the organizations that make up Vía Campesina worldwide were present as special guests: delegates from the Landless Peasant Movement of Brazil, the Peasant League of South Korea, the National Coalition of Family Farmers of the United States, the Federation of Peasant Unions of Indonesia, the National Federation of Women Peasants of Bolivia, the Peasant Union of the Basque Country, the Latin American Coordination of Organizations of the Countryside, the National Confederation of Women of the Countryside of the Dominican Republic, Vía Campesina–Central America, the Bhartiya Kissan Peasant Union of India, the Peasant Network of Northern Thailand, the Assembly of the Poor in Thailand, the Agricultural Workers of the Border of the United States, UNORCA in Mexico, and Union Paysanne from Quebec, Canada.

During the encounter's closing ceremony, which took place in the Tojolabal-speaking community of La Realidad, an invitation was made to a third international encounter, to take place in December 2007, between Zapatista women and women of the world, which will be named after Comandanta Ramona. The struggle of indigenous women in rebellion is in itself a struggle within a struggle, and its small and large accomplishments have had an effect in the entire structure of the EZLN, where there are women comandantas, insurgents, autonomous authorities, health and education promoters, and women in charge of various cooperatives, among other positions. "But we still have a long way to go. There is still a lot of machismo in the communities and it's difficult for women to participate," recognized Tzotzil, Tzeltal, Tojolabal, Chol, Zoque and Mam women during the international encounters held in January and July of 2007. Zapatista women, however, are no longer the same as they were in 1994, and the change, albeit slow, is immense and irreversible.

. . .

The Other Campaign and the Zezta Internazional are moving along. The Mexican government is drifting further and further to the right and resorting with increasing frequency to repress democractic forces of organization and change. But the Sixth Declaration in Mexico and the Zezta Internazional are traveling around the world, walking against the wind and against capitalism. The experience with rebellion and autonomy of the indigenous Zapatistas has found brothers and sisters in the thirty-two states of the country and on all the five continents. And since the road is long and the voyage is only beginning, a few words of hope are in order:

to be continued. . .

ABOUT THE AUTHORS

Gloria Muñoz Ramírez

Gloria Muñoz Ramírez was born in Mexico City and studied journalism and collective communication at the National Autonomous University of Mexico (UNAM). From 1994 to 1996, she worked for the Mexican newspaper *Punto*, for the German news agency DPA, for the U.S. newspaper *La Opinión*, and for the Mexican daily *La Jornada*. In 1997, she left her work, her family, her friends (and other things only she knows) and came to live in the Zapatista communities, where she remained for seven years. Today she writes for the daily *La Jornada* and is a member of the editorial board of its indigenous supplement *Ojarasca*. She is also a member of the editorial board of the magazine *Rebeldía*.

Subcomandante Insurgente Marcos

Subcomandante Marcos is military chief and spokesman of the Zapatista Army of National Liberation. From the first days of the armed uprising, he stood out as the most visible figure of the movement, serving as a bridge between the Zapatista indigenous communities and the world. His rank as Subcomandante subordinates him to the Clandestine Revolutionary Indigenous Committee, a collective command structure composed of comandantes and comandantas from the seven indigenous groups of Chiapas. A guerrilla leader and writer (political essayist, novelist, and poet), his texts have been translated into innumerable languages. He hides his face behind a ski mask, which, together with his ever-present pipe, is part of the internationally renowned mythical and controversial figure.

Hermann Bellinghausen

Mexican writer and journalist, Bellinghausen has published *La hora y el resto*, *Ojos de Omán and De una vez* (poetry), *El telar de los gallos* (short stories), and *Crónica de multitudes* and *Aire libre* (chronicles). He studied medicine at the Nacional Autonomous University of Mexico (UNAM) and since 1994 he has covered for the Mexican daily *La Jornada* everything related to the Zapatista movement. Since 1989 he has directed *La Jornada's* monthly supplement *Ojarasca*, dedicated to indigenous peoples and cultures of the world.

TRANSLATORS

Laura Carlsen

Laura Carlsen is Director of the Americas Program at the International Relations Center (IRC). She has published numerous articles and chapters on social and political aspects of Mexico, and most recently co-edited a collection entitled *Enfrentando la Globalización: Respuestas sociales a la integración económica en México* and co-authored *El café en México, Centroamérica y el Caribe: Una salida sustentable a la crisis.* Before joining the IRC, Laura worked as a freelance writer and collaborator with the Center for the Study of Rural Change in Mexico (CECCAM).

Alejandro Reyes Arias

Reyes migrated to the United States from Mexico in 1978 and lived in Bahia, Brazil, from 1995 to 2004. He is the author of *Vidas de rua* and *Cuentos mexicanos* (short stories) and *A Rainha do Cine Roma* (novel). He is currently a Ph.D. student in Latin American Literature at the University of California at Berkeley and member of the Radio Zapatista collective.

Photo and Credits

Adrian Mealand. 4-5

Angeles Torrejón. 200, 205

Antonio Turok. 2-3, 113, 285

Araceli Herrera. 98-99, 136

Arturo Fuentes. 213, 217, 221, 225

Carlos Cisneros (*La Jornada*). 104, 109

Carlos Ramos Mamahua (*La Jornada*). 218

Christos Stefanou. 12, 24-25

Eduardo Verdugo. 6-7, 255, 260

Elpida Niku. 97, 330

Eniac Martínez. 192, 239, 245

Francisco Olvera (*La Jornada*). 228

Frida Hartz (*La Jornada*). 106, 173

Greg Ruggiero. 16, 333

Georges Bartoli. 150 top, 182

Heriberto Rodríguez. 119, 131, 208, 296

Jesús Ramírez. 10-11, 44-45, 56, 60, 96

José Carlo González (*La Jornada*). 150 bottom, 189, 214

José Núñez (*La Jornada*). 124, 274-275

Marco Antonio Cruz. 110

María M. Caire. 14, 326

Patricia Aridjis. 82

Pedro Valtierra (*La Jornada*). 114 top, 166

Radio Insurgente. 315

Raúl Ortega. 26

Simona Granati. 163, 234, 269

Tim Russo. 233, 249, 273, 279, 326

Víctor Manuel Camacho (*La Jornada*). 17, 316, 319, 323, 329, 335

Víctor Mendiola (*La Jornada*). 114 bottom

Yuriria Pantoja Millán. 50, 68, 89, 94, 129, 143, 196

Photo Editor:
Yuriria Pantoja Millán

Assistant Photo Editor:
Priscila Pacheco